DISABILITY, CUL

Alfredo

Teaching Emergent Bilingual Students With Dis/Abilities: Humanizing Pedagogies to Engage Learners and Eliminate Labels
PATRICIA MARTÍNEZ-ÁLVAREZ

Dismantling Disproportionality: A Culturally Responsive and Sustaining Systems Approach
MARIA G. HERNÁNDEZ, DAVID M. LOPEZ, & REED SWIER, WITH JASPREET KAUR

Discipline Disparities Among Students With Disabilities: Creating Equitable Environments
PAMELA FENNING & MIRANDA JOHNSON, EDS.

DisCrit Expanded: Reverberations, Ruptures, and Inquiries
SUBINI A. ANNAMMA, BETH A. FERRI, & DAVID J. CONNOR, EDS.

A World Away From IEPs: How Disabled Students Learn in Out-of-School Spaces
ERIN MCCLOSKEY

Case Studies in Building Equity Through Family Advocacy in Special Education: A Companion Volume to *Meeting Families Where They Are*
LYDIA OCASIO-STOUTENBURG & BETH HARRY

Intersectionality in Education: Toward More Equitable Policy, Research, and Practice
WENDY CAVENDISH & JENNIFER F. SAMSON, EDS.

Excluded by Choice: Urban Students with Disabilities in the Education Marketplace
FEDERICO R. WAITOLLER

Meeting Families Where They Are: Building Equity Through Advocacy with Diverse Schools and Communities
BETH HARRY & LYDIA OCASIO-STOUTENBURG

Affirming Disability: Strengths-Based Portraits of Culturally Diverse Families
JANET STORY SAUER & ZACHARY ROSSETTI

Does Compliance Matter in Special Education? IDEA and the Hidden Inequities of Practice
CATHERINE KRAMARCZUK VOULGARIDES

Teaching for Inclusion: Eight Principles for Effective and Equitable Practice
SRIKALA NARAIAN

Transition by Design: Improving Equity and Outcomes for Adolescents with Disabilities
AUDREY A. TRAINOR

After the "At-Risk" Label: Reorienting Educational Policy and Practice
KEFFRELYN D. BROWN

DisCrit—Disability Studies and Critical Race Theory in Education
DAVID J. CONNOR, BETH A. FERRI, & SUBINI A. ANNAMMA, EDS.

Closing the School Discipline Gap: Equitable Remedies for Excessive Exclusion
DANIEL J. LOSEN, ED.

(Un)Learning Disability: Recognizing and Changing Restrictive Views of Student Ability
ANNMARIE D. BAINES

Ability, Equity, and Culture: Sustaining Inclusive Urban Education Reform
ELIZABETH B. KOZLESKI & KATHLEEN KING THORIUS, EDS.

Condition Critical—Key Principles for Equitable and Inclusive Education
DIANA LAWRENCE-BROWN & MARA SAPON-SHEVIN

DISABILITY, CULTURE, AND EQUITY SERIES

Teaching Emergent Bilingual Students With Dis/Abilities

Humanizing Pedagogies to Engage Learners and Eliminate Labels

Patricia Martínez-Álvarez

To the teacher candidates and children who shared the Varied Ways of Knowing space with me, and to the staff of the bilingual school, who made it all possible while continuing su lucha diaria (their daily fight): I will be forever grateful for the "hybrid humanizing" moments that sparked while being together and the knowledge we collectively created.

Published by Teachers College Press,® 1234 Amsterdam Avenue, New York, NY 10027

Front cover images: Butterfly by Patricia M via Flickr, Child by Bessi via Pixabay.

Library of Congress Cataloging-in-Publication Data is available at loc.gov

ISBN 978-0-8077-6810-5 (paper)
ISBN 978-0-8077-6811-2 (hardcover)
ISBN 978-0-8077-8160-9 (ebook)

Printed on acid-free paper
Manufactured in the United States of America

Contents

Preface

The Varied Ways of Knowing (VWK) project took place in the Northeastern United States and consisted of an afterschool program for bilingual children that met every week for 2 hours in the bilingual school the children attended during the day. The learning invitations in the VWK came from teacher candidates, most of whom were preparing to teach in inclusive bilingual classrooms, and from the bilingual children, with and without a disability, who participated in the program. I participated in the afterschool program and in the meetings with the teacher candidates, and I was a professor in the program where the VWK project took shape. During our time together, we laughed, became emotional, learned about each other's knowledge, and created new understandings. Above all, despite its complexity, we embraced hybridity in terms of language, culture, and disability and recognized each other's humanity. This book organizes what we learned while sharing the VWK space and offers implications for continuing to ensure more inclusive bilingual education.

The VWK afterschool program was built on the belief that all children, including those identified with a disability, deserve opportunities to maintain their languages and grow to be bilingual and biliterate. This is particularly important for minoritized bilingual children, who come to school speaking languages that are not always prioritized in schools.

While most educators might initially agree with the importance of ensuring that minoritized children learn in their own and in at least the dominant language, what we are seeing in our bilingual classrooms is that, as bilingual children are identified with a disability, their chances to continue to learn bilingually diminish. As part of a commitment to offer playful yet rigorous learning spaces where teacher candidates and children explore knowledge, the program was designed to recognize that learning takes place as much outside as inside schools. The VWK program builds on the importance of putting these different knowledges in conversation with one another. Finally, the VWK was built upon the conviction that all children can learn bilingually when the context is purposefully designed to attend to all their learning identities in balanced ways. A concerted effort, involving the child with a disability, the educators, and communities and artifacts across different social contexts, is decisive in changing the cultural historical practices that continue to impede bilingual children in developing at their own pace and following their own learning pathways.

Grounded in authentic teaching and learning experiences, this book is intended to add to the current understanding of how to create educational spaces that more respectfully and humanely address the needs of emergent bilinguals with a disability in bilingual programs. With that intent, the book is written for researchers in the field of bilingual/bicultural education, inclusive education, and/or disability studies in education; teacher candidates in graduate education programs, especially, those preparing to work in inclusive settings (e.g., Integrated Co-Teaching [ICT] classrooms, bilingual classrooms, etc.); and teacher educators working to prepare teachers for bilingual/bicultural inclusive education settings. The book establishes a conversation among important constructs in the histories of bilingual education and of teaching students with a disability, such as assimilation and ableism, the expansion of identity and agency, and humanistic pedagogies. The issues illustrated, and the tools proposed through this book, are sure to resonate with many researchers and educators who have spent time in bilingual classrooms.

The constructs brought out during the study's analysis and theorization processes are part of critical disability frameworks and cultural historical theory. These can be seen as organizing ideas that are introduced along the book chapters and that can contribute to better understanding children who have been assigned inflexible labels that do not fit them well.

The book starts with three introductory chapters that offer the grounds for understanding the rest of its content. Chapters 4 through 9 then each introduce one construct through illustrative work and conversation samples from a unit taught in the VWK afterschool program. The last chapter synthesizes the theoretical alongside the practical aspects arising from the work and offers implications for progressively expanding bilingual education into spaces inclusive of children with a disability. A brief outline of each chapter is presented next.

The book begins with Chapter 1 discussing tensions surrounding the education of bilingual children with a disability. The chapter offers a literature review focused on the three main cultural historical tensions in this field: the contradiction that manifests in issues of disability identification disproportionality and the consequences that labels pose for minoritized children; the lack of teacher preparation programs for inclusive bilingual education; and the lack of inclusive approaches in bilingual education. To conclude, the chapter offers a vision for bilingual education as a space inclusive of children with a disability.

Chapter 2 introduces the three assumptions grounding the VWK project. These assumptions consist of, first, the belief that all children deserve to maintain their languages and grow to become biliterate; second, the recognition that learning also takes place outside formal school spaces; and, third, the premise that with the appropriate contextual support all children can learn bilingually. The chapter also introduces the afterschool program and the main theoretical ideas guiding its development and the exploration of work and conversations. Cultural historical activity theory (CHAT) informed the design of our program as a hybrid space. Then the emphasis on ensuring everyone participates meaningfully (but in different ways and bringing their own knowledge and practices) is discussed through distributed expertise, Vygostky's (1993) compensation, and the importance of re-mediating (Gutiérrez et al., 2009) cultural historical artifacts that are privileged in schools but that might not work for bilingual children with a disability. Both compensation and re-mediation require that educators allow children to perform different learning identities (Martínez-Álvarez, 2020a) and permit the crossing of figurative boundaries. The collective effort to take actions agentively to address difficulties that arise while learning generates a zone of proximal development, which is collectively rather than individually developed and through which children can begin the healing pathway of *conocimiento* (Anzaldúa, 2002). Lastly, the concept of hybrid humanizing pedagogical moments, which is fully fleshed out in Chapter 6, is also explained in Chapter 2 to familiarize the reader with some ideas that will be used throughout the remaining chapters.

Chapter 3 demonstrates how a project such as the VWK can be documented, including the role of the institution of higher education and the school contexts, and provides information about the participating children and teacher candidates. Twenty-two bilingual children and 15 teacher candidates participated in the project. Together they generated multiple conversations and multimodal products, and the teacher candidates wrote learning notes every week. The teacher candidates met with me for weekly reflective/planning meetings after each session and interviewed with me at the end of each year. Chapter 3 explains how this information was explored and organized for this book.

Chapters 4 through 9 are different, as they discuss the constructs found through the study one by one. Each chapter is guided by a question that is explored through information (i.e., work and conversations) from one curricular unit or project that is described in a Classroom Identity and Knowledge Exploration section. The chapters propose illustrative examples that are discussed using the guiding ideas from Chapter 2 so that researchers, educators, and teacher educators can gain insights about the knowledge that was created and the pedagogies that transpired in the VWK.

Chapter 4 explores issues of ableism, investigating the question: How does ableism manifest in bilingual education contexts with children with a disability? The chapter explains the project of the Yo como Aprendiz (Me as a Learner) Collage. The examples provided concretize the ways through which ableism is embedded in the culture of our educational systems.

The next chapter introduces the issue of assimilation and explores it through the question: How do historical assimilationist efforts manifest when teaching bilingual children with a disability and what opportunities toward inclusive designs might surface? The chapter describes the Lados de Mí (Sides of Me) Project. Through illustrative examples, the chapter surfaces the persistence of historical forms of assimilation and highlights how emergent bilinguals with a disability might be deprived of linguistic and cultural rights (Skutnabb-Kangas & Phillipson, 2010).

After these two issues are discussed, Chapter 6 centers on humanistic pedagogies and entertains the question: How can a humanistic approach assist in making bilingual programs more inclusive of children with a disability? This chapter describes the Capas y Escudos (Capes and Shields) Project. The chapter introduces the idea of hybrid humanizing pedagogical moments to describe moments where hybridity and humanizing pedagogies occur, simultaneously cultivating and nurturing each other.

Chapter 7 asks: What knowledge do bilingual children with a disability manifest while engaging in identity work and learning about disability, and what forms of agency surface as children explore multiple identity possibilities? The chapter introduces the Derechos de las Personas con Discapacidad (Disability Rights Movement) Project and illustrates the need of expanding Freire's (1993) ideas of "conscientização" (conscientization) to raise awareness about disability oppression with bilingual children.

At this point, the book shifts to teaching science and language with bilingual children with and without a disability. Chapter 8 explores the question: How does boundary crossing manifest in a hybrid science learning space with bilingual children with and without a disability and what possibilities for expansive learning surface in this space? The chapter introduces the Contextos Relevantes para Ciencias y Accidentes Geográficos (Relevant Contexts for Science and Landforms) Lessons. The importance of crossing three forms of figurative boundaries is described. These are boundaries between forms of knowledge and practices, disciplines, and formal or informal learning spaces.

The last chapter of this kind, Chapter 9, explores the question: What forms of artifact re-mediation are generated in a bilingual science learning space and what can we learn from the analysis of artifact-mediated activity about teaching bilingual children with and without a disability? The chapter employs information from the Terremotos, Placas Tectónicas, y el Cinturón de Fuego (Earthquakes, Plate Tectonics, and the Ring of Fire) Project to discuss the role of artifact-mediated learning for inclusive bilingual education.

In the concluding chapter, the contributions of the different parts of the book come together. The chapter organizes the implications for progressively expanding bilingual education into spaces inclusive of children with a disability.

We must come to realize the limitations in using labels for categorizing minoritized children in inflexible ways. We instead need respectful practices that enable all learners, who can create and follow their own ways toward learning, with the support of the instructional context and educators. This book provides actual examples illustrating how to do that. It is possible to enable learners with a disability in bilingual classrooms, but it is important to realize that learning along pathways that are not traditionally privileged in schools takes time, persistence, and agentive work. Educators might not directly see the results of their hard efforts to create successful learning spaces for their bilingual children with a disability. For educators, the book has a message: Trust your practice and commitment to create hybrid humanizing pedagogical moments! These efforts will provide possibilities for children with a disability to continue to grow as bilingual, bicultural, and biliterate people.

I close this preface with a note about the terminology I use in this book and with a list of abbreviations that are used in the chapters.

1. **Emergent bilingual (EB):** The term *emergent bilingual* is used to refer to children who have been labeled as English language learners through school processes. The use of EB to refer to children who speak a language other than English at home better captures and highlights their linguistic resources (García et al., 2008).
2. **Children with a disability:** *Child with a disability* is used to refer to those who have been labeled with a disability under the Individuals with Disabilities Education Improvement Act (IDEA, 2004), the current name of the special education law. To be identified with a disability, the law states, the child's performance at school must be negatively impacted. Most children in this study were identified within the "soft" disability categories. These are categories that are of "a less tangible nature—perhaps because of their apparent 'invisibility'—in comparison to physical or sensory disabilities" (Connor & Ferri, 2005, p. 110). Person-first language, as in "children with a disability," is used instead of identity-first "disabled children," to highlight the social aspects involved in identifying a disability in schools, and to recognize and denounce the misdiagnosis of many minoritized children as having a disability. Disability can at times be written with a slash, as in dis/ability, to highlight the continuum across these two categories when assigned to emergent bilinguals and to point to how ability and disability are socially constructed (Connor et al., 2016).
3. In an effort to avoid gender defining expressions, when possible, existing inclusive concepts in English and in Spanish are used. When this is not possible, the letter "x" is used to indicate gender-neutral in both languages because it is a way to avoid binary terms such as Latina and Latino; this ending can be deciphered by screen

readers (in contrast to the use of the at-sign or the asterisk); and it is commonly used among everyday users of Spanish and English in the United States (in contrast to the use of "e" as neutral ending). I invite readers to use whatever gender neutral version they find fits their purposes.

List of Abbreviations

CHAT	Cultural Historical Activity Theory
DSE	Disability Studies in Education
EB	Emergent Bilingual
ELL	English Language Learner
FoK	Funds of Knowledge
IEP	Individualized Educational Plan
ICT	Integrated Co-Teaching
NGSS	Next Generation Science Standards
SETSS	Special Education Teacher Support Services
SLD	Specific Learning Disability
SLI	Speech and Language Impairment
UDL	Universal Design for Learning
VWK	Varied Ways of Knowing
ZPD	Zone of Proximal Development

Acknowledgments

Being able to share the Varied Ways of Knowing (VWK) space with the children and teacher candidates who participated in this project has been a great honor, one made possible by a collective effort. I am beyond thankful to the principal and the staff of the school where the program took place. Thank you to the children and the teacher candidates for the opportunity to get to know you and for your generosity in being willing to explore knowledge, practices, and ways of being in the world alongside me in the VWK. I felt I really knew each one of you so well by the end of the project.

I want also to go back to the time when I first started working with bilingual children who had been labeled with a disability. I owe what I know about bilingual education, and the realization of the humanity that bilingual programs can bring to light, to my first school, Key Elementary School (Arlington, VA). As a brand-new teacher at Key, who was still acclimating to the American culture and language, I was very surprised to see so many Latinx children in special education. I thank the former school principal, Dr. Marjorie Myers, for believing in the 22-year-old teacher who came to her asking for that first job as an inclusive bilingual teacher. I ended up working at Key Elementary for 11 wonderful years. While I can't name them all, I learned about bilingual teaching and learning from those educators, children, and families who accompanied me in that journey.

I would like to acknowledge the contributions of Belinda Arana, who was often alongside me in this effort, and of the four reviewers who voluntarily read early drafts of these chapters. Thank you, Jungmin Kwon, for your thinking, your trust, and your kindness when offering suggestions. You are such a great scholar and friend. You shaped the tone of this book, humanizing it and making it better. Natalia Sáez, thank you for reading my work when you were busy with your own dissertation. I can't wait to read drafts of your publications! Thank you to SooJin Jeon and Estrella Olivares-Orellana for your helpful comments as I made progress and to Ofelia García Otheguy for her loving advice about inclusive language.

When I was at the VWK afterschool program working with the children and the teacher candidates, I thought back to my own children, Luca and Sofía, who were similar in age to those whose work have shaped this book. While discussing education with my husband, Dioni, I made many connections between the learning in the VWK and the learning of my children at home and at their school. Learning indeed is a social endeavor that takes place in different social spaces and crosses boundaries. I thank my family for their commitment to support my passion for bilingual education and for giving and taking in that dance that works so well.

CHAPTER 1

Tensions Surrounding the Education of Bilingual Children With a Disability

When I was growing up in Spain, school was the space where I learned, while my home was the space where I spent time with my family. These felt like two different universes that were strikingly distant and rarely mixed. In my experience, when in- and out-of-school spaces did connect, it was typically because of negative aspects, such as when I was hospitalized in 2nd grade for a good part of the academic year and had to do schoolwork outside of school. Homework was a possible point of association; but this I reluctantly and routinely completed by myself, while sitting in the kitchen as my mother cooked. While in school, I did not have a say in what to study or how to explore it, and seldom felt empowered to express my opinions or to approach learning other than through my school's predetermined tools and artifacts. Content areas in my state-funded school (run by nuns) were strictly separated, in elementary school by class periods and corresponding textbooks, and in middle school by having a different teacher for each subject.

Figurative boundaries among learning spaces and among forms of knowledge or disciplines, alongside a lack of opportunities to enact agency, provoked punitive consequences for those children for whom this traditional way of organizing the educational system did not work. These consequences included, for instance, being belittled in front of classmates or being retained a grade level, as educators and family members blamed children for their difficulties with learning. Once children were situated as not being able to learn, being lazy, or not doing well academically, this disadvantageous learning identity became almost permanent, following them throughout their schooling years. It never occurred to me in my early student days that development also transpires between various spheres of experience. I could not even imagine that knowledge I obtained elsewhere could be valued in schools, or that children's learning identities could fluidly shift, and they could experience being experts or novices, able or not able depending on the learning circumstances (Martínez-Álvarez, 2020a).

When I arrived in the United States and became a bilingual special education teacher, I noticed similar patterns in the public schools on this side of the Atlantic. Not only were children who were progressing differently in school situated as the ones failing in learning, but here in the United States, there was a disconnect between and across the multiple knowledges and spaces that many immigrant children navigated, and little attention was being paid to that critical contradiction. Very early in my teaching experience in the suburbs of Washington, D.C., I realized that this resulted in many Latinx children being categorized with a disability. I taught in a dual-language bilingual school, where most of my students who had been labeled with a disability were Latinx of immigrant background, spoke Spanish at home, and came from low socioeconomic backgrounds. This revealed local disproportionality as, even though the school attracted Spanish-speaking children, it also served a solid proportion of middle-class English-speaking White children. Unfortunately, the disproportionality pattern is also observable at the national level in the United States.

We know that bilingual children come to school with *funds of knowledge* (FoK). Defined as a person's array of resources in the form of knowledge and practices, which are historically and culturally developed over time, FoK can be used for learning (Moll et al., 1992). However, unless schools purposefully endeavor to value and integrate them, these potentially productive assets remain dormant and do not mediate learning, lingering outside but barely contributing to Latinx children's learning identities.

This book is about the varied ways of knowing that bilingual and bicultural children employ for learning and for experiencing the multiple spaces they traverse. Some bilingual and bicultural children (hereinafter referred to as bilingual children) are labeled as English language learners (ELLs) in schools. These children are referred to in this book as *emergent bilinguals* to highlight an additive perspective on their language learning circumstances, although the label of ELL continues to be widely used in public school contexts (García et al., 2008). The different chapters in this book address aspects of the varied knowledges, values, beliefs, cultures, languages, or, in summary, the varied dimensions of the humanity of bilingual children, and aspire to situate and center diversity as the most important tool for learning together.

Regrettably, because of the lack of recognition of the many assets bilingual children possess for learning, and the prevailing comparisons against the unattainable image of the "average" learner that is based on the idea of "normal" as the monolingual White student (Davis, 2006), bilinguals are often portrayed in educational systems as failing. Through biased processes bilingual children are often quite arbitrarily identified with a disability under our special education system (Ortiz et al., 2011). The current federal law guiding special education services for children attending public schools in the United States was established in 1975 as the Education for All Handicapped Children Act. This law is still active, but it has been reauthorized and renamed as the Individuals with Disabilities Education Act IDEIA in 1997 and amended by the Individuals with Disabilities Education Improvement Act or IDEIA in 2004. The law stipulates that any child whose educational performance is negatively impacted by a disability is eligible to receive special education services under one of 13 disability categories (14 if we include developmental delay, which is used only for children in their early years).

Among the 13 disability categories, most bilingual children with a disability are labeled with what can be referred to as the "soft" categories. The soft categories are forms of disability that are socially constructed; they are of "a less tangible nature—perhaps because of their apparent 'invisibility'—in comparison to physical or sensory disabilities" (Connor & Ferri, 2005, p. 110). These include, for instance, specific learning disability (SLD) or speech and language impairment (SLI), labels that have been assigned to over 70% of all emergent bilinguals with a disability in the United States (Office of English Language Acquisition [OELA], 2017).

This book is built on the assumption that the inequities emergent bilinguals with and without a disability experience in educational systems result from "discriminatory structures and practices, as well as un-interrogated beliefs about disability deeply ingrained within educational systems," rather than being within children's bodies and minds (Beratan, 2006, para. 5). It is necessary to better understand how bilingual children who are situated as experiencing difficulties in schools, mediate their learning, and to imagine the collective distributed activity that must take place for respectful bilingual learning inclusive of all children.

This introductory chapter next reviews three cultural historical tensions we currently experience in the education of bilingual children in the United States and offers an overview of the field of inclusive bilingual education. The chapter concludes by expressing a firm conviction of the value of bilingual education as a space inclusive of children with a disability, a view that is at the core of this book.

CULTURAL HISTORICAL TENSIONS IN TEACHING AND LEARNING WITH BILINGUAL CHILDREN

This section describes the three tensions related to the education of bilingual children with a disability. These are: disproportionality in the soft disability categories of special education; the lack of teacher preparation programs for inclusive education in bilingual contexts; and the lack of inclusive approaches for bilingual education. The historical literature around these tensions is discussed to offer perspective on the progress we have already accomplished over time, and on what still needs to be achieved.

ISSUES OF DISABILITY IDENTIFICATION DISPROPORTIONALITY AND CONSEQUENCES OF LABELS

While bilinguals possess linguistic and cultural resources that can be assets for learning, immigrant children have historically been situated as not doing well in public schools throughout the United States. For example, bilinguals are shown not to make expected progress in reading, with only 3% of emergent bilinguals performing at or above a proficient reading level by the end of high school whereas 39% of students who are not emergent bilinguals do, according to the 2019 National Assessment of Educational Progress (NAEP) Report Card (National Center for Education Statistics, 2019). The NAEP (2019) describes the proficient student achievement level as a level of "solid academic performance and competency" over reading rather than as aligned with any grade levels. Similarly, only 13% of all children with a disability perform within or beyond the proficient level (National Center for Education Statistics, 2019). This deficit perspective arises from the use of measurements that fail to recognize the knowledge that these children possess, and also from the lack of culturally and linguistically relevant ways of teaching bilingual children. The view of children with labels as not making appropriate progress is rooted in understanding monolingual and nondisabled children as the "average" learner in our schools. However, with 25% of our public school population being from an immigrant family (Kids Count Data Center, 2019), and 14.4% of total public school enrollment, including 15.5% of all emergent bilinguals, having been labeled with a disability in 2019–2020 (National Center for Education Statistics, 2021, we need to change the way we expect children to perform while learning. We need to improve the ways we collect and analyze available work and conversation samples of children (Cole & David, 2021).

The historical tension of defining bilingual children and children with a disability as underperforming originates in the lack of connections from the resources (i.e., languages, knowledges, practices) that children bring to what is valued in schools. Making connections requires understanding and having familiarity with these linguistic and cultural assets, or at least having interest in learning from the children, but educators instead might readily interpret bilingual children as missing the basics for learning (Greenfield, 2013). These deficit-based processes are related to the cultural understanding of what ability is and looks like. Educational systems have often discriminated against those who did not follow what was perceived as being the "average" when learning. The idea of an average learner is based on the bell-curve shape of a statical representation of children's intelligence levels, often called in psychology the "normal distribution" (Baglieri et al., 2011; Kilinc, 2018). Children who, for instance, do not decode text as fluently as those in their grade levels, speak with an accent different from those who grew up in the United States, or need to move to better learn, are situated as being outside the ideal of "normal". As these children's ways of learning are not favored in schools, they tend not to do well academically. This discriminatory process is referred to as "ableism" and promotes remediation efforts aiming to assimilate children to a more historically recognized image of a learner (Collins & Ferri, 2016).

The historical portrayal of bilingual children as underperforming and the special education disproportionality in the United States are closely connected. Patterns of disproportionality are complex and vary by state and by age and racial group. Currently, a little over 14% of all emergent bilinguals in the United States are identified with a disability. However, in some states such as New York (where 22% of emergent bilinguals are identified with a disability) the percentage is higher (New York State Education Department, 2019, p. 7). When data is analyzed by state, emergent bilingual children might be overrepresented; but this is evident only in the socially created soft disability categories of SLD and SLI (Donovan & Cross, 2002; Sullivan, 2011).

Distinguishing emergent bilingual children who should be receiving special education services is particularly complex along these subjective disability categories, and the 2002 National Research Council Committee on Minority Representation in Special Education reported numerous cases of minorities being misidentified with the disabilities that are connected to language. That is, minoritized children, including emergent bilinguals, have higher possibilities of being identified with these disability categories (U.S. Department of Education, 2015); this was also true of children who receive free and/or reduced-price lunch (Sullivan & Bal, 2013). Equally troublesome is the reported underrepresentation in certain states and age groups. The delaying of the assessment process for identifying bilingual children with a disability when they are learning the language of instruction is problematic, as it might delay the assessment process and take away early services that can be preventive of future academic difficulties (Limbos & Geva, 2001). For instance, emergent bilinguals are underrepresented in the category of emotional disturbance in California (Parrish, 2002) or in general in the early school years (Samson & Lesaux, 2009), which could point to lack of awareness of the right to receive services under the special education law.

While receiving special education services is often perceived as a privilege that can provide better learning opportunities for children experiencing difficulties in school, when emergent bilinguals are identified with a disability, they might not benefit from the consequent services in the same way than their non-bilingual peers. Instead, depending on the state where they live, young bilinguals with a disability might be placed in a more restrictive environments, in terms of number of classmates, at the preschool level or fail to receive services in a timely manner (Zimmerman et al., 2022). As bilinguals receive the disability label, expectations regarding their learning are compromised, promoting less challenging educational opportunities (Shifrer et al., 2013). Relatedly, as bilinguals are identified with a disability, parents might be advised to focus on English-only education programs (Drysdale et al., 2015), and professionals might prioritize the learning of English over bilingual approaches (National Academies of Sciences, Engineering, & Medicine, 2017). In general, emergent bilinguals who have a disability are placed in more segregated contexts than those with the same disability labels who speak English at home (Sullivan, 2011). This includes receiving limited language support (Artiles et al. 2005) and having limited access to long-term bilingual education (Martínez-Álvarez, 2018).

It is no wonder that discourses addressing the progress of bilinguals with a disability are even more negative than those describing children who fall within one of these two categories only. For example, emergent bilinguals with a disability are described as being at-risk of early dropout from school and as having lower graduation rates and worse post-secondary outcomes than other children with a disability (see Kangas, 2020). There is a need to better prepare teachers to understand the learning of bilingual children and the learning of children with a disability simultaneously and to realize how disabled/able and language learner/language proficient labels can become permeable categories, with imprecise boundaries that allow for fluidity of identities. However, the preparation of teachers for addressing these multiple forms of difference is rare. The following section describes this second tension.

LACK OF TEACHER PREPARATION PROGRAMS FOR INCLUSIVE EDUCATION IN BILINGUAL CONTEXTS

The issues surrounding the learning of bilinguals with a disability show that there is a need to prepare educators to attend to the different aspects of these children's educational experience. Bilingual education teachers can address linguistic and cultural needs from asset-based perspectives, and recognize language learning processes and needs. Additionally, they also must be exposed to processing variations typically connected to the soft disability categories, and to ways to facilitate learning experiences for children with such learning differences. On the other hand, special education teacher candidates, who are learning to attend to diversity in terms of (dis)ability and who specialize in attending to individual needs and ways of learning that do not represent the utopian view of the "average" student, must understand about second language learning and bilingual education frameworks.

There are only a few programs in the United States that address these overlapping forms of difference in the preparation of teachers (Wang & Woolf, 2015). Most teacher preparation programs tend to focus on one branch of specialization only (i.e., special education) without connecting with other aspects that impact children's learning (i.e., bilingual education), and ideas developed within one field rarely cross over to other field or take very long to permeate through professional boundaries (see Martínez-Álvarez, 2022). There is also limited research in understanding how to best prepare teachers to address multiple layers of differences with bilingual children (Rueda & Stillman, 2012), but the need to better prepare professionals for the diverse, multicultural classroom has been raised (Gay, 2018; Wang & Woolf, 2015).

Preparing teachers to work in bilingual education with children with a disability is complicated by the different certification demands set by state departments of education and by the conflicting competences, theories, and concerns each field prioritizes (Gallegos & McCarty, 2000). For instance, while special education practices might recommend simplifying or structuring language input, bilingual education principles strive to provide whole language approaches, and the practice of fluently employing the two instructional languages to learn both language and content is pivotal (Cedillo & Covert, 2016; Spear-Swerling, 2006). Furthermore, special education is historically built on medicalized perspectives that prioritize remediation and skill-based instruction, but bilingual education emphasizes the sociocultural context and whole language approaches for learning (Cochran-Smith & Dudley-Marling, 2012). The need for ongoing collaboration where these historical differences are confronted and analyzed in depth when preparing teachers has been highlighted (Ochoa et al., 2014).

Practical experience in schools is one of the most important elements in a teacher preparation program (Ronfeldt et al., 2014). In preparing bilingual teachers to work with children with a disability, it is important that teacher candidates experience bilingual as well as inclusive contexts. While bilingual students with a disability might be taught in self-contained classrooms outside the regular education spaces, there are efforts to serve these children more inclusively. Bilingual classrooms serving children with and without a disability can take different forms, but they all require collaboration among educators (Martínez-Álvarez, 2020b). For instance, one way of serving bilingual children with a disability involves teachers with the special education certification acting as resource teachers, who come into different bilingual classrooms to serve the children with a disability. Other models involve a teacher with both childhood elementary and bilingual certifications leading a class of bilingual children with and without a disability alongside a teacher with the special education certification throughout the day. In this form of inclusive bilingual education, the two teachers work together in what is often referred to as an integrated co-teaching classroom (the ICT classroom model; see Hollinger [2021] for a review of the ICT model and related research). In these inclusive and bilingual classrooms, both teachers could even hold the childhood, the bilingual, and the special education certifications, so that labor can be distributed fluidly in balanced ways.

In bilingual classrooms serving children with a disability, the classroom teacher or teachers will sometimes collaborate with other professionals who organize additional opportunities to learn. For example, bilingual children with a disability might benefit from receiving speech and language or occupational therapy services, which requires collaboration among educators and could be conducted inclusively. That is, teaching children with a disability in bilingual education entails "strong collaborative" possibilities for the multiple educators involved (Hamayan et al., 2013, p. vi). Consequently, preparing teachers for making bilingual programs inclusive of children with a disability must allow teachers to work and experiment while teaching and learning alongside other professionals.

While it has become clear that teachers need to learn to work collaboratively, other competencies that are needed to prepare teachers for inclusive bilingual education have, up to now, not been fully defined. This is because teachers would need to learn content across the disciplines of bilingual education and special education. Furthermore, given the diversity of bilingual children with a disability and their varied ways of learning, it is important to highlight the role of teacher reflection in promoting equity education for all children and in actively negotiating instructional decisions while teaching (Daniels & Varghese, 2020; Tabak & Radinsky, 2015). Alongside the lack of teachers who are prepared to teach inclusively in bilingual education, the lack of inclusive approaches in bilingual programs aggravates the limited access for children with a disability to dual language bilingual programs. We must recognize the historical sociopolitical factors and misconceptions about children's (dis)abilities and be aware of policies that limit their possibilities to learn bilingually. The tension of the lack of inclusive approaches in bilingual programs is described in the following section.

LACK OF INCLUSIVE APPROACHES FOR BILINGUAL EDUCATION

The last cultural historical tension we currently experience in teaching bilingual children with a disability in the United States is the lack of inclusive high-quality bilingual programs. As described below, the tensions in bilingual education are rooted in sociopolitical processes that impact education. While research shows that bilingual education poses manifold benefits for bilingual children with or without a disability and causes no detriment to their development, in practice, bilingual children are being denied opportunities to learn in high-quality bilingual programs when they are identified with a disability.

The United States has a long history of resistance to bilingual education, that is, to having immigrants learn in their home languages while in school. More recently, this resistance has been revitalized as demographic shifts have taken place. Many in the United States felt threatened by this diversity, which led to a movement strengthening English-only ideologies (Pavlenko, 2002). Mediated by complex processes, including racism and monoglossic language ideologies (Flores & Rosa, 2015; Molinar-Arvizo, 2018), English-only policies were implemented in several states at the start of the 21st century. For example, Arizona voters passed Proposition 203 in 2000; its goal was to remove bilingual education programs aiming to teach in minoritized languages (see Fredricks & Warriner, 2016). Likewise, California passed Proposition 227 a few years earlier and Massachusetts approved a similar policy in 2002 restricting opportunities leading to bilingual and biliterate competence for immigrant children (see Kaveh & Sandoval, 2020).

Despite this historical legacy, bilingual education has grown in recent years. In particular, the availability of dual language bilingual education programs has increased over the last 20 years in the United States (Liebtag & Haugen, 2015). Dual language bilingual education programs employ two languages for learning content and this is maintained, at least, throughout the elementary school experience (Howard et al., 2018). These programs distribute the language of instruction in different ways depending on the community's needs (Howard et al., 2003). Dual language bilingual classrooms can include both language learners who speak the minoritized language at home, and those who speak the majority language (i.e., English in the United States) at home, in the same classrooms (two-way programs), or mostly English speakers (one-way programs; Williams Fortune & Tedick, 2008). The emphasis of dual language bilingual education is bilingualism and biliteracy with a cross-cultural focus and strong academic attainment (Palmer, 2007). This contrasts with other bilingual programs such as early-exit bilingual programs, which are transitional in nature because they evolve into English-only education by 3rd grade, providing short-term and restricted access to learning in children's minority language (McCarty, 2012).

Researchers have highlighted how dual language bilingual education is the best option for language learners in our public schools (Genesee, 1994). Well-implemented dual language bilingual programs have for years been shown to provide multifaceted benefits for all, and particularly for bilingual children (e.g., Brisk, 2006; Gómez et al., 2005; Lindholm-Leary, 2001; Thomas & Collier, 2002). For instance, when learning in dual language bilingual programs, children obtain better educational outcomes including language competence, bilingual identities, and positive attitudes toward learning, and they tend to be reclassified as English proficient more often than those learning in English only (Collier & Thomas, 2004). Children's bilingualism can also promote several cognitive aspects connected to learning, such as divergent thinking or creativity (European Commission, 2009), communicative competence (Fan et al., 2015), metalinguistic awareness (Barac & Bialystok, 2012), or executive function (Bialystok & Martin, 2004).

As bilingual children are identified with a disability, opportunities to learn, or continue to learn, in dual language bilingual programs diminish. Research shows that language planning is not always discussed at meetings where the individualized educational plan (IEP), the legal document developed for every child who needs special education, is created (Mueller et al., 2004). As children's disability-related language learning trajectories surface in bilingual families, there is a tendency to search for the cause of perceived difficulties. Unfortunately, children's bilingualism is at times blamed for language delays; parents might be discouraged from maintaining their child's bilingualism, and professionals might recommend English-only learning classrooms (e.g., Kim, 2017; Kohnert et al., 2005; Yu, 2013). Against these common practices, the existing literature suggests that learning bilingually and maintaining their two languages is possible for children with a disability (see Martínez-Álvarez, 2018).

The lack of opportunities to learn bilingually that children with a disability experience is exacerbated by the lack of support systems that attend to the different needs of the bilingual child with a disability. Language learning and special education services are guided by separate policies, resulting in processes that fail to consider both layers of difference (Cioè-Peña, 2017; Schissel & Kangas, 2018). The scarcity of teachers who are certified to teach both childhood elementary and bilingual education and to teach students with a disability mentioned earlier is related to this lack of inclusive approaches in bilingual education (Martínez-Álvarez, 2018). Bilingual programs might not have enough educators that can attend to the varied needs of children with a disability who are language learners, so families are placed in the position of choosing between the multiple identities of their child (Cobb, 2015; Delgado, 2008; Genesee, 2007).

The three cultural historical tensions of disproportionality, lack of integrated teacher preparation programs, and lack of inclusive approaches in bilingual education manifest in a discriminatory process that is taking place in bilingual education for children with a disability. These tensions must be addressed to progress toward the vision of inclusion embraced in the current law guiding special education services, the 2004 IDEA. The law requires equal, free, and appropriate educational opportunities and least restrictive learning environments for children with disabilities. This cannot be achieved if bilingual children are forced to choose between bilingual education and special education as they are identified with a disability. Given the need to create and promote inclusive bilingual education programs and based on the current issues that need to be addressed, I next describe what bilingual education inclusive of children with a disability can look like in our public schools.

BILINGUAL EDUCATION: A SPACE INCLUSIVE OF CHILDREN WITH A DISABILITY

Inclusive bilingual education refers to "the education pertaining to [emergent bilinguals] and [emergent bilinguals] with disabilities within dual language bilingual classrooms" (Martínez-Álvarez, 2020b, p. 305). While this definition might seem straightforward, ensuring inclusive approaches in bilingual education involves several institutional level requirements, alongside strong teacher preparation programs. (Additional information about these different organizational levels can be accessed in other publications that have paved the way for this book, such as Martínez-Álvarez, Under Review, 2020b, and 2022.) This section focuses on aspects directly connected to the classroom experience and the elements that can assist in making bilingual classrooms inclusive of children with a disability.

In imagining inclusive bilingual education and building on the needs highlighted by the cultural-historical tensions earlier identified, I recommend ensuring that schools have dual language programs for all their children rather than having a bilingual stream alongside a non-bilingual stream within their buildings. Likewise, all classrooms should have a co-teaching approach where two teachers work together to serve all children with and without a disability, without creating spaces designed solely for children without a disability or solely for children with a disability. Some ideas for tools and sources that can assist educators and researchers in achieving this follow. The ICT model earlier mentioned could work well for initially extending inclusive bilingual education, but ensuring all classes are equally inclusive, rather than having one class per grade level that serves children with a disability, should be the aim for bilingual schools. Imagining more flexible class arrangements instead of always working by grade level can assist in making the space more inclusive for diverse children as well (i.e., mixed grade classrooms; Martínez-Álvarez, 2022).

Inclusive bilingual classroom instruction must be grounded in culturally relevant and responsive asset-based perspectives (Gay, 2018; Ladson-Billings, 1995), and facilitate hybrid spaces where various cultural practices and knowledges dialectically connect, qualitatively transforming each other (Bhabha, 1994). The inclusive bilingual school curriculum should become a hybrid where home and community knowledge and various literacies and modalities are fostered (Lizárraga & Gutiérrez, 2018; New London Group, 1996). Learning spaces that are hybrid in different cultural practices and knowledges but also in ability allow for permeability across labels and are necessary for inclusive bilingual classrooms. In such hybrid spaces there is potential for "opportunity encounters," as children can fluidly inhabit different ways of being and learning (Martínez-Álvarez, 2020a, p. 3). These encounters might be activities where children can experience being both novices and experts, or language learners and language proficient, within a single period. In these spaces children can enact agency, compensating, to change the direction of the proposed activity toward more successful learning experiences. These practices have the potential to dismantle ableist, assimilationist, and remedial efforts, promoting instead spaces where children learn and inhabit different identities rather than being fixedly situated based on external factors.

Individualized educational plans are developed with extensive input from children's family members and are used to prioritize bilingualism and biliteracy, which are understood as assets within reach of all children. The importance of providing children solid practice in the minority language and in English must be salient in the IEP. Likewise, there need to be spaces for strategic use of translanguaging for mediating high-quality learning experiences for all learners (García, 2009; Martínez-Roldán, 2015). These practices will combine with efforts to foster bilingual and bicultural identities as well as disability identities. In doing so, children can experiment, fluidly fostering strong communities where interdependence rather than independence is promoted (Martínez-Álvarez, Under Review).

Classrooms will center universal design for learning, promoting multiple forms of engaging, representing, and expressing information (Center for Applied Special Technology [CAST], 2018); they will also foster critical work that engages children and their families in recognizing their oppressive circumstances. Freire (1993) referred to such a process of critical awakening to the social, political, and historical circumstances that have led to oppressive conditions as *conscientization*. Inclusive bilingual classrooms will monitor children's response to intervention (RtI) that is culturally and linguistically relevant, and act upon the results by implementing changes to the conditions of learning. Dynamic forms of assessing (Grigorenko, 2009), through which child and adult collaborate to surface knowledge about what they have indeed been taught, and opportunities for self-assessment should be part of the inclusive bilingual space.

The chapters in this book provide examples from the Varied Ways of Knowing (VWK) afterschool program that illustrate some of these different aspects and elements directly connected to the classroom inclusive bilingual learning experience.

CHAPTER 2

Assumptions and Theories in the Varied Ways of Knowing Project

Through my work preparing candidates for teaching in inclusive bilingual education contexts, I realized that the difficulties with learning that many Latinx students experience in school are rooted in the ingrained lack of connectivity across aspects of their lives (i.e., languages, content, knowledge, or spaces). With my input, the program faculty created a new plan of studies in the Program in Bilingual/Bicultural Education to prepare teachers to become aware of issues such as the need to validate and integrate children's resources, and to encourage them to create better learning experiences for bilinguals with a disability. The new program also established a pathway for candidates to work toward the different certifications needed to teach across different settings where bilingual children can learn as they are identified with a disability. That is, teachers graduating from the program could teach in an inclusive bilingual classroom, in a bilingual classroom, in an English-only inclusive classroom, or in a special education context.

To assist teacher candidates in engaging in individual and collective reflection while completing field work and student teaching experiences, I organized an afterschool program called *Formas Variadas de Saber*, or *Varied Ways of Knowing* (VWK). The VWK aimed to better understand how things could be otherwise in schools and to explore the porosity across spaces and disciplines, languages and knowledges, and Latinx children's ways of learning. The rich learning experience created by this afterschool program, which involved bilingual children and bilingual children with a disability, teacher candidates, and professors from the Program in Bilingual/Bicultural Education, helped candidates in exploring outside the constraints of the regular school day as they learned to become teachers. The following excerpt, written by one of the participating teacher candidates, provides a good introduction for this book as it evidences the breakthrough of our humble collective work:

> There were a lot of rainbows, clouds, random arrangements of objects, and hearts. Daniel was cutting a heart with Silvia. When I pushed him a little to say what made him feel good/happy, he said: "a hug from

> my mom" which was so amazing to hear! It has been interesting to see how, at the end of the day, they end up doing what they want in their projects, sometimes regardless of the topic or instructions [. . .] [W]hat has come up while they work has been most rewarding. This has got me thinking that maybe our role should be more of providers of material and activities that are inviting and interesting to them, to then engage them in conversation that will provide us with valuable information about their funds of knowledge. We can "evoke" instead of "prompt." Of course, how we initiate our sessions would still need to be thought of with care and planning. But sometimes it feels like we are trying really hard to come up with a lesson and connect language, culture and the goal of what we would like for them to learn. And more often than not, the results that surprise us the most, is unexpected and evoked by the activity, or has come up in conversation while they are doing the activity [Perla's learning notes; Day 3 of Capas y Escudos].

With these words, Perla (all names are pseudonyms), one of the teacher candidates in the VWK, powerfully described the nature of the learning experience crafted through the chapters in this book. In this excerpt, she captured the process of designing hybrid spaces (in terms of languages, cultures, or forms of meaning making) in our work. Hybrid spaces that embrace humanizing pedagogies surfaced in VWK as tools to support the collective motive of advancing toward inclusive learning for those in the program. Granting instructional value to children's agentive actions while learning allows for experiences between knowledges, disciplines, and spaces, and these crossings of boundaries suggest the permeability of the labels assigned to children in schools.

This book illustrates how certain experiences in the VWK that are described in Chapter 5 as "hybrid humanizing pedagogical moments" created opportunities for children to surface ideas about their knowledge, experiences, and aspirations across social spaces. Rooted in the assumption that bilingual children must be recognized as the "experts of their own lives" (Irizarry, 2016, p. 8), the collaborative work that took place in the VWK afterschool program highlighted the importance of spaces where educators negotiate approaches for humanizing interpretations guided by the centrality of children's agency and their varied ways of knowing and learning.

Before delving into the chapters that illustrate the findings that came out of the VWK afterschool program, this chapter introduces the main theories driving this work. Specifically, the VWK is built upon ideas from cultural historical activity theory (CHAT) and disability studies in education (DSE), and uses several constructs that have been conceived within these frameworks.

ASSUMPTIONS GROUNDING THE VARIED WAYS OF KNOWING PROJECT

The VWK afterschool program at the heart of this book was built upon several theoretically grounded premises and assumptions: first, that all children deserve opportunities to maintain their languages and grow to be bilingual and biliterate; second, that learning takes place as much outside as inside schools, and that it is important to put these different knowledges in conversation with one another; and finally, that all children can learn bilingually when the learning context is purposefully designed to attend to all their learning identities in balanced ways. Consequently, for bilingual children with a disability to succeed in school, a concerted effort involving not only the child with a disability, but also the learning context, including those in charge (i.e., teachers among others), is crucial.

Traditional historical topics that overlap in bilingual education and in teaching students with a disability, such as assimilation, ableism, identity, agency, or humanistic pedagogies, can contribute to better understanding children placed within labels that don't fit them well. These children are exposed to multiple layers of difference, none of which should be dismissed, but which cannot be considered in isolation from each other. Hence, unique approaches must be developed to better understand bilinguals with a disability and their learning across social spaces. This book aims to illuminate the uniqueness of these learners to help prepare caring, invested teachers. The book can also assist researchers aiming to understand how diverse children learn and how best to prepare teachers for complex educational contexts. Furthermore, the book looks at aspects of teaching and learning with children at the intersection of differences, including how disability can be situated as an asset similar to other human differences, such as being bilingual and bicultural.

THEORETICAL IDEAS GUIDING THE PROJECT: A HYBRID AFTERSCHOOL PROGRAM SPACE

The VWK afterschool program was designed as a hybrid space in reference to language, culture, and disability. That is, in reference to language, while teacher candidates primarily used the minoritized language, Spanish, children's communication efforts in any language were welcome. Translanguaging, or the hybrid use of meaning-making while communicating that goes beyond languages to include multiple modes, was hence understood as part of the creative efforts of bilinguals to make meaning and communicate and was analyzed through an asset-based lens (García & Otheguy, 2020).

The program was also hybrid in terms of cultural knowledge. The VWK centered on surfacing and employing children's cultural and historical funds of knowledge (Moll, 2014) for learning additional content and engaging in literacy practices. When teachers document and validate children's cultural resources or funds of knowledge and use them in instruction, interpersonal processes of what Moll (2014) calls "convivencia," or "a mode of conviviality based on forming relations of trust through interpersonal communications between teachers and families" (p. 117), a hybrid space is inhabited. For example, children in the afterschool made decisions about important things to place inside a box that helped them think about the different facets of their identities as part of the Lados de Mí (Sides of Me) Project. Mothers and siblings joined in and they shared about cultural artifacts and assisted the children in making decisions. Similarly, children in the VWK program brought exploratory tasks home, for example by using a digital video and still camera to gather information from their families and by creating conversations about family knowledge in the home and in the community. These experiences exposed knowledge that had been walled out of school and brought it into the educational realm to be used and developed and enjoyed by teachers and students together.

Lastly, in hybridity in reference to disability, children's learning identity in the VWK program was situated as being fluid, and opportunities for experiencing their various identities were purposefully designed (i.e., the Lados de Mí [Sides of Me] Project). This is essential for children who are dually identified (i.e., are labeled as ELLs and as having a disability) as their labels are often fixed, while children's identities are variable. For instance, children could experience what it feels like to be an expert or a novice, a language learner or a bilingual individual, and spaces in between, during the same afterschool program session. This was accomplished in the VWK program as children explored topics that were relevant to them (i.e., Disability Rights Movement Exploration, where they learned about the movement but also designed their ideal inclusive classroom with LEGO pieces), and as they became invested, they took action, enacting agency in ways that built upon and maximized each other's resources. That is, children enacted agency to find pathways to successful learning experiences as they worked with others (Martínez-Álvarez, 2020a).

In one instance during the work in this project, children shared that sometimes they were not understood when speaking or could not explain themselves well for others. They explained how they were at times taking action to defend themselves or how they "put some[thing] random" when asked a question for which they had to give a response. As their strategies and knowledge were recognized and recast as valuable, children could be seen and saw themselves as holders of knowledge and wisdom-bearers. In these kinds of moments, children experienced first being learners, then becoming experts.

Distributed Expertise and Ableism

Distributed expertise, or the "capacity for working with others to strengthen purposeful responses to complex problems," is important in this context (Edwards et al., 2010, p. 31). The idea that learning involves working with others and realizing what each brings to the collective activity is emphasized, from DSE perspectives, as a form of work that relies more on "a relational process of interdependency" than on ideals of independence (Greenstein, 2016, p. 112). The emphasis on independence in public schools in the United States originates in images of learners that resemble what is understood as being "normal." Such emphasis is an effort to assimilate diverse children into the learning experience of White monolingual children who do not have a disability (Slee, 1997).

Historically, education has focused on intervening to "remediate" children who do not align with this image of the ideal average learner so that they could "approximate the norm as much as possible" (Greenstein, 2016, p. 19). This ratifies certain forms of ability as belonging in schools while discriminating against other forms of learning and hierarchically distinguishing between being able or disabled, a process referred to as ableism. Ableism is "rooted in the ideology of normalcy" and it refers to practices that devalue forms of learning and moving that are distant from the ideal of the "average" (Reid & Knight, 2006, p. 19).

When children with a disability cannot match the expectations for independence imagined as being the ideal in education contexts, they are taken elsewhere to a segregated or self-contained space so that they can be cared for (Ware, 2002). From a disability studies perspective, Linda Ware (2002) demands that we "move beyond overly deterministic normalizing discourses of cure and care," challenging educators to "*imagine disability otherwise*" (p. 146). This call for reimagining disability should align with seeing the possibilities that disability brings to the learning space.

Compensation and Fluid Learning Identities

The process of reimagining disability includes Vygotsky's (1993) idea of *compensation* as the way children will agentively take action to change the direction of a learning activity that is not working well for them because of their disability. This can only take place, however, in "opportunity encounters," or hybrid spaces where children might encounter potential barriers, but still move forward toward successful learning spaces as they "were given the opportunity to compensate for their difficulties by enacting different forms of agency" (Martínez-Álvarez, 2020a, p. 4). Allowing children to compensate by mediating their learning-enacting agency recognizes disability and allows for the shifts that are necessary in the instructional space. This process can also be understood as "re-mediation" or mediating one's activity, with the help of a supportive context, through multiple forms of artifacts or tools (Gutiérrez et al., 2009, p. 227). Re-mediation consequently involves hybrid approaches, "a social imagination oriented toward new forms of collective activity and new uses of the technologies of reading and writing" (Gutiérrez et al., 2009, p. 237).

Hybrid spaces foster opportunities for learning as humans intentionally place differing forms of knowing and knowledge in conversation, qualitatively and mutually transforming them (i.e., the individuals and the forms of knowing and knowing) as they take action to surpass initial contradictions (Bhabha, 1994). Hybrid spaces invite and embrace various ways of engaging in literacy involving multiple modes and creative languaging forms (Gutiérrez, 2008; Lizárraga & Gutiérrez, 2018; New London Group, 1996). Similarly, hybrid spaces allow for experimentation with simultaneously occurring identities that might fluidly evolve as children participate in learning invitations (Lizárraga & Gutiérrez, 2018). Such exploration is important for bilingual children with a disability, as it will support a process of conscientization, or learning to realize that their individual experiences are connected to a larger process of oppression and discrimination, which others like them live through (Freire, 1993). Fluid identity exploration can assist diverse children to "better understand themselves, the world and their relations with others in the world, while taking into account the full range of human embodiments and support needs" (Greenstein, 2016, p. 5).

The Path to Conocimiento

Considering the histories of racism and discrimination in the United States, and the long-standing resistance to bilingual education, work in hybrid spaces necessarily involves a level of individual struggle as one enters the uncomfortable space of unfamiliarity around ideas that touch us personally. However, as productive experiences involving collective work are organized, people can enter a pathway toward healing where learning in between forms of knowing and knowledge can take place in multiple directions. This pathway of skillful, sophisticated resistance to assimilationist pressures is described by Gloria Anzaldúa (2002) as the path to "conocimiento" (p. 542). This is a Spanish word that carries two meanings. On one hand, "conocer" in Spanish is a verb that means to meet someone, and on the other hand "conocimiento" is connected to knowledge and wisdom. Learning within hybrid spaces involves a level of uneasiness that connects to these two meanings and that, with respect and validation, can transform into the healing necessary for meaningful learning experiences. For example, as part of the Me as a Learner collage project, children in the VWK created a collage with photographs they had taken and added drawings, post-it notes, and words to illustrate their own learning histories. While working on creating the collage in this hybrid space, Deyanira described her struggle and her anger. These feelings were around her initial learning experiences in kindergarten with writing. She also expressed some hope as she tried to explain that while writing is extremely hard for her, she can now draw as a way to make meaning and communicate. As Deyanira tries to figure out how learning works for her, she enters the path of conocimiento. Just as Galvin (2003) explained how learning to recognize and value disability as part of one's existence can assist in the process of conscientization, learning to be proud of being bilingual and of carrying knowledge that crosses national boundaries must be an important part of learning in hybrid inclusive bilingual spaces. While working in this project, Deyanira was doing both—recognizing her disability and her bilingualism and biculturalism.

Zones of Proximal Development and Boundary Crossing

When taking a cultural-historical view, hybridity can be understood as a space in-between where there is dialogical exchange from which, through exploration and commitment, something new surfaces (Bhabha, 1994, 1996). Such learning takes place along a zone of proximal development that is achieved through actions that are individually enacted but that impact the collective learning experience (Gutiérrez, 2008). Vygotsky (1978) used the idea of the zone of proximal development (ZPD) to explain the long-term learning process individual children go through while developing with the assistance of mediating artifacts and knowledgeable others. However, more recent theoretical work shifts the focus toward the collective activity by analyzing the actions individuals take when experiencing some form of tension while working with others, resulting in a new direction for their shared activity. As people working together encounter contradictions, they experience a "conflict of motives" that acts as a first stimulus to act using an artifact that they select; this artifact acts as a second stimulus, to mediate a new direction for the activity as it is implemented (Sannino, 2015, p. 2). This Vygotskian (1978) process of double stimulation begins with the conflict of motives, which then stimulates the selection of the artifact and the decision-making involved in deciding how to use it, and the final action of using the artifact to address the initial conflict. When this process is fully implemented, there is potential for "transformative agency" as participants convert the conflict of motives they experience into more productive experiences for themselves and others (Sannino, 2015, p. 2). For instance, when children were asked to use clay to represent Manhattan as it was 500 years ago (i.e., the original Mannahatta, as it was called back then), they shifted the direction of the activity and decided to work with the clay in exploratory ways that were not always readily connected to this initial invitation. For instance, one child created a telegraph and another one included a Pokémon as part of their designs. The new space created by their decision allowed them to engage with new artifacts in the form of images they had brought from home and to engage in meaningful conversations.

From this perspective, the ZPD is the "distance between the present everyday actions of the individuals and the historically new form of the societal activity that can be collectively generated as a solution to the double bind potentially embedded in everyday actions" (Engeström, 1987, p. 174). Hybrid spaces hold potential for expansion across a collective ZPD as different forms of learning, knowledge, or practices interact and collide, altering each other. The learning process that follows a sequence of phases that promote actions from individuals as they encounter contradictions, changing their collective activity, is referred to in CHAT as *expansive learning* (Engeström, 1987). Expansive learning requires the crossing of different types of boundaries. *Boundaries* is used in this book to indicate artificial separations across aspects that are represented as dichotomies but are, rather, parts of a continuum. Moments when boundaries are crossed can be opportunities for expansive learning (Engeström, 2001). The VWK explored different types of boundaries, including boundaries between forms of knowledge and practices across cultures and spaces, between disciplines like science or art, and between formal or informal learning spaces.

Critical Agency and Hybrid Humanizing Pedagogical Moments

According to DSE, the capacity to enact agency requires a humanizing pedagogical perspective that embraces "expanded definitions of 'agency'" and "radical notions of what it means to be a 'critical' human being" so that agentive efforts can be recognized and fostered (Erevelles, 2000, p. 32). The ways through which children with a disability enact agency, which can take different forms (e.g., resisting, shifting the direction of the learning activity, acting out, or using augmentative forms of communication), need to be recognized as meaningful opportunities for learning, and they should be fostered in the hybrid space. In the VWK afterschool program, there were multiple instances when hybridity and humanizing pedagogies were enacted and recognized in processes through which these were simultaneously cultivating and nurturing each other. These instances were part of the findings reported in this book and were referred to as "hybrid humanizing pedagogical moments." For instance, during the Capas y Escudos (Capes and Shields) Project, one boy noticed that one of the students from the VWK program, Ana, was going to arrive late. As part of a humanistic approach and in a manifestation of agency, he took action to share this information with others in the program. As Ana arrived, he initiated the process of helping her understand what was happening during that session.

That is, in order to be transformative, different forms of agency need to be recognized and valued. Researchers have elucidated, for instance, the ways children are capable of recognizing how others can be resources for their learning and hence "align [their] thoughts and actions with those of others," which is called *relational agency* (Edwards, 2005, pp. 169). When this ability, at times positioned as copying or needing help, is reformulated from an asset viewpoint, then the child can be understood as productively learning alongside others as they engage in dual tasks to "offer support to and ask for support from others" (Edwards & Mackenzie, 2005, p. 294). Figure 2.1 shows the theoretical constructs in the VWK project at a glance.

This book employs these different theoretical constructs, which have historically been present in the fields of bilingual and bicultural education and teaching students with dis/abilities, to explore topics that surface in the analysis of work and conversations from the VWK project. The constructs contribute to illuminate the topics that overlap in bilingual education and teaching students with a disability and that include assimilation, ableism, identity, agency, and humanistic pedagogies. Raising awareness around the importance of these ideas can contribute to better understanding about how to create high-quality learning spaces for bilingual children and bilingual children with a disability. The last section of this chapter describes the VWK afterschool program and the other components in the project.

Figure 2.1. Theoretical Constructs in the Varied Ways of Knowing Project

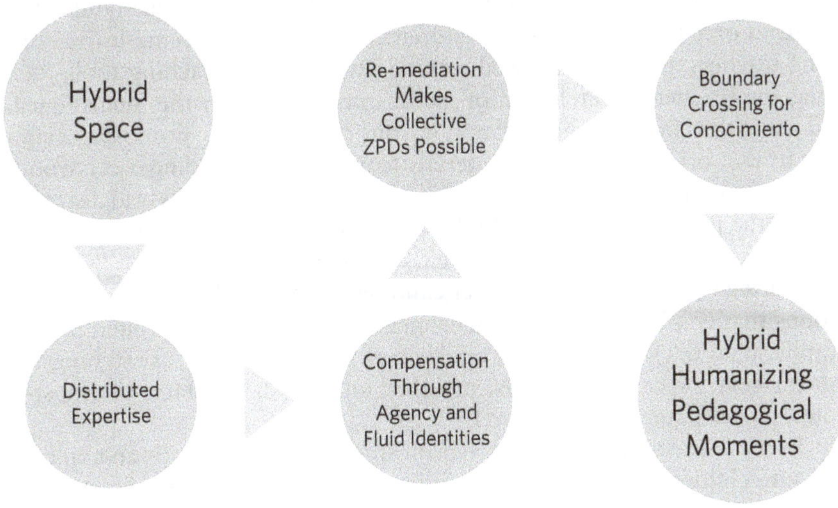

THE VARIED WAYS OF KNOWING PROJECT

The VWK project involved teacher candidates in designing an afterschool program with bilingual children, observing the children during the school day, writing individual reflection notes, and participating in collective reflection/planning meetings once a week. The afterschool program organized as part of the VWK project met for 2-hour sessions once or twice a week depending on the year, and the study lasted for 3 years. The program was designed and implemented by teacher candidates preparing to become bilingual teachers working alongside the professor researcher (author) from the program where they were completing their studies. Dr. Belinda Arana, another instructor and a sutdent teaching supervisor in the program, and SooJin Jeon, a doctoral candidate and an instructor in the program also contributed at various times.

As already mentioned, the afterschool program was conceptualized as a hybrid space. For example, children dynamically moved across languages (i.e., using Spanish, English, or both simultaneously) and the program purposefully recognized and validated other languages such as the presence of Mexican Mixteco in children's homes. Teacher candidates and children also employed different modes within any one session for expressing, demonstrating, or presenting knowledge and practices. These were used as needed for assisting meaning-making and for allowing children to explore spaces where they would feel like experts and novices, or like language learners and bilinguals, within a single activity. This was mediated using children's funds of knowledge in the form of their own transnational expertise (Martínez-Álvarez, 2020a). For instance, children could be experts about terms across languages or across language varieties or from their knowledge about other countries or interests. At times, children could shift from being learners to being teachers and were allowed to take ownership of teaching tools (i.e., using the teacher's whiteboard or chair, interacting with the Smartboard, and using the computer mouse) and lessons or topics (i.e., proposing materials to use, bringing relevant materials from home, or adding a classroom learning center of their interest). To assist with creating hybrid learning spaces, the program provided children with digital photographic and video cameras as a mediator to capture their knowledge and interests.

During the sessions, the teacher candidates proposed instructional invitations that employed multimodal elements (i.e., digital and printed photographs, iPad devices for digital analysis of images and text, searching for information, or creating videos, or other multimodal artifacts like post-it notes, poster paper, markers, etc.).

Every year, the afterschool program started in the fall with an exploration into children's bilingual and bicultural learning identities (i.e., creating a Yo como Aprendiz or Me as a Learner collage [see Chapter 3]). These examinations included learning about different facets of one's identity and realizing the multiple layers that shape who we are (i.e., the Lados de Mí or Sides of Me project where children manifested their identities related to being learners and cultural beings, as participants in family memories and traditions, through the use of cultural artifacts, and as talented in various ways [see Chapter 4]). Explorations about differences of abilities and the relevance of inclusive spaces were part of the fall semester learning experiences (i.e., the Capas y Escudos or Capes and Shields Project invited children to center their strengths as well as their learning differences and those of others [see Chapter 5]). This work included learning about the role of disabled people during the Disability Rights Movement and considering how multiple artifacts mediate learning for themselves and others (i.e., the Derechos de las Personas con Discapacidad [Disability Rights Movement] Project [see Chapter 6]).

The VWK instructional invitations shifted to an emphasis on children's identities as scientists during the spring semester. The projects also included learning about science and investigating what counts as science and what scientists do. Eventually, the program centered on earth science and more specifically on learning invitations related to geoscience. The need for diversity in geoscience and for geoscientists in general, where a growth in employment opportunities has been reported (American Geological Institute, 2009), combined with the professor's prior experience motivated the decision to choose this area. Children of immigrant backgrounds can make multiple connections to their lives within geoscience. For instance, children have experiences with the land and with bodies of water and can explore the knowledge of family members about transnational landforms, increasing opportunities for connecting to existing FoK (Martínez-Álvarez, 2017b; Martínez-Álvarez & Bannan, 2014; Martínez-Álvarez & Hubard, 2015). For example, children in VWR explored home remedies to think about what counts as science and then transitioned to learning about past and present in New York City and the landmarks within and beyond the city to connect to their families' countries of origin (i.e., Contextos Relevantes para Ciencias y Accidentes Geográficos, or Relevant Contexts for Science and Landforms) lessons [see Chapter 7]). Children also learned about earthquakes around the world using multimodal materials they chose and considered the Spanish and English language transfer in this context (i.e., use of slime to demonstrate the movement of plate tectonics and the ideas behind the words "Cinturón de Fuego," literally meaning "Belt of Fire," which is used in Spanish to refer to the Ring of Fire [see Chapter 8]).

Every 2 to 4 sessions, one teacher candidate took the lead in writing out the lesson plan and acting as the main teacher for the day while the rest of the candidates took different roles throughout the lessons and facilitated the small-group work. Families were invited to actively participate in the program through the children's work with digital cameras that were sent home as well as by attending the afterschool session once a month as projects were being finalized. During these family visits, instructional activities were planned for family members to actively contribute. For example, family members were asked to bring a cultural artifact from home, describe a home remedy, showcase a handmade family project, or share their knowledge about landforms in their countries of origin as part of the different instructional invitations.

After every session, the teacher candidates were invited to individually reflect and to write their ideas about the experience in weekly learning notes. We then met for 2 hours each week for the reflective/planning meeting. For these meetings, the candidates shared and reflected collectively about the learning that took place in the session. This sharing took place in a format similar to lesson study where the leading candidate shared first and then each candidate offered their own ideas in a way that resembles systematic inquiry (Yoshida, 1999). The inquiry-based sharing aimed at better understanding what teaching and learning looked like in inclusive bilingual contexts and at surfacing children's knowledge and assets. The meeting also included a planning period when the candidates decided the next steps and instructional activities and prepared materials for the next session.

Chapter 3 provides more information about the methods of the study. This includes a description of the school where the VWK afterschool program took place, and the graduate teacher preparation program where the participating teacher candidates were completing their studies.

Documenting the Varied Ways of Knowing Project

When teaching, we come to realize that children know and come to know in various diverse ways. This idea inspired the name of the project at the center of this book, Formas Variadas de Saber, or Varied Ways of Knowing (VWK). The VWK project consisted of an afterschool learning experience comprising rich work in the form of audio files, written reflections, and photographic materials that were created with a total of 37 study participants (22 bilingual children with a disability, or without a disability label but with difficulty learning, and 15 teacher candidates). As part of the 3-year project, the teacher candidates codesigned an afterschool program for bilingual children with and without a disability, while meeting weekly with the professor, and 1 year with other instructors from the program. The regular meetings were dedicated to look at children's work, reflect about their practice, and discuss new directions (planning/reflection meetings). Most children and teacher candidates participated in the project for several consecutive years.

As mentioned in Chapter 2, the afterschool program was designed as a hybrid learning space along the dimensions of language, culture, and disability. Family members participated in the afterschool sessions once a month and fully contributed to the learning experience with their children and with the candidates. The teacher candidates also observed the children in their regular bilingual classrooms. The book captures the powerful experiences and learning that took place in the VWK afterschool program, the project at the center of every one of its chapters, so that it can be used as a tool for researchers, teacher candidates, and those working to prepare them for the intersectionality classroom.

For the book, I methodically looked at the body of work to better understand how the children mediated their own learning while working in the hybrid afterschool program. I also explored how the children's mediational efforts were connected to the collective components of activity, and to other sociocultural-related instructional aspects. The book reports the ideas that came out of this systematic exploration, illustrating them with work and conversation samples. Grounded in authentic teaching and learning experiences, it adds to the current understanding of how to create educational spaces that more respectfully and humanely address the needs of bilingual children and bilingual children with a disability in programs that foster lifelong bilingual and bicultural identities and aim for biliteracy.

This chapter presents the school contexts and participants, and an overview of the information collected and the process for systematically understanding the work created in the program.

THE ROLE OF THE INSTITUTION OF HIGHER EDUCATION

The VWK project was organized and implemented by a program of bilingual/bicultural education at a large private institution in the northeastern United States. The program had recently created a teacher preparation pathway for candidates to prepare to teach in inclusive bilingual education classrooms. This new stream promoted the creation of additional, less restrictive, experiences with bilingual children and bilingual children with a disability for the teacher candidates.

The program of studies was organized along 2 years and led to a master's degree in education and up to four teaching certifications (i.e., elementary childhood, middle school, bilingual extension, and teaching students with disabilities). As part of the program of studies, teacher candidates were exposed to both CHAT and DSE theoretical frameworks, the theory of multiple intelligences, the concept of multimodality, humanistic perspectives in learning, and research regarding the field of inclusive bilingual education. The candidates were often encouraged, and pathways were created, to make connections between theories and knowledge they were learning in their courses and the afterschool learning experiences. These pathways included the individual reflection, the reflective/planning meetings, and the completion of classroom projects within the afterschool program context.

The program is rooted in asset-based pedagogies that reject prevalent deficit-model thinking about minoritized children (see Gutiérrez & Rogoff, 2003). The learning experience of teacher candidates focuses on realizing the belief that all children can learn if contexts attend to their cultures, languages, and (dis)abilities (Martínez-Álvarez, 2014). The program provides experiences for teacher candidates to act not only as learners but also as researchers that learn from the children, families, and communities they serve in their practice.

THE VARIED WAYS OF KNOWING SCHOOL CONTEXT

The VWK afterschool program took place at the children's dual language bilingual elementary school, located at a diverse neighborhood near the institution of higher education. The school includes mostly children who speak

Spanish at home, with nearly 80% Hispanic (the term used to report school demographics) students; a high percentage of children qualify for free or reduced-price lunch, 30% are English language learners, and 28% have a disability. Given these demographics, this school was an excellent context for student teachers to explore teaching and learning with bilingual children and bilingual children with a disability.

The school fosters biliteracy for all students, including children with a disability. One class per grade level is an ICT (integrated co-teaching) space. This classroom model, described in Chapter 1, includes two teachers who together serve bilingual children and bilingual children with a disability throughout the day. Defined as a 50/50 bilingual program, the school dedicates equal amounts of instructional time teaching in Spanish and in English. Children learn one day fully in Spanish, and the next day fully in English; on Fridays, the instructional time is split between both languages of instruction. As a result, most subject areas are taught in both Spanish and English at this school, while art is always in Spanish and music is always in English.

VARIED WAYS OF KNOWING PROJECT: CHILDREN AND TEACHER CANDIDATES

There were 22 bilingual children and 15 teacher candidates working together in the VWK afterschool program along 3 years. The 22 bilingual children in the program were placed during the day in grades 2 through 5. The children were all Latinx of recent immigrant background and bilingual in Spanish and English. Specifically, students' families came from the Dominican Republic, Mexico, Chile, Guatemala, and Ecuador. All the bilingual children either had a disability as labeled in the school following IDEA (the law currently attending to the rights of children with disabilities) or were experiencing learning difficulties. Most of the children's disability labels were specific learning disability or speech and language impairment, while a few children were labeled with autism or other health impairments in relation to attention.

The 15 teacher candidates were in the first or second year of their program of studies and most of them had been born in the United States and were Latinx. Some of the candidates participated in the VWK afterschool program for 1 year while some did so for both of their 2 years of study. All candidates except for Carmina, who was in the program in teaching English as a second language, were enrolled in the graduate program in bilingual/bicultural education.

Most of the teacher candidates were of diverse backgrounds. Seven of the candidates (Adriana, Juán, Marina, Rita, Samantha, Sebastian, and Silvia) were U.S.-born within immigrant families from Latin America, and Patty was from Puerto Rico. Four candidates (Alicia, Diana, Perla, and Valeria) were first-generation immigrants from Latin America and one (Carmina) from Portugal. Two candidates, Isabella and Rachel, were the only ones who were U.S.-born with no immediate family connections to other countries.

DOCUMENTING LEARNING WITH BILINGUAL CHILDREN WITH AND WITHOUT A DISABILITY

The VWK project provided multiple opportunities for children to creatively and agentively engage in multimodal work. They generated products as they responded to the exploratory activities that the teacher candidates designed, and that are described in Chapters 4–9 under the rubric of Classroom Identity and Knowledge Exploration. Their work included multimodal products created with iPads, the Me as a Learner collage representing their learning identity, the Sides of Me project (a cube representing different sides of children's identities), the capes and shields showcasing strengths and differences made from different materials, and the inclusive classroom model with LEGO pieces. The students participated in whole-group and small-group conversations that were captured to understand their learning processes; children also submitted notebook entries from the afterschool program sessions.

Teacher candidates wrote weekly individual learning notes (typed text and images) capturing their reflections from the afterschool program and other ideas about teaching and learning in bilingual classrooms. There were about 80 to 90 learning notes per year where the teacher candidates wrote detailed but focused reflections in the form of observational notes. The learning notes varied but usually included candidates' insights about artifacts, mediation, disability and bilingualism/biculturalism, and the students' learning, (as well as their own) as they taught in the afterschool.

The weekly reflective/planning meetings with the teacher candidates were also audio-recorded as evidence of the learning experience. The candidates presented a mid-year exploratory project where they were invited to look deeply into the work and reflect about the learning of one of the children. They selected one student for this work based on the frequency of interactions they had with that particular child. They reviewed that child's work for the entire fall semester and answered the following questions during their exploratory work: What is the work telling you about the learning and the knowledge of this student? What does the student know? How is the afterschool program helping this child be their best as a learner? Candidates were invited to support their statements. They organized the results of their explorations using any format of their choice (i.e., Word document, PowerPoint, Prezi, etc.).

Lastly, the teacher candidates were interviewed at the end of every year of participation in the VWK project. The interview lasted about an hour and the questions were grouped into five sets addressing one of the following: (1) learning experience in the VWK program, (2) working with a few sessions in a row and the same small group of children, (3) areas of growth and learning for the candidate and children, (4) describing specific favorite sessions, and (5) their learning about the intersection of bilingualism and disability. The interview ended asking if there were any and other aspects that the candidate wanted to share about the program.

EXPLORING THE WORK OF THE CHILDREN AND THE TEACHER CANDIDATES

The exploration of the work and the conversations with children and teacher candidates during the project involved several rounds of looking across sources of information from various perspectives over time. We started analyzing children's work during our weekly planning/reflection meetings when we looked back at the learning experience during each of the sessions. At the end of every year, I worked with a research assistant to organize and review the work that had transpired during the different sessions of the afterschool program and meetings with teacher candidates. Inspired by constant comparative methods, the annual exploration included multiple stages (Strauss & Corbin, 1990). We created what we called instructional segments, or meaningful parts of the sessions, that related to the shared object of preparing teacher candidates and understanding teaching and learning with bilingual children and bilingual children with a disability. The segments could include discourse from the sessions or from the weekly follow-up meetings, and also images of children's work. In this way, the instructional segments were also multimodal. We then briefly described each of the segments based on content and connections we noticed with the shared object of the VWK project (open coding).

We later connected the initial descriptions to the theoretical ideas guiding the VWK project and new ideas (i.e., codes) were added to better capture the nature of the work as necessary. These ideas included, for instance, re-mediation or compensation, language choices and translanguaging, and manifestation of ableism (Martínez-Álvarez, 2020a).

At the end of the VWK project I used CHAT (cultural historical activity theory) as an analytical tool to further understand the previously identified meaningful segments. For this analysis, I worked with two colleagues in identifying the actions that children and teacher candidates took when confronted with a learning difficulty (i.e., "learning pauses," Martínez-Álvarez et al., 2020, p. 4). Learning pauses are those moments when the teacher candidates described how the ZPD was not achieved for a specific child; that is, when the existing artifacts were not successfully mediating children's learning and so there was a need to take action (identify and use a different artifact) to re-mediate the learning experience (Martínez-Álvarez et al., 2020). Once these learning pauses were selected, the processes (e.g., proposing a new artifact or supporting someone else's agentive actions) through which children and/or teachers re-mediated the difficulties were also extracted. The learning notes that the teacher candidates had written were important in helping to understand and contextualize the learning pauses.

Throughout the periods of systematic review of the work from the VWK project, I worked with research assistants to understand the work through discussion and create the meaningful segments. For each of these stages of systematic review, we created a manual with the names of the initial descriptors (i.e., codes) and added definitions and examples that we progressively finalized. Once the manual had been created, we attached the descriptors to the previously identified segments and then met to discuss our choices, compare descriptors we had assigned, and work out any disagreements, eventually agreeing on a descriptor for each.

Throughout these review processes, and during end-of-program interviews, I shared big ideas with the participating teacher candidates to obtain their feedback (Doyle, 2007). The interview and the mid-year presentation were used to confirm findings from the other sources.

For this book, I went back to the work that had been reviewed and reexamined all the information I had learned during the staged reviews. The chapters in this book highlight the ideas that surfaced from this final analysis stage and from my familiarity with the work in the project.

REFLECTING ON ROLES WHEN WORKING IN BILINGUAL CONTEXTS

When engaging in work with bilingual children with and without a disability, it is important to reflect about one's own experiences and their role and influence in the learning experience. I participated in the afterschool program and in the meetings with the teacher candidates and I was a professor in the program in BBE where the VWK project took shape, so this book is very close to my heart.

I was aware of the implications of my roles in the project and the privilege they granted me as I worked with the candidates and with the children. My position of power, as a professor who had taught most of the teacher candidates in the program, made me cautious of jumping in too quickly or providing too many ideas. Nonetheless, while participating in discussions and attending the afterschool program, I was aware of the impact this could have for the teacher candidates. As I worked with the teacher candidates, I realized that they were at times being careful about what they suggested and the insights they provided. Given the closeness and nature of our relationships that included my sway over their ability to graduate from their master's program, this is a limitation that needs to be acknowledged.

My experiences as an immigrant, as a Spanish speaker, and as a long-term bilingual teacher served as sources of knowledge. My mother is from Galicia, where the Gallego language is spoken; however, given the low status of the language, and other pressures at the time when I was growing up, I never learned this language. This experience resonates with other language hierarchies we see in the United States. Nevertheless, there were many aspects that differentiated my experience from those of the children, families, and teacher candidates in the project. For instance, I arrived in the United States as a young adult holding an undergraduate degree in education. I also arrived with documents that allowed me to safely remain in the country for 1 year, a process that could then be expanded. I aimed to remain aware during this study that the children and candidates in this study each had unique linguistic and cultural histories. Hence, while my practical and intellectual intuition were helpful, I strove to remain open to their own understandings and interpretations as they navigated the activities and learned about teaching in the project.

The last section of this chapter presents the questions explored within each of the remaining chapters and offers a brief introduction to the significance of each topic.

RELEVANT QUESTIONS AND ORGANIZATION OF THE CHAPTERS

The rest of this book is organized into seven additional chapters. Chapters 4 through 9 discuss different findings of the project, while Chapter 10 synthesizes the legacy of the VWK project by highlighting its contribution to the field of inclusive bilingual education. Chapters 4 through 9 each start with an introduction to one of the central topics identified in the analysis process. After an introductory overview, the question guiding the chapter is stated, followed by an exploration of the literature that addresses the central topic within the fields of bilingual and bicultural education and of disability studies. These chapters then use information from one VWK activity, alongside the work the children created, to illustrate ideas around the central topic. Activity invitations, geared at exploring the topic at the intersection of bilingual and bicultural education and disability studies, are included as Classroom Identity and Knowledge Exploration. The sample products from the participating bilingual children, as well as statements generated during the learning activity, are included to illustrate the types of responses one can expect from diverse elementary school–aged children. To guide the reader, I provide below a brief overview of each one of these main chapters.

Chapter 4 introduces the issue of ableism, which is typically connected to critical disability frameworks, and contextualizes it for bilingual and bicultural education. The chapter applies the concept of ableism to bilingual education by unpacking the ableism in metaphors used in bilingual schools.

The fluid complexity of the learning identities of bilingual children with a disability is illustrated using work from children who participated in the VWK afterschool project. The chapter explains the Classroom Intersectionality Connection 4.1, explaining the Yo como Aprendiz (Me as a Learner) collage. Using information from this classroom project, Chapter 4 addresses the question: How does ableism manifest in bilingual education contexts with children with a disability? Chapter 4 ends by concretizing the ways through which ableism is embedded in the culture of our educational systems. The conclusion of Chapter 4 is a call for systems to provide the services children need without having to label them as English language learners or disabled.

Chapter 5 explores the histories of assimilation that connect the immigrant and the disability experiences. To do this, the chapter describes the forms of oppression facing diverse children and the role of assimilation in these processes. The chapter introduces Classroom Identity and Knowledge Exploration 5.1, describing the Lados de Mí (Sides of Me) project. Work generated as part of this project is used to elucidate and discuss the question: How do historical assimilationist efforts manifest when teaching bilingual children with a disability and what opportunities toward inclusive designs might surface? The chapter recognizes that assimilationist efforts are still persistent in today's schools and highlights how emergent bilinguals with a disability might be deprived of linguistic and cultural rights (Skutnabb-Kangas & Phillipson, 2010). The conclusion highlights the importance of understanding our students as human beings who bring what they know and the practices they understand into the educational space.

Chapter 6 centers on humanistic approaches and how they have been taken up in the field of bilingual education and disability studies. The chapter addresses the question: How can a humanistic approach assist in making bilingual programs more inclusive of children with a disability? To help the reader explore this question, the chapter argues for the necessity of humanistic outlooks in the education of immigrant children with a disability and offers examples to understand how to take such a perspective in inclusive bilingual classrooms. The chapter introduces Classroom Identity and Knowledge Exploration 6.1 that describes the Capas y Escudos (Capes and Shields) project. Using products and conversations generated as children worked in the project, the chapter introduces what I refer to as "hybrid humanizing pedagogical moments." Such moments took place as hybridity and humanizing pedagogies occurred simultaneously, cultivating and nurturing each other. These moments are explained and illustrated with work samples throughout the chapter. The concluding sections of the chapter offer the idea of hybrid humanizing pedagogical moments as a tool that can potentially generate spaces for teachers and children to safely explore their multiple ways of being in the classroom and outside it.

Chapter 7 centers on advancing processes of conscientization with bilingual children with a disability. The chapter investigates the importance of identity work and learning about disability through the experiences that took place in the VWK afterschool program. The chapter introduces Classroom Identity and Knowledge Exploration 7.1, the Derechos de las Personas con Discapacidad (Disability Rights Movement) project. Employing work from a series of curricular invitations implemented as part of this classroom exploration, the chapter elucidates the question: What knowledge do bilingual children with a disability manifest while engaging in identity work and learning about disability, and what forms of agency surface as children explore multiple identity possibilities? The chapter shares insights worthy to be considered when teaching about the disability civil rights movement and when exploring children's disability identity. This chapter suggests that minoritized children who do not see certain forms of disability in their schools and classrooms will be surprised by, and curious about, them. From that stance, Chapter 7 proposes that having conversations about varied forms of moving and learning can assist in the process of expanding our understanding of the broad "range of human embodiments and support needs," which, as Greenstein (2016, p. 5) explained, mediates more radical inclusive pedagogies.

Chapter 8 is the first of two chapters addressing the learning of science content in inclusive bilingual education contexts. The chapter uses information from a series of four instructional sessions originally focused on science education but conceptualized from the perspective of expansive learning. It explores the idea of horizontal learning and the boundaries (of knowledges, disciplines, and formal/less formal spaces) that need to be crossed for creating inclusive bilingual spaces. The chapter delves into the question: How does boundary crossing manifest in a hybrid science learning space with bilingual children with and without a disability, and what possibilities for expansive learning surface in this space? Chapter 8 introduces Classroom Identity and Knowledge Exploration 8.1, titled Contextos Relevantes para Ciencias y Accidentes Geográficos (Relevant Contexts for Science and Landforms) lessons. Using work and conversations generated as part of this classroom exploration, the chapter aims to contribute to more comprehensive ways of understanding knowledge and learning with bilingual children with and without a disability.

Lastly, Chapter 9 builds on the ideas introduced in Chapters 6, 7, and 8 to center the critical role artifacts play in inclusive bilingual education. The chapter ellucidates the role of artifacts in mediating hybrid and humanizing pedagogy for expansive content learning opportunities that can lead to identity formation. To do this, the chapter discusses the artifact mediation and re-mediation that needs to occur in inclusive bilingual learning spaces. Chapter 9 explores the following question: What forms of artifact re-mediation are generated in a bilingual science learning space and what can we learn from the analysis of artifact-mediated activity about teaching bilingual children with and without a disability? The chapter employs information from the Terremotos, Placas Tectónicas, y el Cinturón de Fuego (Earthquakes, Plate Tectonics, and the Ring of Fire) project, described in Classroom Identity and Knowledge Exploration 9.1. Through this project, the chapter illuminates the reasons through which, as a result of persistent lack of successfully mediated learning opportunities, bilingual children are often portrayed as failing academically. The chapter ends by highlighting the need to understand children's interests and knowledge as central to the learning of content and as a continuation of canonical knowledge rather than separate from it.

The closing Chapter 10 then reviews the implications of the main constructs discussed in this book for research and for teacher preparation programs (i.e., ableism, assimilation, humanistic pedagogies, learning as a mediational effort, and dialectical relationships between content and language integrated learning). The chapter concludes with a view toward the ways inclusive bilingual education can and must continue to expand as a tool to provide equity education for all children.

I hope the reader finds the chapters helpful in uncovering new ways of understanding the learning of bilingual children with and without a disability, and that this book generates creative and innovative ideas that foster respectful research projects.

The Issue of Ableism in Bilingual and Bicultural Education

Schools have traditionally been organized around the image of an ideal, or average, learner. Such learner is White, speaks the language of instruction at home, is of middle-class economic status, and easily learns to read and write to then acquire new information using their literacy skills. However, this image of the "average" student, promoted by biased intelligence test results and tools such as the bell curve, is a myth (Dudley-Marling & Gurn, 2010). Parents, teachers, and even children understand that we are all very diverse. However, educational systems continue to perceive difference as a threat and respond to it with labels, remediation, and segregation among other discriminatory practices (Annamma et al., 2018). Issues of difference are most salient in highly intense urban contexts, where there are large numbers of students with "a wide range of academic, linguistic, psychological, social, and emotional needs" (Howard & Milner, 2014, p. 202). In fact, in today's complex urban school districts in the United States, such as New York City or Los Angeles, children might in fact carry more than one layer of difference. As a result, some children are identified in educational systems with two or more labels, or are dually identified, with each label involving separate and often contradictory services and policies (Cioè-Peña, 2017).

Children are indeed diverse, and attending to their diversity requires careful understanding of children's needs and the implementation of radical changes in our classrooms. However, educational systems are not typically designed for those who carry multiple forms of difference. The labels, policies, funding, and other rules meant to regulate the ways in which dually identified children are served can cause unintended consequences, such as children experiencing multiple forms of oppression (Crenshaw, 1991). In fact, there are more than 350,000 children who are emergent bilinguals, labeled as English language learners (ELLs) in public schools in the United States, and identified with a disability (Abedi, 2014). Latinx bilingual children labeled with a disability are often placed in more restrictive learning contexts than White monolingual children with the same disability (Skiba et al., 2006). For example, Latinx children identified with a disability might not be allowed to learn in dual language bilingual programs (Kangas, 2017; Martínez-Álvarez, 2018).

As introduced in Chapter 1, dual language is a form of bilingual education where children learn literacy and content in two languages and that aims for "multicultural competence for all students" (Howard et al., 2007, p. 1). As such, a dual language program is an additive bilingual program aiming for bilingualism and biliteracy (Medina, 2017). Learning in additive bilingual programs poses numerous advantages for any child, but its benefits are most salient for Latinx students who speak Spanish in the home and experience bicultural worlds throughout their lives (Collier & Thomas, 2004; Umansky & Reardon, 2014). Research has been showing that children learning in dual language programs become more proficient bilingual speakers, demonstrate more positive attitudes about learning and about their own identities, and develop multiple cognitive and communicative strengths (e.g., Fan et al., 2015; Umansky & Reardon, 2014; Woumans et al., 2015). Additionally, there is emerging empirical work suggesting that children with a disability can indeed learn bilingually and that this causes no additional detriment to their learning and development (see Martínez-Álvarez, 2018, for a literature review).

A related aspect when teaching and learning with children who are dually identified is the deficit discourses their labels carry. In reference to the ELL label, the United States has a history of racism, where languages other than English and related cultures are perceived as inferior (Valencia, 1997). Research has revealed the value of the funds of knowledge that families with immigration histories carry, but these FoK are often not recognized in school curricula and are not well integrated in formal instruction (e.g., Buxton et al., 2015; Calabrese Barton & Tan, 2009; González & Moll, 2002). Hence, emergent bilingual children, also labeled ELLs, tend to underperform in regular school-related assessment, and are consequently perceived as not doing well academically across content areas (Griffith, 2010). In fact, across states, emergent bilinguals tend to have a lower graduation rate than monolingual children. For instance, in New York State, the high school graduation rate for ELLs in 2020 was 46% (students that met the minimum course and credit requirements) with only 2% achieving advanced graduation designation (students that passed a minimum of 8 statewide standardized high school examinations), while for non-ELLs, the graduation rate was 87% of whom 41% received advanced designation (New York State Education Department, 2020).

On the other hand, similar deficit discourses invade educational systems in relation to children with a disability. In 2020, only 62% of the children with a disability in New York State successfully graduated from high school, with only 6% of them achieving advanced graduation designation (New York State Education Department, 2020). Such results have overstressed simplistic skill instruction and drills promoting mechanistic ways of learning and limiting the opportunities of children with a disability for agentive and sophisticated learning (Moore & Klingner, 2014; Vaughn & Linan-Thompson, 2003).

All these issues are at the root of what critical disability scholars call *ableism*. Ableism occurs when certain ways of engaging with the world and with learning in the classroom are privileged over others. To contribute to our understanding of ableism, this chapter explores: How does ableism manifest in bilingual education contexts with children with a disability? The next section explains and illustrates ableism in more depth.

METAPHORS DRIVING BILINGUAL TEACHERS TO ENACT ABLEIST PRACTICES

Ableism is a term used to describe the social and institutional practice of devaluing forms of learning and moving that are removed from what is considered to be the "average" and "rooted in the ideology of normalcy" (Reid & Knight, 2006, p. 19). Specifically, ableist practices discriminate, often inadvertently, against minds which think and learn in untraditional ways, or bodies which move in diverse ways (Freedman & Ferri, 2017).

Ableist practices also take place in bilingual dual language programs where two languages and cultures are recognized and promoted. For instance, a value system can be, at times unconsciously, applied to evaluate different ways of speaking or to favor certain knowledge categories over others. It is important to learn to recognize these and promote more inclusive opportunities to learn in bilingual programs. Ableism has surfaced through commonly used metaphors in my work with teachers working in dual language programs that attend to children with and without a disability. For example, it has surfaced in the use of "grade levels", and in the curricular guidelines their schools had in place, which situated children as lacking, as not learning, and as not making progress (Martínez-Álvarez, 2022). That is, sometimes children are not allowed to move onto the next grade level because they are seen as underperforming despite already having a disability label that grants individualized educational plans (IEPs). In these cases, teachers have often used the idea of not being "on grade level," creating a particular level of rank or knowledge value, to explain their decision-making process.

When talking to bilingual teachers in bilingual schools, I hear teachers' anxiety about meeting the demands of the educational system while at the same time respecting children's abilities and disabilities, languages, and cultures. Schools at times respond by systematically retaining students who did not make expected progress according to their grade level. As a result, conversations around retention of children with an IEP, or in other words, with a disability, often dominated our collective thinking around the children in the VWK program.

For example, bilingual teachers serving children with a disability express preoccupation about grade levels in relation to the children with a disability, as they are often perceived as being several grades behind other peers. I have witnessed teachers reacting against the practice of holding children back one or more grade levels. While this practice could initially appear to benefit children with a disability academically, it might actually harm them in other ways. For example, while children might appear to do better academically when judged against the standards usually applied to the new group of younger classmates, retention might negatively impact their self-esteem and leave a lasting mark on their academic self-concept (Peixoto et al., 2016). Still, teachers often feel uncomfortable with accepting children that are at different levels in the same classroom, or in other words, accepting children with a disability in their general education classrooms. This uneasiness might promote retention practices.

The complexity of the practice of retaining students is connected to the ways schools place children into classrooms, which is by organizing them into similar age groups. Being "behind" would be the case for most of the one-third of the students in ICT classes who have a learning disability if they are compared to an ideal "average" learner of the same age group. This brings along an expectation that all children born in the same year will have similar ways of learning and developing. However, it is difficult to predict the way children will develop as they enter schools. As Greenstein (2016) explained, "[s]uch heavy reliance on age as the main organising factor of school is based on a view of cognitive, social and emotional development as a standardised, almost universal, process that is organised in stages and progresses in predictable and known ways" (p. 92). Currently, when children don't respond to universal expectations for learning, they will be singled out by having them repeat a grade while all the other children move on to the next grade level. Such a strict promotion model stigmatizes children who learn in different ways and who develop along far from average patterns. A more flexible model recognizing the uniqueness of each child and allowing for children of the same age to learn in different ways, as they move through their schooling experience, would assist in attending to this historical issue.

Furthermore, most of the minoritized children's disability categories are connected to language (i.e., speech and language impairment), or to processing information and having difficulty acquiring literacy (i.e., specific learning disability). According to the current law guiding special education services in the public schools in the United States, educational performance must be affected negatively in some way for a child to be labeled with a disability. This is stated in the Education for All Handicapped Children Act of 1975 (reauthorized as IDEA in 1997 and again in 2004), the federal law meant to ensure services for children with a disability. However, teachers might employ a deficit approach to analyze the learning of the children with an IEP (i.e., with a disability) in their class (Kangas, 2020).

As teachers spoke to me about children with a disability in the VWK, they used words such as "behind," "below," or "struggling." The metaphor of a reading level was frequently used to point to the inferior quality of the reading ability of children with a disability. Reading levels in most schools in New York are established through a teacher-administered assessment using the levels from Fountas and Pinnell (1996). Indeed, reading levels for the children with a disability might be, if evaluated by this assessment, far below what is supposed to be the "average." But one must wonder, how can a child be behind or below if we are implementing an individualized plan for him or her specifically? Are we fairly approaching children with a disability in our schools if we keep comparing them to the myth of the ideal learner, and constructing their learning identities as being "behind"?

Teachers in bilingual schools where children with a disability learn have tools to respond to children's difficulties. These tools often take the form of the IEP and placing them in ICT rooms. The ICT classroom has two teachers who can serve the children with and without a disability. Teachers in New York also have the option of providing special education teacher support services (SETSS). SETTS is offered in New York to promote the participation of the student with a disability in the general education classroom. SETSS services might take place inside or outside of the classroom and they include consultation with the student's general education teacher (United Federation of Teachers, 1999). Both ICT and SETTS can be aligned with inclusive possibility contexts when the children receive the services that they need inside the regular education classroom. However, teachers often do not seem to feel that these multiple services and options suffice to help children who are perceived as not being on grade level. Far from appreciating the inclusive possibilities, in their desperation, teachers might recommend a 12:1 classroom option. This, commonly used as a last resort option, refers to a self-contained classroom where there are fewer students with one teacher (in this case 12 children to one teacher). Such a restrictive environment is not aligned with inclusive education frameworks but, unfortunately, if available in a school, this might be an option that bilingual teachers recommend.

Special education systems have been using tools such as the IEP to create personalized plans for children with unique learning trajectories, which are supposed to guide the educational experience of children with a disability. Despite the many years we have been using these tools, in practice, excellent teachers continue to feel the pressure of deeply engrained cultural concepts such as "grade levels" or "curricular standards" that may force them to question whether their classrooms are appropriate for some children (Martínez-Álvarez, 2022). Schools and the teachers that work with children with a disability hence search for alternatives that continue to have damaging consequences such as having the child repeat a grade.

In many schools, self-contained options are still the learning context for children with a disability, who are being pulled out of general education classrooms in order to remediate their disability in special disabled-only spaces. Since the Salamanca Statement on Special Needs Education (United Nations Educational, Scientific and Cultural Organization [UNESCO], 1994) however, there is worldwide awareness of the value of teaching children with a disability alongside their nondisabled peers. This statement is a declaration of commitment, adopted by 92 governments, to inclusive practices in educational systems. Despite worldwide efforts, and the acknowledgment of the value of educating all children inclusively, we continue to question the right of children with a disability to be in our public school classrooms (Bacon & Lalvani, 2019).

Regrettably, the process of exclusion starts even before the child is found eligible for a disability. Even kindergarten teachers have shared with me what they described as the developmental or academic differences they witness in their students, often without realizing that these descriptions are based on cultural images of an ideal learner. Furthermore, as a result of institutional ableist histories and the practices these give rise to, bilingual children who have a disability might also develop unhealthy learning identities based on what they lack or cannot do. Aspects related to identity and how ableism manifests in bilingual education contexts with children with a disability are illustrated next with examples from the VWK afterschool program that took place in the school.

THE LEARNING IDENTITIES OF BILINGUAL CHILDREN WITH A DISABILITY

Work and conversations from the VWK afterschool program are used to illustrate the ways in which the learning of children with a disability is perceived as inadequate when ableist beliefs guide practices, and when teachers, children, and families experience pressure in schools. In the VWK afterschool program, which met weekly in this school for 4 years, the children offered disheartening stories about their past learning experiences that manifested negative self-images.

At the start of the VWK program, children were invited to create a Me as a Learner collage that would help children envision how they learned so that we could better serve them. This is described in Classroom Identity and Knowledge Exploration 4.1. With this collage, the afterschool program aimed at exploring children's identity as learners. Rooted in these initial explorations, children continued to think about themselves as learners and about their early experiences in schools while participating in the afterschool program. This initial invitation thus resulted in numerous insights about learning experiences that were found to be at times painful and often in need of healing.

Classroom Identity and Knowledge Exploration 4.1

An overview of the unit is described in Classroom Identity and Knowledge Exploration 4.1. provided below. The full bilingual description can be found on the product page for this book at https://www.tcpress.com.

THE YO COMO APRENDIZ (ME AS A LEARNER) COLLAGE

Lesson Outline:
Título (title):
________________________ (student name) aprendiendo (learning)
Dibuja/escribe para mostrarte aprendiendo. Usa uno o varios dibujos (Draw/write to show yourself learning. Use one or more drawings).

Protocol:

- Piensa en una ocasión reciente en la que estabas aprendiendo en la clase. Dibuja, escribe, crea un collage para mostrarte aprendiendo en estas situaciones (Think about one recent occasion when you were learning in the class. Draw, write, create a collage to show yourself learning in these situations.)

Main Teacher-Student Conversation:

- Dime acerca de tu trabajo (Tell me about your work).
- ¿Cómo te sentías? ¿Cómo se sentían lxs otrxs (amigxs, compañerxs, maestrxs)? ¿qué hacían? ¿qué decían/preguntaban? (How did you feel? How did others feel [friends, peers, teachers]—what did they do? What did they tell you/ask you?)

The rest of this chapter discusses the experiences Deyanira, Susana, and Jacob shared during their work in the program as they participated in the Me as a Learner collage.

Deyanira: "I Don't Feel Good"

Deyanira was a 2nd-grader in the school when she started participating in the VWK. She had been born in Mexico but was brought to the United States when she was young. Deyanira was a student with an IEP and experienced the learning disability primarily in learning to read and write, but also in math.

In response to the Me as a Learner collage invitation, Deyanira created a multimodal composition, which she started by drawing a female-looking human figure in the bottom middle part of her paper. She then pasted seven pieces of multicolored paper in different shapes using post-it notes we had provided (i.e., a flower, a heart, a speech bubble, several squares, and one piece of paper she created herself by cutting one of the post-it notes provided). She also wrote five sentences, and one word, on these added pieces of paper. From top left to bottom right these stated (italics show untraditional Spanish spelling): "mami te *qiero* mucho mami" (mommy I love you a lot), "Papi te *qiero* mucho" (Daddy I love you a lot a lot), "mami" (mommy), "y *escrivi istorias* de *tipujos*" (I wrote stories of drawings), "yo aprendiendo sope *tipujo*" (I am learning about drawings), "que es *tipujar*" (what is drawing?). Deyanira's collage centered on two themes, the love for her family and the role of drawings in her school learning experience

In an attempt to go deeper into children's identities as learners, the teacher candidates in the afterschool program and I spoke to the children, asking questions while they worked on their collages. Deyanira's interview provided a glimpse at Deyanira's former state of anger related to her learning difficulties as she described her memories of learning struggle as a young preschooler (before she was identified with a disability). The interview also revealed lingering rage remaining in her present learning experience. Here is a partial excerpt from a conversation she had with me:

Patricia: ¿Hay alguna cosa con la que no te sientes tan bien? (Is there anything with which you don't feel so good?)

Deyanira: Que no . . . que no nos dejan . . . que no estoy jugando [. . .] Que no me ponen un check. (That they don't let us . . . that I am not playing so much [. . .] That they don't give me a check.)

Patricia: ¿A veces no te ponen un check? (Sometimes they don't give you a check?)

Deyanira: Fue el viernes que no me ponen un check . . . porque no hice bien las letras, que yo no escuché. Por eso. (It was on Friday that they did not give me a check . . . because I did not do the letters right, that I did not listen. That is why.)

Patricia: ¿Qué tenías que hacer? (What did you have to do?)

Deyanira: Tenías que escribir de . . . tu familia . . . y no me pusieron un check aquí porque no hice bien la letra. (You had to write about . . . your family . . . and they did not give me a check here because I did not do the letter right.)

[. . .]

Patricia: Pero dime ahora. ¿Alguna vez no te ponen check? (But tell me about now. Do they sometimes not give you a check?)

Deyanira: Mmm [affirming], me siento mal. Cuando yo era en kindergarten. (Mmm, I feel bad. When I was in kindergarten.)

As shown here, the beginning of the conversation with Deyanira suggested she was discussing her current experience as a 2nd-grader. Deyanira explained her anger as she yearned for more time to play. She provided more information about her anger as connected to not being able to perform up to the established learning standards. This is shown as Deyanira conceptualized her success in writing as forming the letters well and listening. She expressed her difficulty to do so symbolized by the fact that teachers had not given her a "check." In the last turn in this conversation, Deyanira's difficulty with forming the letters correctly in 2nd grade mixed with memories from her earlier struggles in kindergarten.

I asked her then to tell me about her experience in 2nd grade and here is Deyanira's response:

Patricia: ¿Y ahora en Segundo? (And now in second grade?)

Deyanira: No me siento bien. El Viernes [. . .] no me siento bien porque me piden que escriba y otra vez y otra vez y otra vez. (I don't feel well. On Friday [. . .] I don't feel well because they ask me to write again and again and again.)

Patricia: ¿Y cómo te sientes cuando lo tienes que escribir otra vez y otra vez? (And how do you feel when you have to write it again and again?)

Deyanira: Triste porque no me gusta escribirlo otra vez y otra vez. (Sad because I don't like to write it again and again.)

Patricia: ¿Qué no te gusta de eso? ¿Crees que te ayuda a aprender? (What don't you like about that? Do you think it helps you learn?)

[. . .]

Deyanira: No me siento muy feliz porque escribiendo y escribiendo y después estaba llorando. Bastante trabajo hacerlo. Lo estaba haciendo en clase allá, cuando yo era en kindergarten [. . .] Y mi mami después me recogió y después la maestra ya no me regañó. Solo me dijo que escribiera y escribiera y escribiera. (I don't feel very happy because writing and writing and then I was crying. A lot of work to do it. I was doing it in class there, when I was in kindergarten [. . .] And my mom then picked me up and after that the teacher did not scold me anymore. She only said to me that I write and write)

As she went back and forth in her description of a struggle that centered on the need to write and her perceived inability to do so in the expected way, Deyanira repeatedly spoke of "a lot of work," and of "not feeling well," feeling "sadness," and crying "a lot." Furthermore, in the last half of this exchange, Deyanira spoke of her painful experience across the grades as she was asked to write it "again and again."

I prompted her once more to think about how her experience was different now, to which she explained the following:

Patricia: ¿Y ahora en Segundo? ¿Ya mejor? (And now in 2nd grade, is it better?)

Deyanira: Mmm [wondering]. En inglés tampoco. Era lo mismo. (Mmm. Not in English either. It was the same.)

Patricia: ¿Qué pasaba en inglés? (What happened in English?)

Deyanira: Ah era más dificil. Porque en inglés era más difícil la escritura y solo podía dibujar y dibujar. Quería dibujar, no quería escribir poque me va a costar mucho trabajo. (Ah, it was more difficult. Because in English it was more difficult to write and I could only draw and draw. I wanted to draw; I did not want to write because it was going to be a lot of work for me.)

Patricia: ¿Y por qué dibujaste a tu mamá? (And why did you draw your mom?)

Deyanira: Porque quiero aprender de ella. (Because I want to learn from her.)

In this excerpt, as Deyanira brought her consciousness back to her present experience in 2nd grade, the focus of her anger shifted to her process of learning English as being "the same." She explained how in English writing was ever more difficult and brought back the safety net of drawing to communicate.

Throughout this conversation, there is some indication that Deyanira perceives her struggles as somewhat solved as she aimed for a path of healing toward Anzaldúa's "conocimiento." This was indicated by how she, at times, states that she "was doing it in class there" and explains that it was when she "was in kindergarten." She also used the past tense and sentences in her description of her kindergarten experience such as "I was doing it in class there, when I was in kindergarten," and this consistency seems to try to highlight that this took place in the past, and hence hints at it maybe being over.

However, this is not fully clear in the second part of her sharing, when, at times, she also let us know that this struggle and her anger were still very much going on now ("I don't feel well"). Throughout her narrative Deyanira expressed hope as she tried to explain that while writing is extremely hard for her, she can draw to make meaning and communicate. She is figuring out how learning works for her, and in this discovery there is potential for healing. Uncovering how best she is a learner is part of the pathway toward conocimiento.

Simultaneously, she clearly positioned her family at the center of a more successful learning experience, not only as part of her collage, but also as she described her mom saving her from her painful kindergarten experience ("my mom then picked me up and after that the teacher did not scold me anymore") and ended explaining that she wanted to learn from her. As Deyanira explains through her comments how the school nevertheless prioritizes writing or learning English, or how she can learn from her mom (expressed in her reference to wanting "to learn from her") because she has knowledge that is left outside of her school experience, she brings issues of ableism in bilingual education to the front.

The collage, when situated alongside Deyanira's interview responses, suggests that Deyanira is in the path of *conocimiento*, a term used by Gloria Anzaldúa (2002, p. 542) to describe the healing path toward learning and knowing. This Spanish word "conocimiento" has multiple meanings, including the ability to learn but also the process of getting to know a person (see the dictionary of the Royal Spanish Academy at http://dle.rae.es). Anzaldúa meant it to have these two meanings in reference to the experience of anger and then the process of overcoming it when immigrants and other communities living borderland experiences learn about others and begin to heal so that they are more ready or able to learn (Anzaldúa, 1987/2007). While feelings of anger can be inferred from Deyanira's words, she seems to be entering a path to healing as she reveals her ability in telling stories with drawings. This ability is mediated by her disability (primarily her difficulty with the mechanics of reading and writing and thus her interest in communicating using drawings). As Deyanira agentively explained, "I wanted to draw; I did not want to write"; her concrete realization of the modes that make learning difficult for her and those through which she can best learn allows Deyanira to feel she is a competent learner (i.e., to rethink her identity as a learner).

Ableism surfaces in this context through the privileging of different aspects. For instance, it is apparent in the favoring of traditional learning modes, as traditional writing is privileged as the mode Deyanira should use. It is also evident in the push for learning the English language as Deyanira describes how in 2nd grade and with English, "it was the same." There is also a hint at different knowledges as Deyanira expresses her desire to learn from her mother; this knowledge that comes from outside the classroom should be recognized and brought in as valuable for learning in this bilingual space. When only certain knowledge is valued in schools, a form of ableism manifests as White children from middle-class backgrounds who typically share a series of values and "normalized" cultural repertoires are, often invisibly, given an advantage. Deyanira's agentive protest through this interview opens opportunities for potential change and transformation (Sleeter, 2001).

Susana: "They Said That I Don't, Like, Get What the Teacher Say"

Susana's case is also used to illustrate aspects related to identity and how ableism surfaced in the bilingual classroom with children with a disability. Susana was an older Latina 3rd-grader in the afterschool program. Labeled with a disability, Susana often manifested anger when invited to engage in academic work she did not find easy to complete. She was retained in kindergarten, but the afterschool team did not know about her having repeated that grade, because up to her second year in the program, she had never mentioned it. However, in a session when we were working with slime to simulate processes of erosion (slime was a particular favorite of Susana's), a conversation took place between myself, Susana, and Carolina. Carolina was another child participant who was of Susana's same age but was in 4th grade. The conversation changed our assumptions and showed how much having to repeat a grade can impact children:

Susana: Do you have daughters?
Patricia: Tengo una niña de nueve años, de cuarto [. . .] (I have a nine-year-old girl, in fourth grade [. . .])
Carolina: Yo estoy en cuarto. (I am in fourth grade.)
Susana: I don't know why. I'm supposed to be in fourth grade but I don't know why.
Carolina: Why are you supposed to be in fourth grade?
Susana: I don't knooow, because, my mom said that I didn't fail, I didn't fail kindergarten but she said that, um, my teacher said that I didn't still get what they're teaching and then she said that I had to restart kindergarten again and that's why I'm in third grade.
Patricia: ¿Tú te acuerdas de eso? (Do you remember that?)
Susana: Yeah, cause, um, I passed but, um, I, I passed but, um, I, I passed but, um, they said that, they said that, my teacher, they said that I don't, like, get what the teacher say, like, cause before, um, um, before, when I, the first day of school, the first day of school, I used to be really shy, and (it's going to get dark) and aaah, they say, I'm like, they was talking but I didn't get what they were saying, so . . .
Carolina: So, they were talking to you in Spanish?
Susana: No, they were, were you in Ms. [last name of kindergarten teacher] class?
Carolina: No, my sister was.
Susana: I was in Ms. [last name of kindergarten teacher] class.
Patricia: ¿Y tú te acuerdas? (And do you remember?)
Susana: [nods head yes]
Patricia: Y cómo te sentías tú cuando . . . (and how did you feel when . . .)
Susana: I felt happy but I didn't get like, I didn't get [teacher's] math problems and reading, that was like the hardest thing for me.
Patricia: ¿Eso era muy difícil? (that was very hard?)
Susana: Mmm, in kindergarten so that's why.
Patricia: Bien, estás en tercero, y ahora ¿cómo te va en la clase, en tercero? (Good, you are in third grade and now how are you doing in your class, in third grade?)
Susana: It's good.

Patricia: O sea que ¿fue una buena idea lo de kindergarten entonces? (So, then it was a good idea what took place in kindergarten then?)
Susana: I finished my story.

In this conversation, when confronted by a girl who, despite being her age, is in a higher grade, Susana timidly shared about having been retained in kindergarten. As shown by numerous hesitations, pauses, and the sudden ending to the conversation, Susana was having a difficult time speaking about this knowledge she had about her early retention.

Attempting to conserve some of her dignity, Susana explained early on in the exchange how she had "passed," which she repeated twice, and blamed her retention on the fact that she was "really shy." However, she then added that she couldn't "get" what teachers and others were saying, pointing to a possible difficulty with oral language processing or comprehension. Being described as "shy" by teachers at times also results in the perception that a child is not as academically developed as those who are more outgoing. This is because children might show limited oral participation, often because they lack the confidence to use their language publicly (Coplan & Evans, 2009). In fact, in the United States and other North American countries, being less socially adventurous and shy often translates into negative outcomes (Rubin et al., 2006).Teachers' perception of children as shy is associated with lower performance on literacy and attention in the early grades (Rudasill et al., 2013).

Her classmate Carolina, hearing Susana explain that she "didn't get what they [the teachers] were saying," immediately assumed that language was the issue, rather than a disability or something else (i.e., learning preference or personality), as she wondered whether they were talking to her in Spanish or not. This showed the awareness of these children in how using only one language (i.e., English) can cause miscommunication. It also highlighted the issue of the overlapping, often intersecting, identities of language learning and disability. When Susana explained that it was not because of the actual code used to communicate, she provided additional information on her difficulties, this time in math problem solving and in reading, pointing to that as being "the hardest thing to me." Susana hinted at her anger toward the end of the conversation when, asked whether she thought that what took place in kindergarten (being retained) was a good idea, Susana suddenly declared the story "finished" in her closing sentence.

Ableism manifests when children's preferred ways of communicating (nonverbal over verbal, for instance) are not all valued equally. In this case, Susana's self-description as being "shy" and her explanation of how she could not "get" what teachers were saying both suggest ableism had a role in the decision to keep her in kindergarten for 2 years. These aspects that Susana brought up can be part of language acquisition process manifestations for bilingual children who are learning the language of instruction, who might be silenced if the medium of instruction is only English or if the classroom is highly teacher-centered (Cole, 2013).

There are different ways of manifesting intelligence that are all interconnected. Children vary in their ways of making meaning and might demonstrate strengths along the intrapersonal or existential intelligences, if they are more insightful or philosophical, rather than interpersonal intelligence, which tends to manifest in more actively engaging in social interactions (Gardner, 2006). These preferences might also impact children's participation patterns in class. The decision to have children repeat a grade is often guided by comparisons to the image of the "average" learner and it can be understood as being a manifestation of ableism, particularly when considering the learning of emergent bilingual children with and without a disability.

Jacob: "There Isn't Any Spanish at Home So It's Very Difficult for Him"

For children whose families lost their Spanish over the generations (at times even within one generation), and who do not use Spanish in the home, the process of learning Spanish is very different from how it is for those who come speaking Spanish (Lindholm-Leary, 2018). However, everyone in a bilingual program is a language learner in one way or the other. Those who speak Spanish in the home need to continue to learn English, and the same is true for those who speak English in the home; they need to learn Spanish. Even children who grow up speaking both languages will show varying competences in each of their languages. There should be space for all these different learners to learn and develop in bilingual classrooms. Bilingual teachers might still compare the Spanish levels among different children and might expect those who do not use Spanish at home to be able to master both languages quickly. However, it is important to keep in mind that learning a language is a lifelong process and that for most children, acquiring a language up to a comfortable competence to be able to study academic content takes at least 5 to 7 years (Baker, 2006).

Jacob was a child whose family originated partially in the Dominican Republic and partially in Africa. Being a second-generation immigrant, Jacob's mom had lost most of her Spanish at an early age. In addition, he had an IEP and experienced difficulty with processing information impacting his reading development. While his not speaking Spanish at home was well known, and teachers knew about Jacob's reading disability, they would still situate him as lacking when speaking about his learning in their inclusive dual language program.

Jacob's English bilingual teacher in his 3rd-grade classroom described him as someone who did not identify as Latinx, and as consequently having a lot of difficulty with the language. Identity, rather than being fixed, is a fluid construct that evolves and is formed and reformed in a context of meaning (Holland et al., 1998). Jacob's teacher had suggested that as he was in a bilingual school, maybe his Dominican identity should have been more marked than it was; still, he had drawn a Dominican flag in school as reflecting part of his identity. His bilingual teacher had canvases painted by the children displayed around their classroom that we admired during the after-school sessions. The canvases were the product of an invitation to represent their culture. As part of his canvas, Jacob had drawn a small Dominican flag, showing that he did identify with this part of his heritage.

Children in the class would translate for Jacob often as he searched for help, but teachers interpreted this translation assistance as getting in the way of Jacob's acquiring fluent Spanish. That is, his efforts at mediating his own meaning-making by asking others for translation, a form of agency that demonstrates his understanding of the resources other children could offer, were instead seen as a problem. These ideas seem to suggest that in this bilingual classroom, the expectation is that children have more knowledge of Spanish than Jacob, who is thus situated as lacking. This contrasts with a critical disability perspective that highlights the role that the classroom and school contexts have in provoking learning barriers. For instance, disability studies scholars suggest that excessive emphasis on independent learning is a form of ableism and does not align with what we know about how learning happens (Savarese, 2020, as cited in Hastings Center, 2020). In fact, within CHAT frameworks, knowledge and development are not things that are discrete or acquired by individuals but rather take place as people shape and are shaped by the social context where they are learning (Wertsch, 1998). In this sense, the relationship between individuals and their context and learning community is one of exchange (Engeström, 1991). This means that when children engage in working with others, they will most probably divide the work into smaller tasks that individuals can collaboratively accomplish as they progress toward accomplishing their larger activity. This process will result in more possibilities for participation and for taking multiple roles in the activity at hand, resulting in learning and development (Roth & Lee, 2007). Learning should be based on the interdependence among children who benefit from working together, rather than on independence.

In the collage Jacob created for the VWK program, he pasted images that he had taken around the school. Among these, Jacob included a photograph of a world map where children and teachers had placed a pin to mark their countries of origin, as well as a photograph of a painting displaying both the American and the Mexican flag. In a related activity, when drafting notes about his talents, Jacob wrote "Sing School Math Baile" (Sing School Math Dance), using the Spanish word for dancing. The image of the map and the flags speak to Jacob's transnational awareness. His translanguaging event could be connected to Jacob's knowledge of the Dominican culture and the role of dancing for Dominican people. Independently from the personal connection Jacob made with these pieces of work, we can see that, while working in the afterschool program, he manifested his appreciation for multiple cultures, including his Dominican heritage, and used both of his languages. His work in the afterschool program hence contributed to the teacher candidates' developing an appreciation for Jacob as a multicultural and multilingual child. The recognition and appreciation of the identity of heritage language speakers in bilingual programs is important as it is an aspect which influences children's maintenance of their bilingualism (DeCapua & Wintergerst, 2009; Martínez-Roldán & Malavé, 2004).

Strict expectations about what identifying with a certain culture should look like or what those identifying with a culture should do, promote a form of ableism that is rooted in a misunderstanding of culture as a fixed trait. Cultural group traits cannot be applied directly to individuals in fixed ways, as life trajectories always vary among members of those perceived as a group. Rather, as Gutiérrez and Rogoff (2003) have elucidated, cultural practices need to be understood as merely what they are, "proclivities of people with certain histories of engagement" (p. 19). As has been historically highlighted by multiple scholars, more flexible understandings of culture that are contextualized in the particularities of individuals should be centered (Gay, 1995; Nieto, 1999).

This also applies to language. While Jacob's family might have lost their ability to communicate in Spanish regularly in the home, they are still fostering his bilingualism and biculturalism by choosing to enroll him in a dual language program (Tse, 2001). This decision showed an important level of commitment from a family with a child with a disability. Professionals might erroneously discourage bilingual education when children experience difficulties in school (Martínez-Álvarez, 2018). Furthermore, language ableism surfaces, as teachers expect a child to have acquired higher levels of Spanish just from having been in the bilingual school since kindergarten. Considering the different labels that a child like Jacob carries, however, illuminates a learning experience subjected to multiple forms of oppression, both inside the school system and outside in the larger society as he goes through his elementary years in the United States. Specifically, in Jacob's case, he is a male of color, one of his parents is Latinx and the other one is African American (which situates him at the intersection of two linguistically and ethnically diverse communities), and he also carries a high-incidence disability label. Aspects connected to these layers of difference can help explain the disparities teachers claim in his bilingual/bicultural performance and learning. As we judge children's language and their learning potential based on societal expectations and culturally created parameters without considering forms of oppression, including institutional discrimination, we risk engaging in language ableism. It is ableist to expect children to demonstrate cultural traits, including language, that have been historically developed within contexts that are so different from those of bilingual children with transnational family histories.

The cases of Deyanira, Susana, and Jacob illustrate the schooling experiences of bilingual children who have a disability. The children's work described in this chapter also shows their awareness of these layers of difference, and the presence of these forms of oppression in their school lives, including ableism, as they tried to make sense of their developing identities as learners.

CONCLUSION

These different examples surface ableist beliefs in education. We are embedded in a culture that compares children to each other and to the ideal of an average learner. It is very difficult to realize how engrained these are in our education systems. Disability is socially constructed as a deficient state and as a negative label, and messages communicating these perspectives are present in all school practices, in the literature, and in our cultural discourses (Baglieri & Shapiro, 2017). Unfortunately, as shown, children internalize deficit discourses about their own disability (Lalvani & Bacon, 2019).

Scholars have even question the use of any labels, as these force fixed identities in children without considering the sociocultural and institutional factors mediating those labels (McDermott et al., 2006). There is a controversial disproportionality of emergent bilinguals in the high-incidence disability categories in the United States (U.S. Department of Education, 2015), and educators are presently struggling to differentiate mild disability from language acquisition processes (Klingner & Eppolito, 2014). Issues of disproportionality show how labels commingle with race, language, class, among other markers (Lalvani & Bacon, 2019). The language practices of Deyanira, in relation to her writing ability (i.e., "I did not do the letters right"), and of Susana, for her perceived shyness and lack of understanding of the oral language (i.e., "I don't, like, get what the teacher say"), and of Jacob for the expectations placed on him, are situated as being deficient as elucidated in these descriptions. However, as this chapter has elucidated, emergent bilinguals' language practices can be perceived as "atypical" (i.e., deficient). This happens if we understand "typical" as the monolingual practices of White children, growing up in middle-class families, whose cultural practices are well-aligned with those that are valued in educational systems. Children growing up with two languages and cultures engage in translanguaging, or creative ways of using languages for communicating, or for meaning-making in schools (García & Wei, 2013). Bilingual children, including those with a disability, are diverse and develop these different languaging practices depending on multiple factors such as their history of exposures to their languages or experiences in connection to their countries of origin (Brisk, 2006). Historically, bilingual children's language practices have not been privileged, or even seriously considered, in educational contexts. Rather, bilingual children's ways of using language have been stigmatized (Flores & Rosa,

2015). Lack of understanding of language development when working with bilingual children who have a disability manifests language ableism. As a result of language ableist processes, instead of learning from immigrant bilingual children's ingenious experimentations with words across languages and modes (Heath, 1983; Wei, 2011), their linguistic practices are evaluated as deficient. This is evident in the ways systems and many educators describe and remediate the language of emergent bilinguals with a disability.

Could educational systems provide the services children need without having to label them as English language learners, or disabled? Inclusive education aims for this goal by continuing to promote universal designs for learning (Broderick et al., 2005; Reid & Valle, 2004). The concept of universal designs for learning and its proposal to consistently integrate multiple forms of engaging, representing, and expressing information while teaching (Center for Applied Special Technology [CAST], 2018), however, has not been clearly operationalized and its potential has not been explored consistently in bilingual contexts. It is important that we create contexts in schools where children with and without a disability can engage in meaningful conversations about differences and about knowing and learning to know, ability and disability, and other diversity factors. The following chapters continue to offer views into the experience of bilingual children with a disability and the impact these multiple labels have in their lives and education.

CHAPTER 5

Teaching Children With Multiple Labels

Manifestations of Assimilation and Turning Points

Young bilingual children of immigrant background, who have a disability, are exposed to the consequences of multiple simultaneously occurring layers of oppression throughout their schooling experience. Schools might see children with a disability as a monolithic group, but many of these children carry other layers of difference (e.g., being language learners or having an immigrant background). The complexity of carrying multiple layers of difference might impact the way bilingual children embrace their disability identity and the services they receive in school. For instance, children might acknowledge being bilingual but not having a disability. Or they might receive special education services in school while having to give up bilingual education (Martínez-Álvarez, 2018). It is at the intersection of these multiple dimensions of children's identities that oppression takes place, and where group membership might become contested and problematic in multiple ways.

PARALLEL PROCESSES OF ASSIMILATION: BEING BILINGUAL AND HAVING A DISABILITY

To situate the need for a humanistic approach in teaching and learning at the intersection of differences, this chapter explores the question: How do historical assimilationist efforts manifest when teaching bilingual children with a disability, and what opportunities toward inclusive designs might surface in a hybrid space? The chapter begins by discussing the histories of assimilation that connect immigrant and disability experiences, as well as the resulting forms of oppression facing children who are seen as learning along multiple forms of difference. The chapter then offers the experience of Andrés and Deyanira to showcase the expansive views that the teacher candidates embraced while working with them in the VWK afterschool program, and the opportunities their renewed perspectives offered for inclusive spaces. After that, Susana's experience is introduced to illustrate how assimilation pressures from simultaneously occurring layers of difference manifested, and the possible turning points that might be created through projects that invite children's fluid knowledge and identities into schools.

ASSIMILATIONIST PROCESSES IMPACTING CHILDREN OF IMMIGRANT BACKGROUND

Many countries around the world share early histories of rich multilingualism and multiculturalism. Eventually, such legacies often shift to a search for one nation and, consequently, one language. This is the case of the United States. The United States has a rich and diverse cultural and linguistic early history, with a multitude of American Indian languages spoken in the 15th century (Grosjean, 1982). However, as the Europeans arrived, there was a shift favoring a more unified vision, mostly grounded in the English system and practices (Tyack, 1981). While the United States has never adopted an official national language, assimilationist forces based on racist and classist discriminatory practices valued and, hence, promoted European languages at the cost of indigenous languages (Crawford, 1999; Heath, 1976).

Traditionally, there has indeed been enormous resistance to providing solid bilingual education for children of immigrant background. The educational context in the United States during the 19th century can be described from a multilingual perspective as "permissive," but not "set up to actively promote bilingualism" (Ovando, 2003, p. 4). Ovando (2003) explained, however, that this perspective shifted at the end of the 19th century when, particularly starting early in the 20th century, the new approach was to have immigrants assimilate into the United States culture, and thus the English language. The 20th century has been plagued by an English-only emphasis, with legislation restricting bilingual education being passed in several states, and by an anti-immigrant sentiment that remains today (García & Sung, 2018). This new era was rooted in nationalist discourses exemplified by United States President Theodore Roosevelt who in 1919 wrote that "we have room for but one language here and that is the English language" (1919, p. 2). In the 21st century, political leaders such as United States president Donald Trump have emphasized similar monolingual ideologies. In a 2015 interview he said, in response to a question from ABC journalist Tom Llamas, "We're a nation that speaks English. I think that, while we're in this nation, we should be speaking English [. . .] Whether people like it or not, that's how we assimilate" (ABC News Politics, 2015). These discourses are part of the history of the United States and remain very present nowadays, as a general anti-immigrant sentiment is being politically disseminated.

The 1968 Bilingual Education Act, which was dismantled and renamed with the 2001 No Child Left Behind Act, briefly promoted bilingual education for minoritized communities. However, states soon developed English-focused educational approaches while resisting more linguistically inclusive designs (García & Sung, 2018). Examples are the passage of Proposition 227 in California in 1998 and of Proposition 203 in Arizona in 2000, with other states following with similar anti-bilingual efforts. As a result, bilingual education has been reframed as dual language education focused on the benefits of learning in two languages for English-speaking students, and solutions such as short-term bilingual programs have instead been promoted for minoritized or immigrant children (García & Sung, 2018; Lindholm-Leary, 2001).

Today, the schooling experience of bilingual children of immigrant background often continues to center on cultural and linguistic assimilation (see Salazar, 2013). Attempts are made to teach children who do not conform with existing norms to adopt such norms, setting the White middle-class student as the standard (Warikoo & Carter, 2009). In fact, the goal of education for minoritized communities is culturally presupposed to be the achievement of similarity; that is, of assimilating minority children so that they end up being more like those from the White middle class (Rist, 1977, as cited in Warikoo & Carter, 2009). This is illustrated by studies showing how the schooling experience of immigrant children is often subtractive of their cultures and languages, because of school tracking through labeling, anti-immigrant climates, and linguistic bias (see Valenzuela, 1999).

ASSIMILATIONIST PROCESSES IMPACTING CHILDREN LABELED WITH A DISABILITY

The idea of "normality," or of the existence of the average learner, promotes disability as a deficit needing to be remediated and resolved (Davis, 2006). Historically, families or the community were, even when unwilling to do so, in charge of caring for people with a disability. These people were left out of education and out of society because they were considered as being unemployable (Brown, 2017). However, beginning in the early 19th century there was a rise in segregated institutions to care for disabled people and isolate them "as far from society as possible," with a clear medicalized orientation (Brown, 2017, p. 488). More recently, as people with a disability have claimed their right to be part of society, efforts to force them to assimilate into what is viewed as "normal" have dominated their learning and living experience (Slee, 1997). Working with children with a disability in schools has historically involved an effort to minimize differences by teaching those who did not fit the average learner to "approximate the norm as much as possible" (Greenstein, 2016, p. 19).

When children failed to fit the perceived norm, they were segregated to specialized classrooms or institutions, where they could be "cared for" (Ware, 2002). Nocella (2008) explained how "disability has been the justification to kill, test on, segregate, abort, and abandon" (p. 77). The political historical dominance of the image of what an "able" learner should look like has been used to "reify the ideology of normal" (Annamma et al., 2013a, p. 1280). The image of the able student has hierarchical associations, which gives power to those recognized as "normal," while situating the others as in need of care and relegating them to a lower place at multiple levels in society (McDermott et al., 2006). Special education systems have historically situated disability within the individual child, rather than realizing the complexity of sociocultural and historical factors that create disabling learning spaces for children (Slee, 2001). This pathologized view of disability as within the individual, which is linked to the medical model, is then consequently addressed via interventionist and remedial approaches aiming to minimize differences (Slee, 1997).

Today, with the relatively recent inclusive movement, which is meant to challenge "the ways in which educational systems reproduce and perpetuate social inequalities," there are efforts to include children with a disability in general education settings (Liasidou, 2012, p. 168). Still, mediocre progress has been accomplished so far in this terrain, and the need for a more radical approach has been highlighted (Greenstein, 2016). As Slee (2001) explained:

> Our starting point ought not to be the question how do we move the special sector into the regular school and thereby overcome exclusion? This is assimilation. More properly we ought to commence with an interrogation of the formation of regular and segregated schooling as a first step towards a different educational settlement, the inclusive or democratised school. (p. 388)

In a sense, given the emphasis to focus inclusive education research and practice on disability in the United States, other identities might be disregarded (Harwood & Humphry, 2008). For example, the identity of disability might be prioritized over that of being bilingual for children learning at the intersection of these differences, for reasons such as service provision conflicts or popular misconceptions about the learning potential of children with a disability (Martínez-Álvarez, 2018). As part of this depreciation of certain identities over others, schools often continue to demand that children with a disability assimilate to the existing general educational system, rather than creating spaces where their diversity can be celebrated and embraced to its fullest (Kilinc, 2018).

From a historical standpoint, then, both bilingualism and disability share points in time when assimilation was the aim; this perspective is still very much present in the 21st century. When children are labeled in schools both as English language learners and as having a disability, these assimilationist perspectives collide, and new forms of oppression are produced. For example, despite the multiple benefits that bilingual education offers to students of minoritized backgrounds, when bilingual children are labeled with a disability, they are less likely to learn in high-quality bilingual programs where they could become bilingual and biliterate (Martínez-Álvarez, 2018). Where a child is allowed to learn in their home language in school, this may be treated as remedial, with the home language merely used until the child develops enough English to transfer to monolingual contexts (see Martínez-Álvarez, 2018). Furthermore, parents who speak other languages in the home might be asked to provide input only in English if their child is identified with a disability, which is another manifestation of assimilationist efforts (Kim, 2017).

INTERRUPTING PROCESSES OF ASSIMILATION

During the teaching and learning effort in the VWK afterschool program, teacher candidates often discussed the languaging and cultural practices of children in expansive ways, which could be situated as a form of resistance to counteract assimilation. Work and conversations from several of the instructional invitations in the afterschool program supported this idea. In particular, the Lados de Mí project (in English, Sides of Me) involved children in a five-session identity exploration undertaking, during which teachers often reflected about children's languaging, as well as their fluent identities and cultures. However, the project also served to make visible subtle ways in which assimilation takes place in schools regarding bilingual children with a disability. While actions during the project also manifested assimilationist processes, efforts like exploring multiple identity layers using themes, or including talents and family memories, facilitated through the Lados de Mí program described below, held the potential for turning points to ensue. I next offer an overview of the project, and then present work to illustrate these findings.

The Lados de Mí (Sides of Me) project consisted of a multisided depiction of the many layers of children's identities. Children represented their ideas of themselves as learners, and of their cultures, family memories, and talents, by painting, drawing, and/or writing on four pieces of stiff paper, each representing a side or "lado" of a cube. The four papers were then folded into a cube or box that could open and close. The children later chose family and personally relevant artifacts to place inside the finished box. This instructional invitation, proposed by Sebastián, the Colombian American teacher candidate in the project, is explained in more detailed in the description below, Classroom Identity and Knowledge Exploration 5.1.

Classroom Identity and Knowledge Exploration 5.1

An overview of the project at the center of this chapter is described in Classroom Identity and Knowledge Exploration 5.1. provided below. The full bilingual description can be found on this book's product page at https://www.tcpress.com.

THE LADOS DE MÍ (SIDES OF ME) PROJECT

Day 1 of the project—Side 1: Exploring identity as a learner with the prompt "mi lado como aprendiz" (the side of me as a learner)
Day 2 of the project—Side 2: Exploring identity as a cultural being with the prompt "mis culturas" (my cultures)
Day 3 of the project—Side 3: Exploring identity using family traditions and memories with the prompt "recuerdos de familia" (family memories)
Day 4 of the project—Side 4**:** Exploring identity by surfacing talents with the prompt "talentos" (talents)
Day 5 of the project—Inside the Box, Family and personally relevant artifacts

CHILDREN'S EXPERIENCE: EXPANSIVE VIEWS CROSSING IDENTITIES AND CULTURES

The Lados de Mí project provided opportunities for the candidates to reflect not only upon language in this bilingual space, but also about children's fluent identities and cultures in relation to learning. The work of both Andrés and Deyanira are good examples of this finding.

Learning Identities Beyond Figurative Boundaries

On the first day of the project, Sebastián, the Colombian American teacher candidate who led the explorations for the Lados de Mí project, documented Andrés's work as follows (italics added to show untraditional Spanish spelling):

> He quickly was able to draw and write a caption for each idea. He wrote: "viendo videos" (watching videos), "viendo a otras personas" (watching other people), "la *ecuela*" (la escuela; the school), "*gugando gegos*' (jugando juegos; playing games). He was excited to show me [. . .] Andrés always continues to surprise me; he is creative, sensitive, and almost always on point. It is great to see these children thrive and

> demonstrate their knowledge in different ways. It makes me think of how powerful it would be if we had more activities/lessons that would allow students to flourish as learners in the general ed[ucation] classroom. [Sebastián's Learning Notes; Day 1 of Lados de Mí]

Andrés's response to the invitation to show the side of himself as a learner is shown in Figure 5.1.

With his words, Sebastián captured aspects of his own learning as a teacher candidate and what he perceived as being interesting in Andrés's work. In this note, he included phonetic aspects of the child's idiolect, or Andrés's distinctive language expressions that can expand linguistic and semiotic

Figure 5.1. Andrés's Response to "Mi Lado Como Aprendiz" (The Side of Me as a Learner)

resources (Bloch, 1948; Otheguy et al., 2015). This is worth noticing as an opportunity toward linguistically inclusive spaces because the candidate accepted Andrés's choices as they were instead of replacing them with prescribed standard versions. Additionally, through his work, as documented here, Andrés demonstrated his awareness about learning taking place across multiple social spaces (in school and outside of it), and through different modalities (playing and watching). In this way he was figuratively crossing not just physical boundaries, but also boundaries about what learning is and looks like.

The crossing of the figurative boundaries also allowed children to explore learning across languages, as discussions that were often left out during the school day took place. For instance, Patty wrote about Deyanira's response during the invitations as she explained:

> I then asked [Deyanira] about the languages in her home, and I asked about Spanish. She then told me that no, that I should know this [her family not only speaking Spanish at home], and I asked her about Mixteco. She said that yes, that's what they speak in at home. I told her that [this] was a great idea to add to her learner identity ideas, and that it would be great if she could teach us some words in Mixteco. [Patty's Learning Notes; Day 1 of Lados de Mí]

In this excerpt, Patty situated Deyanira's Mixteco as an asset and she showed that she considered it to be an important part of Deyanira's learner identity and that she welcomed it in school. Likewise, Sebastián's reaction to Andrés's work focused on positive aspects of his work as he interpreted it as "creative," "sensitive," and "on point." In this way, Andrés was described from a strength-based perspective as thriving. The work that both teacher candidates documented presented an opportunity to go beyond the traditional binaries of inside and outside school, or everyday and academic concepts or discourses (Moje et al., 2004).

Expansive Views of Children's Agency, Languaging, and Cultures

During Day 2 of the project, the group explored the different cultures children carried. As Sebastián worked with Andrés, they generated ideas more typically recognized as part of the Mexican culture such as drawings showing "las posadas" (religious Mexican festivals), "tacos" (a traditional Mexican dish made of a fried tortilla), and "la bandera Mexicana" (the Mexican flag). They also came up with words they enjoyed in Andrés's family, from within their Mexican roots and beyond like, "¡Útala!" (Wow!), "Chismoso" (neighborhood gossiper), "Sonic," "Supersonic," and "Video Juegos" (video games). Sebastián explained his own learning during the planning and reflection meeting, as he said, "I got to learn a new phrase, "¡Útala!", which I guess is like a, it's kind of like a dang it [Wow!]. Like in Mexican slang." With this exchange, Sebastián demonstrated an expansive perspective on language as he recognized his own learning of the language Andrés's family employed.

Patty, on the other hand, wrote about Deyanira's interest in China, which the candidates had not expected to be part of this session's exploration of cultural repertoire.

> Deyanira was still very upset she couldn't share about what she knew of China. I told her that she could share now what she knew, and she talked more about the law of having only one baby [. . .] When it came time to share more about her own Mexican culture, I was very surprised to see that she wasn't sure of what to add or where to start, and I had to prompt her towards different things. I knew about her, so she could share more. I asked her how she knew so much about China, and she said that her mom talks to her about it. I noticed a lot of the students were very in-tuned with the idea that culture = flags. I told her a flag could be both a surface level and deeper level if we are relating to what the flag [means]. [Patty's Learning Notes; Day 2 of Lados de Mí]

In this excerpt, Patty indicated her surprise as Deyanira expressed her knowledge and interest in the Chinese culture, initially staying away from her Mexican roots. She then tried to get Deyanira to express ideas about Mexican culture, when she was going in a different direction, and so she explained how this required prompting. The last part of the excerpt showed Patty's own reflection about the superficial and the deeper levels of culture. Patty situated flags as a superficial aspect of culture, but also as objects that could be open to deeper analysis. In this way, the activity facilitated spaces for more expansive views of culture.

It was here that Deyanira shared additional ideas that more clearly aligned with Patty's expectations, as she wrote:

> I then asked her if there is any food she likes eating with her family. She started sharing about mole [a word rooted in the Aztec Nahuatl word "molli," meaning mixture] and told me it was a very spicy sauce they eat with their tortillas. Last year when I did a case-study with her, she taught me how to dance La Cumbia Mexicana [the Mexican version of a kind of dance music similar to salsa, originally from Colombia]. I asked if she could share more about that with me [. . .] She started dancing Cumbia and seemed to enjoy herself very much while doing so! I told her that is another thing she could definitely add to her ideas, as it is a part of her culture. [Patty's Learning Notes; Day 2 of Lados de Mí]

Here, Patty celebrated Deyanira's ideas and performing abilities, which she "definitely" interpreted as "a part of her culture."

However, when Deyanira illustrated her ideas on Face 2 of the cube, Patty said, she had "painted circles of different colors." Patty asked Deyanira about this choice, and the girl told her that "the more olive green represented her mother." Once Patty realized there was meaning behind Deyanira's art, she accepted her decision to only draw circles of different colors (see Figure 5.2).

In addition to discussing culture in expansive ways, the teacher candidates showed their own learning process while working with children, generating opportunities toward inclusive spaces. The work Deyanira generated also revealed how children might not respond to proposed invitations in traditionally expected ways (see Figure 5.2). This process also manifested during Day 3, which is described next, as children were asked to share their "recuerdos de familia" (family memories).

Language and Immigrant Experiences as Cultural Artifacts

During Day 3 of the Lados de Mí project, Sebastián described how Andrés drew himself "cooking at home with his mom. He drew his family playing the game Uno. And went on to tell me a long story about his dad coming home late Christmas Eve and hearing jingles for Santa." These ideas were clearly recognized by Sebastián as family memories. Right after these more figurative representations, however, Andrés also painted a series of circles, similar to those Deyanira had decided to create the previous week (a favorite of the children as they enjoyed exploring and mixing the primary colors to obtain new shades). As shown in Figure 5.3, Andrés then added the names of Ninja characters from the Ninjago children's show (i.e., "*jay,*" "Kai," "*Zayn,*" or "Cole")

Figure 5.2. Deyanira's Representation of "Mis Culturas" (My Cultures)

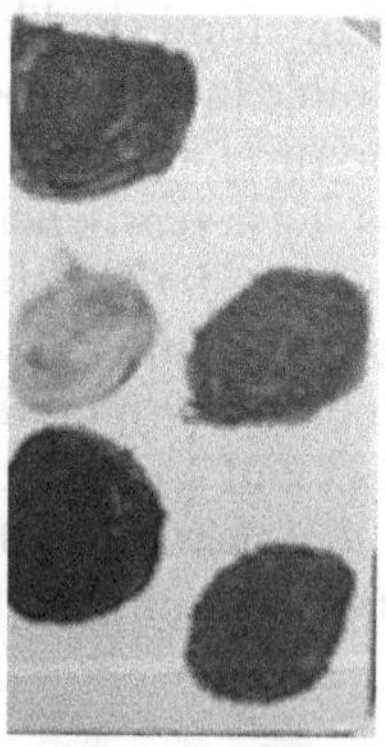

Figure 5.3. Andrés's Responses to "Recuerdos De Familia" (Family Memories)

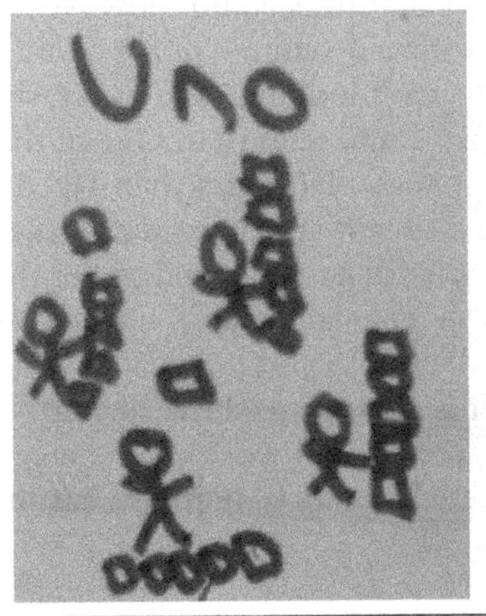

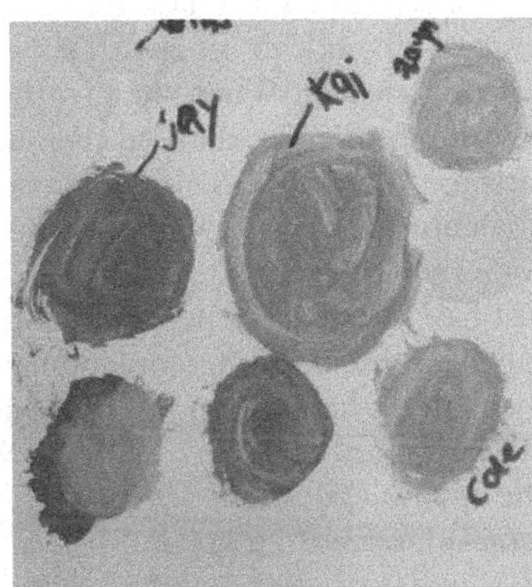

Sebastián was surprised by this second drawing and challenged Andrés to explain the connection of the ninja-named circles of paint to his family memories. He wrote that Andrés had "explained that this was a show he would watch with his family." Andrés also pointed out the yellow shape at the top left of his art, and explained that this represented his baby brother, and added his name next to it. In this way, Sebastián realized that the ideas that he had assumed did not relate to the given prompts were actually based on a family memory.

The information involving Deyanira and Andrés suggests that, while children's initial responses might appear to adult eyes as meaningless or unrelated to the assignment at hand, it is important for children to have the space to enact agency as part of the learning process. The active and engaged listening that Patty and Sebastián demonstrated acted as a tool to "center children's agency," allowing children to decide what they "would or would not like to express" (Kwon, 2021, p. 105), creating opportunities for more inclusive spaces.

Patty described how Deyanira's curiosity about China resurfaced during this Day 3 of the project. This was mediated by visits from two teacher candidates from the same graduate program, who were Chinese and attended the VWK afterschool program to learn about the children. Sebastián had invited these visiting teacher candidates, who took a course with him. Patty wrote:

> Deyanira looked at the back of her cuaderno (notebook) and saw that there was some Japanese writing, but she thought it was Chinese. She then started yelling to Sebastián's friends: "*¡China, China, China!*"

> (Chinese [person], Chinese [person], Chinese [person]!) to get their attention, and I had to remind her that [this is] not how we respectfully talk to others, so she then started yelling *"¡amiga, amiga!"* (friend, friend!). When she saw they weren't looking over to her, she went up to them and asked them if they could read that. One of the girls told them no because it was in Japanese. Deyanira then asked if it's not the same as Chinese, she didn't really understand that they were two different languages. Sebastián's friend explained to her that, just like she speaks English and Spanish (two languages), Chinese and Japanese are two different languages. Deyanira communicated with them all on her own in English, and it is great to see how curious Deyanira is about other cultures. We just need to work on the way she always calls them "*chinas*" (Chinese [persons]). [Patty's Learning Notes; Day 3 of Lados de Mí]

In this excerpt, we can once again witness how the children went beyond the Latinx cultures to explore other cultures and how they explored new knowledges. Patty recognized the value in Deyanira's curiosity and praised her ability in English. Simultaneously, she also interpreted Deyanira's actions from an educated adult's perspective, giving a stereotyped interpretation to the way Deyanira called the teacher candidates "China" (Chinese [person]). From a raciolinguistic perspective, which centers on ways in which language, race, and social class intermingle, resulting in damaging interpretations of minoritized children's languaging as inappropriate or inferior (Flores & Rosa, 2015), Patty's reaction to Deyanira's words can be read as a misinterpretation of her culture and language-mediated actions. Such a reaction to Deyanira's words appeared to be rooted in Patty's unconscious interpretation, given that she is a Puerto Rican graduate student whose father is college-educated, and while privileged in some ways, might have herself experienced linguistic violence while in the United States (Fallas Escobar & Treviño, 2021). Hence, Patty's reaction could have resulted from a combination of her linguistic experiences infused with features of class, race, and culture that Deyanira carried.

Deyanira demonstrated sincere interest in the two teacher candidates who were Chinese, and who were visiting for the first time. She also was learning about Japanese and Chinese being different languages, something Patty also recognized as valuable. Likewise, discussing ways in which we might respectfully refer to (or call on) people from varied racial backgrounds is important. Such exploration can be fruitful for minoritized children, opening additional opportunities for inclusive learning, if carried out in a safe space where culturally different ways of referring to racially diverse people are recognized as such, rather than misinterpreted, and discussed as part of an asset-based perspective.

Patty quickly redirected this initial exploration toward the topic of family memories at the center of the session. She wrote about how Deyanira was "having such a hard time with this transition." This is something to be expected given Deyanira's excitement toward learning more about China. It was clear that the candidates aimed to eventually redirect children's conversations toward the program's agenda for the lesson, even while initially trying to offer some time for children's enactment of agency in relation to the direction of the session.

Patty explained that, once she had moved the conversation back to family memories, Deyanira, talked about how "she likes to teach her sister how to write and read." Patty explained that she had asked Deyanira "if she teaches her [sister] Mixteco too," but Deyanira had said "that no, little kids can't learn Mixteco," excerpts which showcase more information about how Deyanira used and perceived Mixteco in her life.

At this moment Patty noticed that Deyanira became emotional, and explained how she shared about the few family members who lived in New York, but how most of her cousins are in Mexico. As the sharing continued Patty wrote:

> I asked if [Deyanira] still speaks with her family in Mexico, she said "a veces" ("sometimes") pero que "no puedo ir allá porque no tengo papeles, porque te acuerdas ya . . . necesito papeles . . . verdad? No te dejan ir a otros países, but no nos dejan viajar" ("I cannot go there because I do not have papers because you remember already . . . I need papers . . . right? They don't let you go to other countries, but they do not let us travel"). [Patty's Learning Notes; Day 3 of Lados de Mí]

Patty, a Latina herself, recognized Deyanira's understanding of lack of "papeles" ([immigration] papers) as barriers for her to be able to go back to Mexico to see her family. In this sense, Patty's background assisted her in particular ways, sometimes to facilitate an asset-based interpretation of Deyanira's knowledge and languaging as in this case, and other times to do the opposite (as illustrated by Patty's interpretation of Deyanira's use of "China" [Chinese person] to call on the student teachers from China).

In the current context, Patty empathized with Deyanira, as she wrote about what she said to her:

> [E]spero que eso lo cambien pronto (I hope that they change that soon), and [Deyanira] said "sí, que cambie muy pronto" (yes, that it is changed very soon). I asked her how it makes her feel, she said, "mi primo me quiere ver [. . .] le mandamos una foto" (my cousin wants to see me [. . .] we sent him a picture). [Patty's Learning Notes; Day 3 of Lados de Mí]

At this point, the conversation took a turn as Deyanira understood the impact that politics had on her personal experience as an immigrant. At the time of this interview, Trump was president of the United States and Patty captured Deyanira's awareness of his stance on immigration:

> [S]he said, "hace tiempo [que fui allá], pero sí, ya no vuelvo por Donald Trump, ojalá que se vaya. Espera que se cambie para que la gente dice . . . ah, ¡por fin!" (it's been a long time [since I went there], but yes, I don't go back anymore because of Donald Trump, I hope he'll leave. Wait until it changes so that people would say . . . ah, at last!) I said: "y para que la gente pueda ir . . ." (and so that people can go). Yazmin replied: "viajar . . . lo que quieran" (travel . . . whatever they want). [Patty's Learning Notes; Day 3 of Lados de Mí]

Despite the fact that President Trump was a powerful figure, and was elected the president of the United States, Deyanira realized that many people do not support his deficit discourse about immigration. She suggested with her words that people in the United States would be very happy when he stops being president. She also placed her dream of going back to visit her family and Mexico on a timeline coinciding with Donald Trump's ending of his presidency term. Deyanira's knowledge is rooted in her status and her positionality as an undocumented student living in the United States, who came as a toddler into the country.

Her contextual experiences provided Deyanira with expertise in this topic that should be used in the classroom for further learning, and which can be a mediator to situate her as a knowledgeable learner, promoting an inclusive space.

Children's Talents and Knowledge

For Day 4 of the project, the children were invited to explore their "Talentos" (talents). The introductory part of the session invited children into the life of Celia Cruz through Monica Brown's 2004 book titled *My Name is Celia/Me llamo Celia: The Life of Celia Cruz/la Vida de Celia Cruz*. The teacher candidates discovered that the children did not know about Celia Cruz. However, they noticed the children's knowledge about other Latinx artists such as Frida Kahlo and Selena. Patty wrote in her notes after this session:

> I then asked the girls to talk more about Selena because I knew that was a singer they've said previously they were familiar with, and we started talking about her songs and played one of them. Deyanira then mentioned how Selena's dad died, and that Selena also died. I thought Sebastián handled explaining how Selena died well [. . .]. [Patty's Learning Notes; Day 4 of Lados de Mí]

In fact, Deyanira expressed her talents for painting and dancing, which had been mediated by her connection to Frida. Patty explained this in her notes:

> I could see in her demeanor that [Deyanira] was so fascinated by the paint and the colors [. . .] She has mentioned before that she loves painting and that she relates to Frida, so I think painting is good for her. She started painting musical notes because dancing Mexican cumbia is one of her talents (which, I'm sad we didn't do more of this week; the girls really enjoy it). [Patty's Learning Notes; Day 4 of Lados de Mí]

The topic of exploring one's talents went onto a very different direction for Andrés. For this face of his cube, Sebastián explained how he had told him that "he was not going to use any colors and just write his talents on the last side of his cube. He wrote '*Matematicas*' (Matemáticas; mathematics), 'Arte' (Art), 'decorar' (decorating), '*cosinar*' (cocinar; cooking), and 'lavar' (washing [clothes])." Sebastián felt that the piece looked unfinished and convinced Andrés to add some color to his work as described in his writing: "I eventually was able to coax him to add color and explain to me why he chose some of these" (see Figure 5.4).

With or without color, Andrés identified, once again, the multiple talents he carried, crossing traditionally established boundaries as he identified aspects within the academic world (i.e., mathematics represented with a computation problem), a multimodal learning talent (i.e., art), as well as other things he learned and practiced in the home or the community (i.e., decorating, cooking, or doing laundry).

Figure 5.4. Andrés's Responses to "Talentos" (Talents)

This session was key in situating the children as knowledgeable and as carrying strengths to be used for classroom learning. Information across sessions in Lados de Mí highlighted the importance of allowing children's enactment of agency, and how knowledge that adult educators might expect Latinx children to have might not be what their specific funds of knowledge are. As shown through the work by Andrés and Deyanira, this project provided opportunities for the candidates to reflect upon languaging, as well as children's fluent identities and cultures in relation to learning. In order to create opportunities for inclusive spaces, it is important for bilingual teachers to be ready to learn from the actual knowledge of their students, and follow their lead in their lessons, even when the unexpected manifests in children's work.

Susana's work, presented next, was conversely much less positively received by the candidates, who were initially challenged by the girl's agency and at times resorted to deficit perspectives to interpret her actions. The tension that surfaced as this took place resonated with processes of assimilation. Day 5, which was the last day of the project, when parents joined the VWK afterschool program, included a possible turning point that is worth exploring. Work illustrating Susana's engagement and the candidates' reactions to their interactions with her are discussed next.

A CONTRASTING EXPERIENCE: SUSANA'S AGENCY AND LEARNING IDENTITY

While some children were generally described in expansive terms in relation to academics and learning in bilingual contexts, as seen in the teacher candidates' learning notes, this was not immediately the case when working with Susana. As mentioned in Chapter 4, Susana was a girl who had repeated kindergarten and had been labeled with a disability.

Susana's Identity and Belonging: "Why is Susana in Varied Ways of Knowing?"

Susana was a second-generation Latinx who was situated as an English speaker with a disability from the beginning of the VWK afterschool program. She was also situated as being sad or little communicative. For instance, on Day 1 of the project, Perla, the Chilean teacher candidate, wrote the following in her learning notes: "She [Susana] seemed intrinsically sad. I asked Patty if she knew what was wrong and she said that she is usually that way." After the same session, Rachel wrote about this exchange with Susana: "I spoke to Susana, but she only replied in head nods or shrugs. Patty later told me that she was English-dominant and if I had known that I might have spoken differently to her." Here Susana is initially capturing the candidates' attention, but not in ways leading to positive interactions.

Rachel explained how Susana had also taken a deficit view about herself during the session. The teacher candidates played a short video clip showing children denouncing stereotypes in the United States about children of color and immigrants as part of the Day 1 activities. The candidates then used this video to explore the children's identities through the sentence "I am . . ." adding the things they felt they did well. Rachel recorded Susana's answers to this invitation. "Susana said, 'I am nobody.' I then asked her what she could do well, and she replied 'nothing.' I told her how she clearly spoke well, and she could understand Spanish and speak English. Susana [answered] 'I don't talk Spanish.'" Rachel then continued describing Susana in positive terms as she negatively responded to several of her questions, but then the candidate eventually concluded in her learning notes that "Susana [. . .] does not see herself as a Spanish speaker." In this way Susana had been, early on in the afterschool program, situated as an English speaker with, so far, little positive connections with the candidates.

During Day 2 of the project, the candidates decided to introduce a song to open up every session from then on. They chose the song "Buenas Tardes" (Good Afternoon) by J. L. Orozco, a popular Mexican children's singer and author. Some of the children had heard the song and were happy to follow along. However, Sebastián, who was the lead teacher during this session described how he had heard Susana say, "This is first grade." Patty also captured Susana's reaction to the song as she wrote:

> When Sebastián gave Susana the lyrics sheet and he turned his back to keep giving out the lyrics sheet, she threw the paper across the room and said, "I don't need this." I got the paper and told her that wasn't nice, and we talked for a minute on how we need to be respectful. [Patty's Learning Notes; Day 2 of Lados de Mí]

Given Susana's lack of success in school as demonstrated by having repeated a grade and having a reading level considered to be below her grade placement, she could have been trying to protect herself from material that, while might have been at her reading decoding level, could be, in fact, seen as infantile for 3rd- and 4th-graders. However, Patty at this point rebuked Susana's behavior as not being "respectful." The meaning of the Spanish word for education, *educación*, goes beyond the mere transfer of academic knowledge to create identities and ethical and cultural values with the intent to prepare good people, and it includes addressing rules for living within one's society (Sánchez, 2022). The emphasis on showing respect to adults therefore is probably part of Patty's values as well as those of the other Latinx teacher candidates who had grown up in Latin American countries (Hopewell & Abril-Gonzalez, 2019).

From then on, Susana continued to be described from deficit frameworks. Rachel wrote how, later in the lesson, when ideas about "culture" were being explored on Day 2 of the project, she had done the following:

> [I] asked Susana about her culture. She would repeatedly tell me, "no hacemos nada" (we don't do anything) and things to that effect. She drew a picture with lots of squiggles and said it was "her imagination." I asked her how imagination played a part in her family, but she would just say things such as, "I just want to paint." [Rachel's Learning Notes; Day 2 of Lados de Mí]

Indeed, as this excerpt illustrates, many of the children in the afterschool aimed to just enjoy the paint rather than readily representing anything in particular. Such playful exploratory spaces, which are not sanctioned by formal curricular endeavors, can open possibilities for children to playfully explore their multiple identities (Lizárraga & Gutiérrez, 2018). However, in the case of Susana's work as interpreted by Rachel, this was not the case. Rachel ended her learning notes writing the following: "Why is Susana in Varied Ways of Knowing? Does she benefit from [it]?" With these questions, Rachel situated Susana not only in the way she had been categorized up to this moment, namely as an English speaker or as a reluctant learner, but also as not belonging to the VWK afterschool program.

In a sense, this child who acted differently from the candidates' expectations was positioned, through Rachel's words, as not benefitting from the program because she would not assimilate and engage in the activities in the ways others would do. This was even though the VWK afterschool program was created for bilingual children with and without a disability, children just like Susana, who do not typically follow the idea of the "average" learner that is promoted in most educational spaces.

Things did not get much better over the next few sessions. For Day 2 of the project, Rachel wrote in her learning notes the following concern in relation to Susana and her need for assistance:

> If Susana is refusing to work, I would not be able to devote any time to [her]. In truth, Susana may need a one-on-one for this program. I think Perla is a great one-on-one for her, and she did such great work with her this week. I do fear for Laura [another student], though, and her getting left behind or feeling forgotten. [Rachel's Learning Notes; Day 2 of Lados de Mí]

This description characterized many others in the candidates' learning notes where children who demanded more adult time or attention were described as taking time away from other children. It seems that the candidates were aiming to ensure all children received an equal amount of time from adult educators, and that the same kinds of things were provided to help them learn. This can also be interpreted as another effort to assimilate learners, because if you demanded more time than the other children, then, once again, you did not belong. As shown above, Rachel was worried about not giving enough attention to Laura and had decided that Susana should not be in her group (as shown by her emphasis on the need for one-on-one attention and her suggestion that this task was best assigned to Perla).

Maybe based on Rachel's suggestion in this previous session, and her sharing of this perspective during our reflective meeting, Perla did focus on working with Susana during Day 3 of the project. In her learning notes after the session, Perla described how the session was particularly difficult for her and for Susana. This started from the time they were grouped together as a pair. Perla explained:

> Sebastián announced the teacher–student pairings [or groupings for other children]. I told Susana, "¡Vamos a trabajar juntas de nuevo hoy!" ("we are going to work together again today!"). To what she said, muy amurradamente y de brazos cruzados (in a sulk and with arms folded) "NO!!" And so, it begun . . . [Perla's Learning Notes; Day 3 of Lados de Mí]

Perla's words closing this paragraph were "And so, it begun," which summarized the back and forth they experienced during the session, as her efforts to work with Susana were met with her resistance; Susana often answered with negative expressions, and even ran out of the classroom as Perla followed her.

The time we spent in the school was full of Susana's acts of resistance, a form of agency she manifested as she was placed in a pair learning group with Perla. Susana's resistance during the session could be her form of reacting to the conflict or tension she was experiencing, when she was assigned to a learning group in a pair instead of in a small group with other children like everyone else. She could have been sensing that working in a separate group with only one teacher candidate was a form of exclusion from the afterschool program, and maybe was also wondering whether she belonged there.

It is interesting that Susana was typically described in her regular day class as not very active (based on the candidates' visits to day classrooms), but she clearly took more and more action, even if it took the form of resistence, in the afterschool sessions as time passed. Still, Susana's volition created a clear conflict for the candidates, particularly for Rachel and Perla, as she enacted her agency in ways that seemed to disrupt her own engagement with the proposed learning experiences. While she was still engaging in the proposed learning experiences, these very different ways of engaging were not recognized or valued as such by the teacher candidates.

Accommodating and Controlling: "[B]ueno, ¿lo quieres o no? Porque si no, lo guardo"

During our reflection and planning session that week, we decided that Perla would bring playdough for Susana to use, with which she could soothe herself when feeling angry, or as an object to have in her hands for fidgeting (Susana really enjoyed slime and playdough). This was quite successful, and Perla wrote extensively about it in her learning notes after Day 4 of the project, "She (Susana) had blue slime in her hands, and I asked her if she wanted to put hers away since she was going to use the [playdough]. She said, 'yes' so I gave her a bowl to put it in." In this excerpt, Perla set rules for Susana, which she followed without any complaints. Then, as Susana expressed her interest in writing her name on the container of the playdough, Perla continued to set limits and they engaged in a small struggle with Susana as she tried to set conditions for using the playdough and maintaining control (in a way, once again resisting to assimilate):

> She said she wanted to write her name on them [the containers] but I told her "no," that this was not "her" [playdough]. That we got it because she had asked for it/needed it to fidget, but that it belonged to the afterschool for anyone who needed it. She didn't seem happy about that and tried one more time to say it was hers. Without engaging much, I asked her: "bueno, ¿lo quieres o no? Porque si no, lo guardo" (well, do you want it or not? Because if you don't, I put it away). So, then she stopped and took it. [Perla's Learning Notes; Day 4 of Lados de Mí]

We can observe here that Susana really had little space for any individually initiated volitional action, even actions that could be more acceptable for the candidates in the afterschool program. It seems that as Perla tried to avoid less tolerable volitional manifestations, which she had witnessed the previous week, she also became more restrictive with Susana than what we were typically being with other children in the sessions (since this space was designed to be a less restrictive context than the day school).

Toward the end of her notes, Perla brought back the already familiar idea that she did not feel comfortable with giving something to one child who needed it, but not to another. This was explained as follows:

> I felt bad for [him] because he wanted to play with [playdough] and I had to tell him that maybe later I could give him some, that it was for "fidgeting purposes really, not for playing." He is such a sweet boy, and he always has such a positive attitude and avidly participates in whole group sessions, that I felt really bad telling him "no ahora, pero tal vez más tarde . . . Ella lo necesita como fidget" (not now, but maybe later . . . She needs it as a fidget) and all while he gave me this

> look, eyes wide open and very "resignados" (resigned). The truth is, I would have given it to him, but was afraid the situation would result in everybody asking for [playdough] and being distracted (some even more distracted) [. . .] I felt I was being unfair to him. [Perla's Learning Notes; Day 4 of Lados de Mí]

These words show how uncomfortable Perla felt about providing Susana with something the other children did not have, even though this had served to mediate her learning, and not anybody else's. That is, the other children did not need an external artifact to mediate their learning at that time, but Susana did. Examples of similar circumstances were present in other sessions and throughout learning notes as well (either in the form of an artifact or in the form of additional attention), highlighting an area that is worth further exploring when working with teacher candidates.

Additionally, the words Perla wrote reflect numerous positive statements about the other child, who is described as "sweet," having a "positive" attitude, or "avidly" participating. Similarly, as shown in Andrés's and Deyanira's cases, other children were generally described in very affirming ways, while references to Susana, who did not follow the rules or resisted them, were mostly deficit-oriented and highly negative, always focusing on what was going wrong.

While Day 4 went more smoothly, and the playdough really helped Susana, she still expressed that "she hated the 'Buenas Tardes' (Good Afternoon) song," as Perla wrote in her learning notes. It is important to point out that Susana had been complaining about this song being childish for three sessions now, but no action had been taken to address her concerns.

At the end of this session Perla wrote that her goal with Susana was "to help her change her attitude/demeanor when asking for things she wants or doesn't [. . .] to try to explain to her the difference in attitude between 'angrily demanding' something, and 'asking' for something" (quoted from her original notes). In a way, Perla was continuing to ask Susana to change her way of speaking to belong in our learning space.

A TURNING POINT: "[SUSANA] IS A VERY STRONG GIRL FOR SHARING THAT WITH ALL OF US"

Susana's family, unfortunately, did not come to the afterschool family visit on Day 5 of the project. Despite the physical absence of her family in the classroom, the last day of this project was also an important turning point for Susana. For the first time, the teacher candidates wrote in very positive terms about her and expressed deeper understandings about Susana's feelings and circumstances outside of school. The opening into Susana's worlds that this session provided suggests that family visits and integration into our classrooms not only benefit the children whose family members are able to come, but also reveal a lot about others who might not have anyone attend.

As explained earlier, the families were asked to share an artifact that was important for them, and to explain why it was meaningful. When Susana's turn came, she was ready. She had brought a small stuffed animal. Rachel explained her sharing with these words in her learning notes:

> Susana's sharing was the most surprising and also extremely deep. She shared a tiny stuffed animal [. . .] She said that [a close family member] had died [. . .], and this was a toy she had given to Susana. I wanted to cry in that moment, and although extremely sad, Susana was able to express her feelings missing [the person]. It was really beautiful, and Deyanira gave her a hug. [Rachel's Learning Notes; Day 5 of Lados de Mí]

As shown by the description of this sharing as being "deep" and "beautiful," among others, there was a much more positive tone as the teacher candidates discussed Susana's work during this session in comparison to previous ones. Other candidates like Patty highlighted "how open she was" and described her as "a very strong girl for sharing that with all of us," similarly using mostly affirmative descriptions about Susana after this day's meeting ended.

There were other productive experiences during this session after Susana had spoken about her loss. Sebastián, who was leading the session, explained how:

> Susana asked if we could play a game in which everyone shares where they are from, and what they like about it (the place or their culture). I told her that we would play the game after everyone shared; she seemed very happy about this. [Sebastián's Learning Notes; Day 5 of Lados de Mí]

The group did play the game that Susana suggested in this excerpt, and her volitional action opened spaces for additional sharing with the family members that were present. Rachel summarized it as follows: "I am so glad Sebastián went with this because the mothers all shared as well, and the kids were excited to play Susana's game."

An important aspect of this last session of the project, and part of the turning point as well, was how the emphasis on recognizing Susana as a Spanish speaker was renewed. This is shown through Rachel's words, as she noticed how much Spanish Susana had used: "Susana shared in Spanish today as well. Sebastián would ask her a question in Spanish and then sometimes repeat it in English. When he started in English, Susana would change to English but often changed back to Spanish." Importantly, while Susana was described as persisting in using Spanish, it was Sebastián who often repeated his words in English for her.

Sebastián was reflecting about this in his own learning notes: "Sometimes, I do not even notice when I switch languages, or that I do it more often with Susana [. . .] I am wondering why I am doing so, and if I should be concerned of this habit when I begin teaching (hopefully) next year in a bilingual school." For many bilingual teacher candidates like Sebastián, who grew up in the United States, language competence is very high in both languages. Because of this, it is often the case that Latinx teachers growing up in the United States communicate best through translanguaging, and this was a characteristic way of speaking that he also had.

During the reflection and planning meeting, he explained his effort to offer as much Spanish as possible to the children: "So, I am trying to like, you know, [unclear] be more cognizant of like how they [can be] speaking Spanish. I don't mind if [they] speak to me in English, but then always like repeating [the] thought in Spanish for the rest of [children] as well." His reflection about switching to English more with Susana was also an important one, as it might have been impacted by deficit views about Susana's Spanish and could, once openly recognized, be addressed more effectively. Rachel put it this way:

> I think we [should] use as much Spanish as possible with [Susana]. If we don't say the questions in both languages for Deyanira [child situated as Spanish speaker in the program], we shouldn't do it for [. . .] Susana, in my opinion. [She has] proven [herself], especially Susana today, that [she] can express [herself] very well in Spanish. [Rachel; Planning/Reflection Meeting; Day 5 of Lados de Mí]

The teacher candidates really shifted directions in this session with Susana in a most critical way. This process of shifting is worth exploring further as a tool to mediate more holistic understandings of children for teacher candidates during their teacher preparation programs and a tool to break away from subtle but persistent assimilationist processes. Inviting children to bring an artifact through which to share something that was important for them and their family, alongside the explorations stimulated by the Lados de Mí project, eventually generated an opportunity for a space inclusive of Susana as a unique learner.

While there were moments of tension after this project ended, and Susana continued to be very agentive in ways that were not always fully understood by the teacher candidates, they also began taking more productive inclusive perspectives about Susana's learning and ability to communicate in Spanish. For example, during a later session (part of the second semester in the year), Susana brought some of her homemade slime to the afterschool program. Patty highlighted this in her notes:

> Then Susana came up to me and greeted me very excited because she brought the slime she made! She said that you need Tide and an activator [. . .] She told me I should play with it but then it got stuck on my hands and she cleaned my hands for me which was really nice of her. [Patty's Learning Notes; Consequent Session]

The positive shift in the teacher candidates' reports about Susana is very noticeable and happened across all learning notes.

During the beginning part of the session, when several options were given for children to choose where to work, Susana asked the teacher candidates if visiting a "center about slime" with her could be one of the options. The teacher candidates agreed to this, and they set up a space for "Susana's center" as one more activity to do during the session. Sebastián noticed the work in this center when Deyanira joined Susana's activity. He explained, "Susana and Deyanira were talking to each other quite nicely; occasionally they would have disagreements about sharing Susana's slime. She colored her slime pink! [. . .] she [Susana] was in a good mood." These words show a positive tone in talking about Susana that was very rare in earlier sessions. By facilitating a hybrid space, the candidates were able to direct Susana's energetic agency toward a space of possibilities for her growth and belonging, which were more readily understood by the teacher candidates, in the afterschool program.

CONCLUSION

The Lados de Mí (Sides of Me) project highlighted issues of inequity through pressures to assimilate, which are inevitably, at this point in time, often taking place when teaching bilingual children with a disability. It also highlighted the importance of the process, and of seeing our students as human beings who bring what they have into the educational space. It is for us to uncover who they are and what they know and can do, and elevate it to the level it deserves, while making radical changes in our everyday decision-making processes (Martínez-Álvarez et al., 2020).

While, over time, there was some light at the end of the tunnel, for half a year the program had functioned within limited views about cultural and linguistic identities of children like Susana, which promoted assimilationist efforts. As children were situated as Spanish or English speakers, and as deficit views about their learning guided the decision-making process, the afterschool program space reproduced some of the patterns and inequities present in society as well as in the educational system (Chaparro, 2019). It was evident that children do internalize the identities others shape for them, but they also resist them and take action to dismantle restrictive patterns (Mackinney, 2017).

There were two ways in which Susana's disability label appeared to result in additional consequences in this dual-language context, what Vygotsky (1993) referred to as secondary disability or the additional issues provoked by the society's responses to a child's primary (i.e., labeled) disability. These two consequences of having a disability included on one hand lack of bilingual development despite being in a bilingual program, and on the other hand the development of negative perceptions about their own ability to learn.

In reference to the first issue arising from being labeled with a disability, some children with a disability were described as not really growing in their bilingualism, particularly in Spanish, even while learning in dual-language bilingual programs. This unfortunate secondary consequence took place despite the fact that research is showing that children with a disability can indeed learn bilingually (Martínez-Álvarez, 2018). That children with a disability are not given enough opportunities for growing bilingually suggests larger processes threatening equity in the bilingual education of these multiply-marginalized children (e.g., a tendency to prioritize English when speaking with children who have a disability, less focus on their language learning, or more emphasis on their disability-related services while sacrificing services specific to language learning). That is, for language learners, being labeled with a disability seems to end up provoking the secondary consequence of losing, or not advancing, in their home-language competence. While bilingual development is a long-term process, it is important that educators take responsibility and maintain a hopeful view about language learning and identities as being fluid and dynamic, and as dialogically shaped through cultural artifacts (Bartlett, 2007).

While the educators in the VWK fought hard to foster children's Spanish identities, other learning efforts that prioritized meaning-making over language or identity development led the teacher candidates to switch to English at times. In the end, the learning experience was about meaning, which is fostered through effective communication, but it was also about bilingual identity, which is assisted by Spanish language competence. This balance is a very important one to center when working with minoritized children with a disability. As Alma Flor Ada (1975) explained:

> If bilingual bicultural education is to fulfill its goal [. . .] [w]e must be able to provide future generations with a command of their language and culture as adequate as the command we are demanding they obtain of the dominant language and culture. (p. 11)

That is, an expansive view about language as not a nice skill to have but an essential part of the minoritized child's identity (Haque, 2017), including for those with a disability, is central in these efforts. Otherwise, it is easy to give up and favor practices that eventually promote assimilation.

The second way in which Susana's disability appeared to have provoked additional consequences in this dual language context was in reference to negative perceptions of ability, resulting in resistance and low self-views that consequently impacted learning. In the case of Susana, her history of failure in school (i.e., having repeated a grade and having been identified with a disability that requires evidence of underperformance) manifested in the way she acted, often beyond what was "within the limits" in the afterschool program. As Susana attempted to take control and explore other possibilities for her learning, her agentive behavior challenged the teacher candidates, who responded with additional efforts to control her. This process manifested historical assimilationist educational efforts. Eventually, given the less restrictive context in which the program was situated, the candidates did try to generate some options for her volitional success, but while continually trying to keep things within the educators' control.

An interesting finding in relation to Susana's learning was in reference to how the teacher candidates, even though preparing to teach children with a disability, felt uncomfortable with the idea of providing some children with artifacts or means they needed to be successful, while not granting them to those who truly did not need them. However, artifacts that precisely mediate their learning are what can help children with a disability the most. Research shows that young people with a learning disability who were most of the time in inclusive classrooms identified the willingness to customize instruction by individualizing it without making comparisons across learners as an effective pedagogical skill that inclusive teachers should develop (Connor & Cavendish, 2020). This is an important aspect of learning processes awareness that should be further explored, as it could potentially assist teacher candidates in becoming more prepared to help children whose unique differences require specific tools and services. Redirecting the focus toward optimizing everyone's learning, rather than on providing everyone with the "same" tools or services, should be clearly established.

The perspective embraced in this chapter acknowledged assimilation as a historical process that is persistent in today's schools and highlighted how emergent bilinguals with a disability might be deprived of linguistic and cultural rights (Skutnabb-Kangas & Phillipson, 2010). Educational institutions must make efforts toward more consistently taking on the responsibility to foster the linguistic and cultural rights of children with a disability by monitoring instances when historical assimilationist tendencies in education manifest and working to dismantle them. This must happen whenever we encounter children, and at whatever level of competence or abilities they have built up, or of which they have been robbed, when they cross our paths. Otherwise, the linguistic and cultural rights of children with a disability would not really be protected when learning bilingually, and the inclusive spaces that are needed in bilingual education might not materialize.

CHAPTER 6

Humanistic Perspectives in Inclusive Bilingual Education

There have been different takes on humanistic perspectives in education, such as Kant's classical humanism in which he asserted that education is to help individuals in achieving what is good civically and emphasized the importance of the method of reason. Dewey's naturalistic approach focuses on the child as a means to social progress and his view of schools as "the child's habitat" and "embryonic" communities (Dewey, 1915, p. 15). However, most of the work around humanizing pedagogies in the context of inclusive and/or bilingual education embraces perspectives rooted in Freire's critical radical approach (see Chatelier, 2015, for an overview of humanistic perspectives).

In order to situate the need for a humanistic approach in teaching and learning for inclusive bilingual education, this chapter entertains how humanistic approaches have been discussed and investigated in both the field of disability studies and the field of bilingual research in education. The chapter claims that, in both contexts, there are multiple similarities to be analyzed. For instance, in both fields, there is the call "to humanize the lexicon that litters academic spaces, which is often presented through the discourse of whiteness" (Salazar, 2013, p. 122). There is also the shared imperative to build "humanizing research in ways that privilege the co-construction of knowledge, human agency and voice, diverse perspectives, moments of vulnerability, and acts of listening" of the children and teacher candidates involved in it (Kinloch & San Pedro, 2014, p. 23). Guided by the question, How can a humanistic approach assist in making bilingual programs more inclusive of children with a disability?, this chapter argues for the necessity of humanistic outlooks in the education of immigrant children with a disability and offers examples to understand how to take such a perspective in inclusive bilingual classrooms.

THE SIGNIFICANCE OF HUMANISTIC PERSPECTIVES WITH BILINGUAL CHILDREN WITH A DISABILITY

While children are highly diverse, we mark certain differences and identities with labels emphasizing the need to remediate. This process removes so much of children's humanity in schools, as their identities and ways of learning are situated as problems and deficiencies. The tendency to force bilingual children and children with a disability to assimilate discussed in Chapter 4 manifests the efforts within educational systems to remove those aspects that make them who they are as learners, aspects which make them unique and varied. These aspects include languages other than English, cultures that differ from the majority vision and practices, or forms of making meaning or learning that do not match the ideal image of the "average" learner (Davis, 2006). Both bilingual education and critical disability scholars have stressed the need to foster humanizing pedagogies to achieve a more holistic and inclusive learning experience (e.g., Erevelles, 2005; Fránquiz et al., 2019; Greenstein, 2016; López, 2019).

Humanizing Approaches in Teaching Children With a Disability

When addressing disability, a humanizing perspective contrasts with the medicalized approaches which have dominated the field of special education where the emphasis is on "curing" the person with the disability (see Cochran-Smith & Dudley-Marling, 2012). Greenstein (2016) explained how understanding disability should center on social spaces rather than the practice of "developing ever more intricate biological and psychological models" (p. 18). A humanizing perspective helps in understanding disability as a social construct, "a social and political phenomenon," rather than an individual trait located in the child's body and mind (Greenstein, 2016, p. 17). Erevelles (2005) explained how, while "disabled people acknowledge the reality of their bodily differences; they nevertheless contend that the experience of being disabled is related to how they are treated in the social contexts they live in" (p. 428). The institutional emphasis is typically on normalizing those who do not neatly meet the image of the ideal learner, or, as an alternative, governing them in ways that limit their capacity to act (Greenstein, 2016). Governing the lives of those who are perceived as in need of care aligns with capitalist ideologies through which some populations can be excluded because of their lack of desirability from an economic neoliberal standpoint (see Erevelles, 2005). Similarly, in K–12 schools in the United States, the curriculum and related evaluation processes are used to predict employability and economic productivity. Erevelles (2005) described this as follows:

> Using the results of these evaluative tests based on standardized norms, students are segregated on the basis of their 'natural' abilities and labelled 'gifted', 'regular', or 'special', and assigned to different curricula that educate them for their designated slot along the social division of labour. (p. 433)

In this sense, some topics, such as reading certain written texts or learning math, are recognized in the national curriculum whereas others like learning minoritized languages or engaging in artistic or creative processes are hidden (Erevelles, 2005). Certain forms of knowledge are hence privileged in the process, creating and fostering power hierarchies based on who possesses what is most valued (Morgan, 2000). This is an aspect which has been highly criticized by the disability community, given that inclusion aims at helping "*all* children to learn and participate in meaningful ways" and at "creating a nurturing learning community where everyone belongs and everyone benefits" (Valle & Connor, 2011, p. 65). The capacity to enact agency is also part of a humanizing perspective which is underlined by scholars of disability studies in education. These researchers highlight the need for exploring "expanded definitions of 'agency'" and "radical notions of what it means to be a 'critical' human being" so that these can be recognized and fostered (Erevelles, 2000, p. 32).

Helping children learn in meaningful ways while allowing them to enact agency involves positive views about disability, which are yet to be recognized in today's school and social discourse. It is important that the curriculum includes explorations about human differences and specifically about the constructs in the continuum along ability and disability from critical perspectives (Valle & Connor, 2019). Likewise, taking a humanistic perspective when teaching and learning with children with a disability requires forms of knowledge that open new ways of being so that all children can actively participate in class and eventually in the world (Greenstein, 2016). As Greenstein (2016) explained, situating some children as able to learn and acquire special powerful knowledge while others are not allowed to enter this dignified space fosters societies guided by meritocracy and hierarchies.

When preparing teachers for the inclusive classroom, humanistic approaches can broaden understandings of what types of competences and knowledge are needed to teach young people who are labeled with a disability and the essential role of flexible and universal learning approaches to designing curriculum. The apparently highly specialized knowledge that has invaded the world of special education makes other teachers feel unprepared to work with children with a disability (Alderson & Goodey, 1998). Teachers in the general education classroom often request specialized services for those children who bemuse them in their classroom if they believe there are professionals, other than themselves, that have the knowledge they lack and that could help these children better learn. Greenstein (2016) says, "The usefulness of this specialized knowledge to the actual teaching of students with SEN [special education needs] is questioned by many researchers in the field of education" (p. 45). Humanistic approaches focus instead on helping children understand themselves, and others, as powerful learners who make different contributions to the shared goal of participating to learn together, contributions that are all to be equally valued. Such approaches highlight caring relationships and types of knowledge that take different forms, accepting multiple ways of expressing and receiving information and other aspects of the world in which we live (approaches that reflect the guidelines of Universal Design for Learning or UDL; see Hall et al., 2012).

Humanizing Approaches in Teaching Bilingual Children

In similar efforts, and with closely comparable concerns, the field of bilingual education emphasizes the need for humanizing pedagogies. Just as in critical disability studies, in bilingual education humanizing pedagogies are viewed as a tool to break away from the assimilationist trends in schools, especially when working with bilingual children of immigrant background. Bilingual research in education scholars explain how, when thinking of humanizing education, it is important to be wary of the fundamental purpose of educational systems, which is to ultimately "assimilate and stratify subjects" (Chávez-Moreno, 2020, p. 218). The main concern is how immigrants and other minoritized communities, "who are not immigrants but are still Othered," have been dehumanized in the United States context through policies and practices that situate them as outside the system and promote negative attitudes toward them (Chávez-Moreno, 2020, p. 216).

In bilingual education research, and in more recent work in fields of critical disability studies, humanizing pedagogies have been inspired by the work of Paulo Freire. In his *Pedagogy of the Oppressed* (1993), Freire proposed a process of re-humanization in pedagogy. According to Freire (1993), "the only effective instrument is a humanizing pedagogy," one where the teacher "establishes a permanent relationship of dialogue" with the bilingual students with a disability (i.e., the oppressed; p. 50). In a humanizing pedagogy, Freire (1993) explained, "the method ceases to be an instrument by which the teachers [. . .] can manipulate the students [. . .], because it expresses the consciousness of the students themselves" (pp. 50–51). That is, children are at the center of the teaching and learning process and the curriculum is molded to validate and integrate children's interests, disability, and funds of knowledge (Moll et al., 1992), while prioritizing trusting relationships (Zisselsberger, 2016). A dialogical approach to quality multicultural literature can help teachers enact humanizing pedagogy that engages their students in "reflection and action upon the world in order to transform it" (Fránquiz et al., 2019, p. 382). In other words, humanization involves the process of becoming active and creative participants in the world (Freire, 1993). The efforts of teachers who embrace humanizing pedagogies "must coincide with those of the students" and must embrace "the quest for mutual humanization," in ways that demonstrate "trust in people and their creative power" (Freire, 1993, p. 56). As Freire explained, the process of humanizing must involve teachers and children in the mutual work of occupying vulnerable positions.

López (2019) called for educators to disrupt patterns of systemic violence in educational institutions and offered several examples of this in the literature. Specifically, his examples included selecting texts beyond the traditional canon so that children's critical reading is prioritized and the "ability to read rigorously serves as a function of their engagement" (Peel, 2017, p. 109), or moving away from redirecting student behaviors and from the integration of law enforcement in schools that promotes "a culture of control" (Monahan, 2009, p. 123). A culture of control imposes on children the identities of either "victims or criminals" as their primary experiences in schools (Monahan, 2009, p. 133). Engaging in projects that are inspired by youth participatory action research tenets that connect to the community and that the youth are passionate about is yet another way to disrupt systemic issues (Irizarry, 2016). These tenets include the understandings that children are knowledgeable about their lives, that institutions can be altered, and that deficit views of minoritized youth need to be reconceptualized (Irizarry, 2016). While López (2019) claimed that the classroom is not a place to do the transformative work that is necessary for a more humanistic world, humanistic pedagogies should certainly be implemented in schools as a means to disrupt systemic violence.

Embracing humanizing approaches in classrooms can help validate and integrate the linguistic and cultural knowledge and practices of children, but also place focus on the attitudes and dispositions of teachers (Fránquiz & Salazar, 2004; Huerta, 2011). Teachers who embrace humanizing pedagogies are often described as those who "believe that marginalized students (due to race, economic class, culture, or experience) differ in how they learn, but not in their ability to learn" (Huerta, 2011, p. 39), and see language as linked to identity and as a means to positioning children as agents (Zisselsberger, 2016). When working with children who are both minoritized and labeled with a disability, there is a need to consider the different ways of being able alongside other forms of difference. As teachers practice humanizing ways of being and learning with children, they also need to help children acquire the practices of the dominant culture (Huerta, 2011). Such processes must be complementary and additive, so that children's existing knowledge and practices continue to expand and are not expected to eventually disappear or be replaced (Valenzuela, 1999). In summary, while pedagogical content knowledge is important, teachers' ongoing reflection and their understanding of the relevance of their moment-to-moment decision-making is essential in humanizing approaches (Daniels & Varghese, 2020; Martínez-Álvarez et al., 2020). Teachers need to understand and reflect upon their own position within histories of oppression, attaining a more humane understanding of themselves and children and of how they can address oppression (Chávez-Moreno, 2020; Freire, 1993).

It is at the point when the potential of mutual qualitative change is imagined that humanizing pedagogy connects with the idea of the hybrid space, which is described next.

Hybrid Spaces and Humanizing Pedagogy

The third space or hybrid space is situated as a "space of radical openness" (Soja, 1996, p. 84). When taking a cultural-historical view, hybridity can be understood as a space in-between where there is dialogical exchange from which something new surfaces (Bhabha, 1994, 1996). A postcolonial perspective on learning at hybrid third spaces highlights its contradictory nature and the need for mutual change to take place, which can be viewed as a form of collective ZPD (Gutiérrez, 2008). As introduced in Chapter 2, Vygotsky (1978) used the idea of the ZPD to describe the long-term development process that is possible within individual children with assistance from artifacts and people. However, in CHAT the idea of the ZPD has more recently been used to help us understand collective learning experiences. That is, the ZPD is described as the "distance between the present everyday actions of the individuals and the historically new form of the societal activity that can be collectively generated as a solution to the double bind potentially embedded in everyday actions" (Engeström, 1987, p. 174). Hybrid spaces hold potential for expansion across a collective ZPD as different forms of learning, knowledge, or practices enter into contact and collide, altering each other. Gutiérrez (2008) described learning spaces as incorporating "multiple, layered, and conflicting activity systems with various interconnections," which she talked about (drawing on Goffman, 1961) "as the 'under life' of the classroom" (p. 152). Attending to these spaces, Gutiérrez and her colleagues (1999) documented short-term cycles of learning with potential for larger transformation. They also highlighted how "tension between play and learning" is part of hybrid learning taking place (Gutiérrez et al., 1999, p. 298).

This tension between play and learning is furthered by Lizárraga and Gutiérrez (2018), who illustrated how minoritized youth "used hybrid practices to express playful fluid identities and navigate spaces as nondominant youth who teeter on the boundaries of expert and novice roles" (p. 41). Using a critical event captured in the home of a Latinx working-class family, the researchers highlighted how "building powerful literacies involves the centering of dispositions and practices that thrive on the boundary—spaces that are not always sanctioned as educational" (Lizárraga & Gutiérrez, 2018, p. 38). Martínez-Álvarez (2020a) added that spaces not always sanctioned as educational can be playful but still rigorous, and highlighted how these spaces "validate the knowledge and practices of the minoritized communities being served, which might not be immediately perceived as academically sophisticated in educational institutions" (p. 6). Working with Latinx bilingual children with a disability, I proposed the expression *opportunity encounters* to refer to "hybrid spaces where children encountered some challenges but were able to compensate and move forward," allowing them to inhabit *nepantla*, a space where multiple cultures and knowledge are put into contact impacting each other in qualitative ways (Martínez-Álvarez, 2020a, p. 3). Opportunity encounters are fundamental in embracing humanizing pedagogical principles as they can help us leverage disability as an asset—as part of the natural variability among humans just like being bilingual and bicultural—and better understand how we can attend to children learning at the intersection of ability, language, and cultural differences (Martínez-Álvarez, 2020a). The following sections use information from a series of 3 days or sessions when the teacher candidates in the VWK afterschool program explored children's assets and knowledge by implementing a unit called Capas y Escudos (Capes and Shields). A brief outline of the different parts of the project, which took place along a 3-week period, is provided next.

THE CAPAS y ESCUDOS (CAPES AND SHIELDS) PROJECT

An overview of the unit is described in Classroom Identity and Knowledge Exploration 6.1. provided below. The full bilingual description can be found on this book's product page at https://www.tcpress.com.

Classroom Identity and Knowledge Exploration 6.1

The Capas y Escudos (Capes and Shields) Project

Day 1 of the project: Introduce the idea of powers; begin creating ideas to make a cape.

Day 2 of the project: Continue exploring strengths, talents, and differences using *Por cuatro esquinitas de nada* (Four little corners) by Jerome Ruillier.

Day 3 of the project: Design a shield that shows what makes you feel better and protected when you are feeling sad, lonely, frustrated, etc.

PLAYFUL SPACES AS TOOLS FOR HUMANIZING PEDAGOGIES

This section describes the work of the children with the teacher candidates in this three-session project, to illustrate playful learning spaces as tools to foster humanizing pedagogies (Lizárraga & Gutiérrez, 2018). While working in the project, children's knowledge and assets were validated and integrated as identities intersected fluidly. Children engaged in critical thinking and learning, worked in hybrid spaces as they created their capes and shields, and experienced what I refer to in this chapter as "hybrid humanizing pedagogical moments," which took place as hybridity and humanizing pedagogies occurred simultaneously, cultivating and nurturing each other.

Humanizing Pedagogies, Agency, and Critical Thinking

The multimodal texts the teacher candidates chose to introduce the Capas y Escudos project included the book *Por cuatro esquinitas de nada* (Four little corners) by Jerome Ruillier (2014) and the video clip titled *What would Christmas be without love?* by Erste Bank (2008). These texts generated interesting critical discussions and propelled the children into their own critical work and identity exploration. Following are illustrative samples from the discussion that took place while reading the book.

The children really enjoyed the read-aloud of the book that the teacher candidate leading the project (Perla) had selected for Day 2 (session 2). The apparently simple book, titled in Spanish *Por cuatro esquinitas de nada* (Four little corners) by Jerome Ruiller (2014), tells the story of a group of circles and a square who like to play together. When it is time to go back to the big house, only the circles fit through the door, which is circular. The book engages the readers in an exploration of possible solutions for this problem until, rather than fixing the square, they fix the door, and all shapes can go through it and enter the house.

During our discussion, we arrived at the point when the problem of the story, the square not fitting through the circular house door, was revealed. Here, Perla stopped reading and wondered out loud with the children. She asked them how the cuadrado (square) might feel because he can't fit in and asked for their suggestions so that the square could be included, and for the circles to find a way for the square to enter the house.

The teacher candidates captured the responses during the discussion. For instance, Isabella noticed how one boy had said, "[E]l cuadrado no siente bien [aunque] puedes ser tú solo [ser diferente] y eso es bueno" (the square does not feel good [although] you can be yourself [be different] and that is good) [Isabella, Learning Notes; Day 2 of Capas y Escudos]. This response focused on the square not feeling good and highlighted the boy's understanding that being different is not a problem, but an asset ("that is good"). Silvia captured additional responses, such as another boy who, she explained, had "suggested for the circles to call the circle police" and another girl who had said, "maybe the square could bend its corners" [Silvia's Learning Notes; Day 2 of Capas y Escudos]. These responses took the group on to considering changing the square to fit the other shapes. However, this did not align well with the idea of how being different was not the problem at the center of the story. Children also connected to the resources they knew from the school and outside it, and suggested to maybe call the police, as members of their communities, to help them find a solution.

One girl, an 8-year-old 3rd-grader named Mirella, started, while Perla was doing the read-aloud of this book, using the standing whiteboard that was placed near the group in the class. As Perla stopped to ask the questions, teacher candidate Isabella, who was initially worried about Mirella's engagement and attention, realized that she was actually thinking and participating through the whiteboard that she was using. Isabella explained this with the following words:

> As we entered the classroom, she [Mirella] immediately went over to the white board in the back and began to draw. I asked her about her drawing, and she began to explain it to me. Perla called the students to the carpet, and I told Mirella we needed to go to the carpet, but she should leave her drawing where it was and go back to it when she wanted. For the carpet time, I gave her a squishy that she could manipulate as she sat. When Perla asked how the cuadrado (square) might feel because he can't fit in, Mirella drew her response on the whiteboard behind her. I had gone to grab my notebook during this time and came back to see her writing on the board again; at first, I didn't realize she was sketching her answer and I almost redirected her to the whole group, but then I observed her drawing and saw she was depicting a square folding in its corners to become a circle. I positively reinforced that she was drawing her response, and in whole group, told Ms. Perla about it so she could reinforce as well. [Isabella's Learning Notes; Day 2 of Capas y Escudos]

This important entry captures the learning of the teacher candidate as she realized that by enacting agency, Mirella was mediating her learning and thinking through the whiteboard. She made this discovery as she recognized that she had initially tried to take Mirella away from the whiteboard onto the carpet, and later she explained how she, once again, "almost redirected her to the whole group." This is an essential moment of humanizing pedagogy, because as children engage in agentive actions to mediate their learning, these will not be successful unless they are encouraged and permitted by the educators in charge (Martínez-Álvarez, 2020a). Furthermore, it is important that teachers learn to move away from constantly redirecting behaviors in schools toward embracing children's mediational volitional actions in order to break the current "culture of control" (Monahan, 2009, p. 123). This event shows the negotiation that can take place in hybrid learning spaces where teachers and children collaborate to create more inclusive and humanizing opportunities.

As part of Day 2 of the project, Isabella also noticed in her learning notes how another boy said—going back to the discussion about the square who wouldn't fit through the door—how "pueden construir una casa para el que es más grande, para que los redonditos y los cuadraditos pueden entrar juntos, para que el cuadrado no siente mal" (they can build a house for the one that is bigger so that the little circular ones and the little square ones can go in together so that the square does not feel bad) [Isabella's Learning Notes, Day 2]. In this response, the child focused on changing the house, rather than the square, a more inclusive perspective that is rooted in the child's understanding that we need spaces where difference is welcome, and one can maintain their uniqueness and still belong.

As the children and teacher candidates heard and processed each other's contributions, Perla pointed out the importance of noticing (as explained in Silvia's learning notes), "that the issue wasn't with the square but the door!" Silvia wrote how at this point, "all of the kids seemed excited, especially the ones who suggested for the circles to create a bigger door" [Silvia's Learning Notes; Day 2 of Capas y Escudos]. However, most children had not suggested this option and were indeed intrigued by the idea. The suggestion of building a bigger house certainly went in this direction of expanding opportunities for access, and was widely celebrated at this point, as an even more inclusive suggestion that the one in the book, where the door is cut to include the four corners of the square.

This discussion that accompanied the read-aloud engaged children in critically processing the text. The meaningful text the candidates had selected clearly connected with children in important ways and mediated their engagement leading to a rigorous reading experience (Peel, 2017). Such experiences, as López (2019) has highlighted, can alter the systemic violence minoritized children experience in educational institutions, by drawing on children's experiences and their expertise while simultaneously expanding knowledge.

Humanizing Pedagogies and Children's Work: "We can 'evoke' instead of 'prompt'"

This section discusses the work that the children created while making the actual capas y escudos (capes and shields) in the project. In doing so, it provides examples of the processes that humanistic pedagogical perspectives can facilitate and the multiple identities that can manifest within this kind of work. It also showcases ways to interpret the potential of these experiences in the inclusive bilingual classroom. The learning notes of the teacher candidates help interpret and contextualize the exploration of the children as the candidates wrote about the work being done and described how the children themselves spoke about their process and productions.

In an entry during the second day of the Capas y Escudos project, for instance, Silvia wrote about one of the girls, Cynthia, who had been absent during the previous session. She explained how Cynthia hesitated when she was beginning the work but quickly came up with ideas. Silvia described this as follows:

> Cynthia wasn't there last session so she needed to begin a new cape, but she quickly got to work. At first, she didn't know what to put [as her powers] and then I reminded her it didn't have to be academic. I gave her the example of math being my power but also taking care of my dog is another power of mine. From there she came up with the idea that her power is playing with her grandmother. She quickly began to add more ideas such as being lovable and being a good friend. [Another child] also said that she is a good drawer and she quickly added that to her cape as well. [Silvia's Learning Notes; Day 2 of Capas y Escudos]

In this excerpt, Silvia demonstrated her awareness of a possible reticence on Cynthia's part to identify power among school subjects. In this space, aspects typically considered as academic and those not formally recognized as such were mixed; Silvia made sure to make this explicit to Cynthia, which reinforced the idea of the welcoming of a hybrid space. This allowed this girl to add "playing with her grandmother" as a power. Cynthia had drawn her grandmother wearing heels and jumping rope with her as part of her work in a prior session and she brought this idea back while adding to her cape. Cynthia worked conscientiously throughout the session to catch up, and her final cape design is showcased in Figure 6.1.

Cynthia's cape work, mostly written with words and a few symbols, centers on aspects of her emotional intelligence, such as "soy una experta a ser muy amorosa" (I am an expert at being loving; top left), "a ser una amiga buena y amable" (at being a good and kind friend; lower left), "amo a mi familia" (loving her family; one from last to the right side in the center), and

Figure 6.1. Cynthia's Cape Showing Her Powers

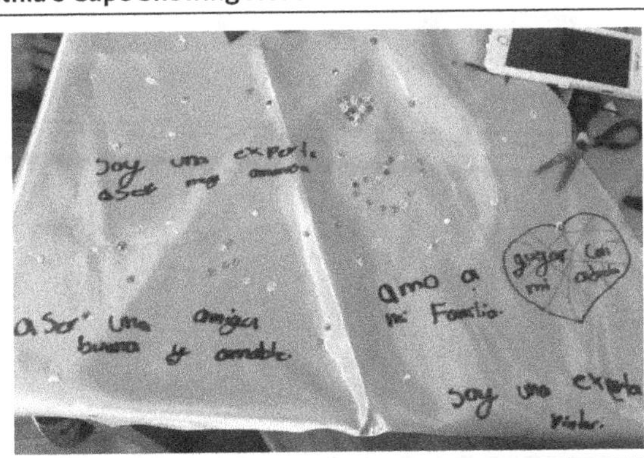

"*gugar* con mi *aduela*" (playing with her grandmother), which is inside a heart shape decorated by a shiny gem and with a background pattern of green wiggly lines (right side). Cynthia also added, when a classmate verbally complimented her with one more power, "soy una *expeta* pintar" (being an expert at painting), in the lower right side of her cape.

Another child, Luis, also captured teacher candidate Silvia's attention and she wrote about how he had incorporated the "idea of Math but also included video games" [Silvia's learning notes; Day 2 of Capas y Escudos]. Silvia explained that she had "asked him what kind of video games he likes, and he added pictures of characters from Minecraft" [Silvia's learning notes; Day 2 of Capas y Escudos]. This resulted in the cape shown in Figure 6.2.

Luis's cape included not only words but also symbols and drawings. He wrote Math three times in different sizes and colors, but also expressed this same power with a big drawing of a calculator and with two equations (bottom left and top right), and a multiplication sign. His cape also included elements that connected to his power with video games. For this, he chose to draw a small console, to write "games, *viedo*" (games, video), and the example of one popular game, "Minecraft" (Mojang, 2011). He also drew two video game characters using different colors and wrote the word "*cpeeper*" for creeper, one of the main figures in Minecraft (Mojang, 2011). Three stars of different sizes were included at the top and bottom of the cape design.

During the Day 3 of the project, the children created their shields to complement these capes. Mirella's work (Figure 6.3) was fully symbolic and captured the attention of Isabella who wrote about it in her learning notes. Isabella explained:

> I asked Mirella what the different symbols on her shield represented (she had a heart, a zig zag, an M, and a black square with cut-out hearts). She explained that the black square was for "mis amigos" (my friends),

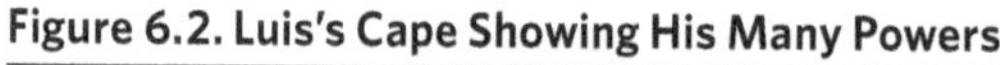

Figure 6.2. Luis's Cape Showing His Many Powers

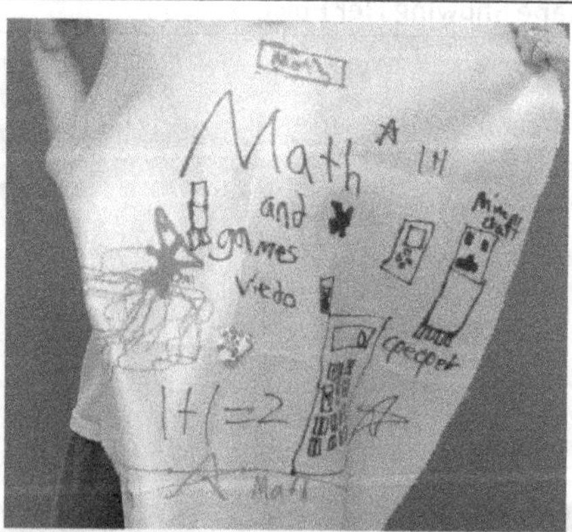

Figure 6.3. Mirella's Shield Showing What Makes Her Feel Protected

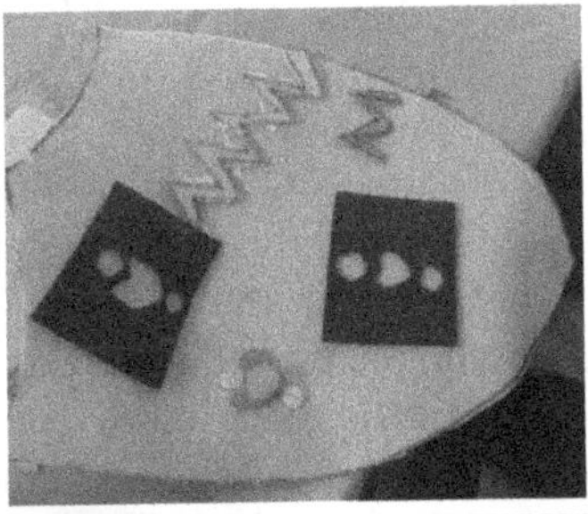

the heart "es para mi familia, they love me" (it's for my family, they love me), the zig-zag was because "I like to feel cool" and the M was "me for myself." [Isabella's learning notes; Day 3 of Capas y Escudos]

Mirella's shield, as she explained, integrated friends, family, and a desire to "feel cool," all while centering herself through the capital letter "M," the initial of her first name. The careful work and balance in the colors and the cutouts on the shield show how hard Mirella worked in designing her shield to showcase resources that help her feel better and protect her when she experiences anger, sadness, loneliness, or frustration.

For Jimena, another one of the participating girls, the emphasis while creating her shield was on love. She created the shield and accompanied it with a plastic bag selecting materials she liked and that she felt could not fit well on the shield. Her shield and bag are shown in Figure 6.4.

Figure 6.4. Jimena's Shield and Bag Showing What Makes Her Feel Protected

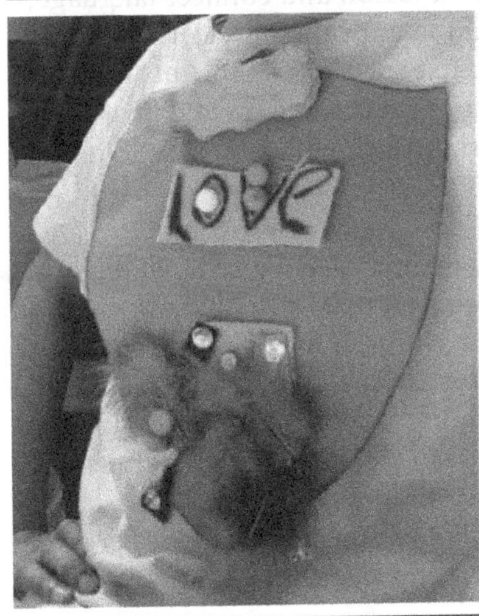

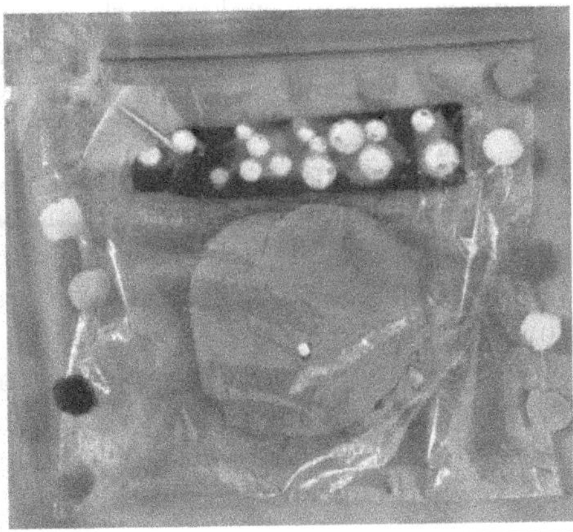

Jimena focused on working with materials and including whatever textures she liked on her final products. The word *love* is written in big black letters on a separate piece of felt fabric, and, as shown in Figure 6.4, she had cut out spaces to add three pompoms in different colors. The pink piece of clay appears in both of her designs as well, as if symbolizing a cloud, part of what she can use to feel protected.

As shown, at times the products the children created were mediators for artistic experimentation and, as explained in the next subsection, the resulting product was not always the most important part of the experience. Rather, the hybrid experience facilitated by this humanizing space provided opportunities for children to surface ideas about their knowledge, experiences, and aspirations in and out of school. This is summarized by Perla in her learning notes from Day 3 as follows:

> There were a lot of rainbows, clouds, random arrangements of objects, and hearts. Victor was cutting a heart with Silvia. When I pushed him a little to say what made him feel good/happy, he said: "a hug from my mom" which was so amazing to hear! It has been interesting to see how, at the end of the day, they end up doing what they want in their projects, sometimes regardless of the topic or instructions [. . .] [W]hat has come up while they work has been most rewarding. This has got me thinking that maybe, our role should be more of providers of material and activities that are inviting and interesting to them, to then engage them in conversation that will provide us with valuable information about their funds of knowledge. We can "evoke" instead of "prompt." Of course, how we initiate our sessions would still need to be thought of with care and planning. But sometimes it feels like we are trying really hard to come up with a lesson and connect language, culture and the goal of what we would like for them to learn.
> And more often than not, the results that surprises us the most, is unexpected and evoked by the activity, or has come up in conversation while they are doing the activity. [Perla's learning notes; Day 3 of Capas y Escudos]

I found the important conversations and actions that Perla is highlighting in her learning notes, through which children offered valuable information about themselves and their learning while working in less sanctioned educationally spaces, to be critical. The conversations and actions manifested children's creativity and recognized them as "experts of their own lives" (Irizarry, 2016, p. 8). These processes can help dismantle the deficit perspectives typically guiding education decisions about minoritized children with a disability. The work of the children highlighted the importance of creating spaces where educators employ humanizing approaches and interpretations, focus on children's agency, and attend to children's varied ways of knowing and learning. Through her words, Perla demonstrated a humanistic perspective as she trusted the "creative power" of these young children, which is fundamental in embracing a humanistic perspective (Freire, 1993, p. 56).

I put forth the phrase "hybrid humanizing pedagogical moments" to describe this form of conversing and taking action in a mutual respectful exchange. The idea of "hybrid humanizing pedagogical moments" can be explained by the following closing Perla included in her learning notes for the last session of the project: "The activity that we provide is almost like an 'excuse' or the means by which we obtain a lot of the valuable information of their funds of knowledge" [Perla's learning notes; Day 3 of Capas y Escudos]. Examples of hybrid humanizing pedagogical moments are next further illustrated to conceptualize them more clearly.

Hybrid Humanizing Pedagogical Moments

The written learning notes of the teacher candidates illustrated the level of humanity that surfaced during this project. For example, Silvia's notes after Day 2 of the Capas y Escudos project opened with a description of how some of the children who typically worked with Rita, a teacher candidate who was absent in this particular session, were very sad that she was not going to be there. Silvia wrote:

> The first thing I noticed was the disappointment on Jimena's face when she realized Rita was not at the afterschool [program]. In an attempt to cheer her up I asked her if she wanted to make a video for Rita so I could send it to her. We made the video and [several children] made a guest appearance to say hi to Ms. Rita. [Silvia's Learning Notes; Day 2 of Capas y Escudos]

This exchange showed the importance of really seeing the human beings in the afterschool program, here shown through the understanding and empathizing with children's need to express their feelings in the absence of one of the afterschool members. Creating a video for Rita acted as a mediator for "human agency and voice" (Kinloch & San Pedro, 2014, p. 23), that helped address the conflict of missing Rita. The video connected the in- and out-of-school worlds and most probably helped Rita, on the receiving end, feel missed while she had to be away.

Another example illustrating moments of hybrid humanizing pedagogy came from one of the children. Isabella highlighted in her notes how the boy had made Ana, one of his afterschool program classmates who was joining the session late, present in thought when she was not there in body. Isabella described it as follows:

> As [boy] was working, he clearly remembered Ana's presence from last week and said, unprompted, "Ana's gonna come here, she's gonna be late, so everyone's gotta be prepared." It was great to see him thinking about his peers and their presence even when they weren't there yet! [Isabella's Learning Notes; Day 3 of Capas y Escudos]

Here Isabella captured, and awed, at the boy's noticing of Ana, who was going to be joining late. This boy remembered from the previous session that Ana was going to arrive late on this day, and he made sure to keep a mental note on that, which he then was ready to share with others. In this way, he created a hybrid of the in- and out-of-session space that was ready to welcome Ana even before she was there. Isabella also explained later in her notes how, "When Ana did arrive, [the boy] immediately started to help her with [making] her shield and shared some of his strategies (you need to hold the felt in place for the sharpie to work, etc.)" [Isabella's Learning Notes; Day 3 of Capas y Escudos]. The connection and attention children offered to other children and adults during the afterschool program, even when they were not in the classroom, manifested in these different moments and highlighted the hybrid of worlds and the humanizing pedagogies in the program.

The calm and flexible hybrid humanizing spaces that the teacher candidates were able to foster alongside the children also provided opportunities for expansive conversations where the children brought up both traditional academic concerns and preoccupations alongside those concerns that are not typically recognized as academic or as belonging in school. This is shown in the following entry from Silvia's Day 3 learning notes:

> As we worked, we had many interesting conversations. Victor told me more about his family and his interests. He said that Fortnite makes him feel happy. He also expressed his dislike for school and doing work. Luis spoke to me about his sister, his family, the dog him and Andrés [his brother] want, and how he went up two levels in guided reading and much more. As me, Luis and Victor worked and talked, Andrés was very concentrated on his shield and didn't say much. [Silvia's Learning Notes; Day 3 of Capas y Escudos]

This excerpt summarizes the easy flowing topics of the conversations, or humanizing "acts of listening," that took place (Kinloch & San Pedro, 2014, p. 23), as children worked in this less sanctioned space of the afterschool program. It shows the actual hybridity of topics in children's lives, which crosses the imaginary lines of the in- and out-of-school topics and spaces.

While some children preferred to concentrate on their work first and then talk about it (i.e., Andrés), and this was respected, others spoke about things that were important to them as they engaged in the creative work. These moments of creative work often led to critical topics. For instance, Silvia highlighted this follow-up exchange involving Victor and Luis. Victor was a child with a disability who was placed in 2nd grade but was at a reading level lower than that of his classmates (according to the school guided reading levels). Luis was a child with a disability who had made a lot of progress along the reading levels during this year. As shown, Victor had stated earlier that while Fortnite, a popular video game, made him happy, he "disliked schoolwork." Silvia wrote about how the conversation happened.

> When Luis spoke about his progress in guided reading, Victor seemed to get quiet. After some time, Victor stated that he was at a level C before coming to his current class and he actually went down two levels and is now at a level A. He seemed hesitant to speak about it, but he continued. Luis then said that he wouldn't be at a low level if he tried a little harder. [Silvia's Learning Notes; Day 3 of Capas y Escudos]

In this part of the conversation that Silvia described, Luis initially placed the responsibility for becoming a better reader on Victor, who, he explained, needed to try "a little harder." It is often the case that schools, through those within that space, situate a lack of progress on the children's shoulders. It is no wonder that Victor would express that he did not like school if he is seen as regressing and maybe not trying hard enough. This perspective, however, does not fully recognize the role of the learning space and the contextual factors that might be negatively impacting children's reading, as well as the (at times limited) way reading is conceptualized and measured in schools. However, through this moment of Victor's "vulnerability," part of "humanizing research" work (Kinloch & San Pedro, 2014, p. 23), Luis realized the impact of his words on Victor. He consequently revised his perspective, realizing that he might have been unfair. Silvia explained how this part of the discussion took place with these words:

> [Luis] began to stammer because it seemed like he thought he may have hurt Victor feelings by saying that. He began to say "I don't want to be mean like, you know, because, you know" I jumped in and looked at Victor and asked him how that made him feel. He replied that it made him feel bad. I looked at Victor and in a caring but serious way I said "Victor, I know it may seem difficult because you have a lot to catch up on, but you can do it, you can get to where you need to be, but you can't stop trying, you can't give up." He didn't say anything, but he looked at me and it seemed like what I said to him meant something. After saying that, Luis joined in and told Victor that he could do it, he just needs to work for it. [Silvia's Learning Notes; Day 3 of Capas y Escudos]

Luis's hesitation and Victor's reaction highlighted how emphasizing the child's responsibility for their own lack of progress can hurt children's self-images and confidence, as they might be already trying what they perceive to be their best. However, the discussion ended up in a similar direction where Victor is placed as merely having "to work for it." It is important that educators recognize that even when children work their hardest, the ways in which reading is taught in schools might not favor their ways of learning, or children might not know the path that could lead to them making more progress. As Freire (1993) explained, teachers' and children's efforts must coincide and they must together aim for "mutual humanization" informed by each other's' feelings and perspectives (p. 56).

This chapter aimed at exploring the ways through which a humanistic approach can assist in making bilingual programs more inclusive of children with a disability, as children's agency and critical thinking are facilitated through playful spaces where teacher candidates can "evoke" instead of too directively prompting students to do work in predetermined ways. The cases presented here illustrate the process of taking a humanistic approach to hopefully inspire teacher candidates in facilitating the type of collective ZPDs needed for such transformative learning to occur. Humanizing pedagogies call for the recognition of the role of the classroom context and institutional factors, as much as the role of the children themselves as they are provided with tools and artifacts to be able to mediate their learning (Martínez-Álvarez, 2020a).

CONCLUSION

Based on the analysis of work from the three-session exploratory work of the Capas y Escudos project, I proposed in this chapter the term "hybrid humanizing pedagogical moments" to describe those moments where hybridity and humanizing pedagogies occurred simultaneously, cultivating and nurturing each other. The moments took place in the less sanctioned educational space of the VWK as children revealed valuable information about themselves and their learning that integrated different social spaces, and that allowed for the exploration of multiple identities, or, in other words, that centered their humanity. The center of the activity at the hybrid humanizing pedagogical moments shifted away from the lesson's intended product or learning objectives, toward the unexpected and unscripted mutual learning of the teacher candidates about the children, and the children about teachers, classmates, and the world. Hybrid humanizing pedagogical moments involved the recognition of the role of the classroom context as well as institutional factors. They highlighted the agentive role of the children themselves who could potentially mediate their own learning (i.e., Victor's perceived reading lack of progress), express their feelings and voice across in- and out-of-school worlds (i.e., the creation of a video for Rita), or humanely attend to and/or anticipate the potential needs of those inside and outside of the classroom (i.e., the boy attending to Ana's needs). Hybrid humanizing pedagogical moments took place within calm and flexible spaces and led to "acts of listening" (Kinloch & San Pedro, 2014, p. 23) and expansive conversations about topics typically considered as being of both academic and less academic natures. These moments manifested the hybridity in the lives of bilingual children labeled with a disability, which goes beyond a single learning space (i.e., outside school), and were enacted in different ways. For instance, at times, children conversed as they engaged in the activity, while at other times, like with Andrés, they demonstrated ideas directly through their work or after finishing it; some revealed more of their preoccupation about school topics while others preferred to focus on images beyond school. This inclusion of ideas across spaces is a central point because it could be that, as David Kirkland (2014) found, when working with marginalized children "the location of their literacies wasn't in a classroom" (p. 179). The hybrid humanizing pedagogical moments were full of creative collective learning potential: learning involving multiple spaces that are often perceived as being separate, and learning that is both unexpected and humanizing.

I hope this chapter and the illustrative work included within it can assist future teachers in planning for activities that are means toward the kinds of conversations and humanity that we experienced in the afterschool program space. Strictly limiting school time to cover a standard curriculum might risk downplaying the importance of more open spaces where unexpected and unscripted mutual learning can take place. The caring relationships and knowledge that fluidly surfaced in this space are accepting of multiple ways of expressing and receiving information, which, as suggested in UDL approaches, is key when working with children with a disability (Hall et al., 2012). Hybrid humanizing pedagogical moments might give teachers and children the space that is needed to safely explore their multiple ways of being in the classroom and outside it.

CHAPTER 7

Exploring Disability With Bilingual Children

Inclusive education, understood from a radical perspective, requires going beyond addressing the technical aspects of schooling (e.g., schedules, groups, or resources; Greenstein, 2016). It demands a school reform focused on equity and social justice for children who have historically experienced exclusion in learning and social contexts (Bacon & Pomponio, 2020; Slee, 1997). Radical inclusive education highlights the need for "supporting children to better understand themselves, the world and their relations with others in the world, while taking into account the full range of human embodiments and support needs" (Greenstein, 2016, p. 5). From this perspective, providing opportunities for children to explore their multiple identities and how these impact learning is an important aspect of an inclusive agenda. In the case of bilingual children with a disability, identity work involves multiple layers as there is a need to attend to children's bilingual and bicultural characteristics and disability-related uniqueness.

Simultaneously, a radical inclusive education must embrace approaches where children can begin the process of conscientization (Freire, 1993). According to Freire, conscientization refers to children's learning to understand that what might seem to be their individual issues as learners are connected to the issues of other minoritized people, and to the limitations placed on them in the contradictory social contexts they navigate. This process creates pathways to foster children's sense of agency and to develop collective understandings of their oppressive circumstances, stimulating significant questions and learning (Greene, 1988). Teaching the histories of disabled and immigrant peoples as part of the school curriculum and recognizing the knowledge both bilingual children and children with a disability bring to school becomes fundamental in inclusive bilingual education contexts. However, these histories are seldom recognized or valued in educational institutions. Rather, systems have historically understood bilingual children from deficit perspectives (Greenfield, 2013; Martínez-Álvarez, 2020b), ignoring their perceptions, knowledge, and practices (Kangas, 2020). Only dominant literacies that privilege reading and writing modes and particular texts representing the majoritarian culture and social practices have been historically valued. Prioritizing dominant literacies (Barton & Hamilton, 2012) while rarely teaching the collective story of others like disabled activists (Bacon & Lalvani, 2019) or hardly recognizing various ways of making meaning have created hierarchies of learners. While Freire did not directly center disability, bilingual children with a disability must become aware of these oppressive processes following their own unique processes toward conscientization (Gabel, 2002).

To assist in advancing processes of conscientization with bilingual children with a disability, this chapter investigates the importance of identity work and learning about disability through the experiences that took place in the VWK afterschool program. This chapter employs work and conversations from a series of curricular invitations implemented in the VWK afterschool program. Through these invitations, bilingual children with a disability worked with teacher candidates in exploring the origin of the services that disabled people have the right to receive to ensure a free and appropriate education, and the role of the disability civil rights movement in making this happen. Curricular invitations included creating their ideal classroom using LEGOs and clay materials. The chapter investigates the questions: What knowledge do bilingual children with a disability manifest while engaging in identity work and learning about disability, and what forms of agency surface as children explore multiple identity possibilities?

The following sections offer an overview of the research attending to aspects of identity with children with a disability and with children who are bilingual and bicultural. Then the chapter discusses literature addressing the relevance of teaching about disability and exploring multiple identities. Before presenting information collected during an exploration of disability with the bilingual children in VWK, the chapter offers some theoretical ideas from CHAT that have the potential to contribute to our understanding of disability as an asset and as an identity.

IDENTITY AND DISABILITY

The process of creating an inclusive learning space entails understanding disability as a form of identity, a positive aspect of one's experience, which is part of the place one occupies in the world (Gabel, 2002). Recognizing and naming disability is hence important to ensure that children with a disability are not always compared to the standard of the ideal learner, against which they are constantly perceived as lacking (Annamma et al., 2013a). When compared to a standard image of a learner, the ability of children with a disability to be self-determined and exert agency might end up being restricted (Petersen, 2009). DSE scholars work toward developing practices to "honor disability diversity and promote an understanding of disability as a positive and prideful identity that young children can associate with" (Erwin et al., 2021, p. 6).

Unfortunately, children's agentive efforts to identify in multiple ways may not always be appreciated, or even recognized. Children with a disability might express autonomy in ways that are perceived as inappropriate in our restrictive schooling contexts, such as the nonverbal actions of crying, yelling, or hugging (Gabel, 2002). These actions might also be interpreted as manifestations of a biological "impairment" when coming from children who are labeled with "learning difficulties," impeding the analysis of the sociological epistemologies that are at their core (Goodley, 2001, p. 225). Gabel (2002) suggested, "Rather than thinking about voice as the use of conventional literacies to represent the self [. . .] consider voice as any attempt, even unrecognized or difficult to interpret attempts, to represent the self, regardless of whether they are enacted in conventional ways" (p. 190). Such an approach can assist in understanding the critical forms of agency in which children with a disability constantly engage (Gabel, 2002; Petersen, 2009).

In a study examining the way in which disability is present in published work informed by critical pedagogy frameworks, Gabel (2002) found that ability diversity is often either ignored or minimized in this body of work. Researchers have compared the absence of considerations of ability discrimination (i.e., ableism) to the way colorblind racism or language-based discrimination might be ignored in classrooms, making it difficult to envision what is needed to transform oppressive forces (Bonilla-Silva, 2020; Erwin et al., 2021; Román et al., 2019).

For our classrooms to be inclusive spaces, there is a need to provide opportunities for the flexible exploration of multiple identities, something achieved through responsive and child-centered experiences (Erwin et al., 2021). This is the case for children with a disability and for those who are minoritized in other ways, such as bilingual and bicultural children of immigrant background.

BILINGUAL AND BICULTURAL IDENTITY

Bilingual children need purposeful opportunities to explore their multiple identities in flexible ways just as much as children with a disability do. Minoritized children bring rich knowledge and valuable practices to school, and these assets ought to be not only validated but also integrated into the curriculum (Martínez-Álvarez, 2017a). When children's resources are employed for formal learning, opportunities for renewed academic achievement and identity development are created (Martínez-Álvarez, 2020a). For instance, research showed that when teachers embraced "translingual pedagogical approaches," honoring and leveraging their students' vast linguistic repertoires, opportunities to enact agency, and identify as being bilingual and bicultural, expanded (Zapata & Laman, 2016).

Research looking into identity explorations with bilingual children demonstrated "the interplay between language, literacy, and identity" and suggested that language and culture act as resources that can be continually developed while in schools (Lynch, 2018, p. 129). Lynch's (2018) case study of a newcomer child learning in a transitional bilingual 3rd-grade classroom revealed that bilingual and bicultural children whose knowledge is recognized and integrated into school can experience what it is to feel as an expert and can continue to grow as the strong learners they are. The knowledge to which children are exposed as they navigate the social spaces they experience and that are accumulated and pass onto new generations, children's FoK, are fundamental for healthy and fluid identity work (González et al., 2005).

While bilingual and bicultural children carry multiple identities and are highly diverse, they might be perceived as all sharing the same practices, knowledge, or ways of learning, among other dimensions. In a study looking into the identities of 18 diverse youth who were undocumented, researchers found that the participants experienced "frequent assaults on their identity" and felt "continuously essentialized by unfounded stereotypes" and by the "monolithic identity" of having no legal United States documents (Chang et al., 2017, p. 201). The study highlighted the need to construct pathways of "critical hope" for children focused on a strength-based perspective that uses the capital they possess, rather than on the obstacles they face (Chang et al., 2017, p. 211).

While understanding minoritized children's FoK is important, mere understanding is not enough. These FoK need to be employed for learning and expanded to create new knowledge if they are to be useful in schools. Otherwise, children's assets and resources will remain in a secondary role in education. That is, FoK become part of one's identity work as they are used to define oneself, transforming into what is referred to as *funds of identity* (Esteban-Guitart, 2014). According to Esteban-Guitart (2014), funds of identity include the artifacts children create and use from their FoK and that mediate the constitution of their human identity (language, beliefs, flags, objects, school tools, talents, skills, ways of being, etc.). Succinctly put, identity development and learning with bilingual and bicultural children necessarily involve consideration and integration of children's FoK into the regular curricular experiences.

MULTIPLE IDENTITIES AND BILINGUAL CHILDREN WITH A DISABILITY

Children who bring bilingual and bicultural resources and children who have a disability have been separately documented as experiencing marginalization in educational institutions and in other social contexts (e.g.,

Coakley-Fields, 2019; Petersen, 2009; Suárez-Orozco et al., 2010; Valenzuela, 1999). Consequently, children who are simultaneously bilingual and have a disability are often multiply marginalized (Annamma et al., 2013b). For instance, bilingual children who are labeled with a disability are frequently situated as having low educational outcomes (Trainor et al., 2016), might be subjected to negative expectations about their development (Kangas, 2020), and might spend more time in segregated spaces than other children with a similar disability (Sullivan, 2011).

Relatedly, many of the bilingual children who are identified with a disability might be misclassified due to inappropriate referrals, lack of educators with expertise in bilingual children's development, or biased assessment processes (Ortiz et al., 2011). As a result, issues of both over- and under-identification of bilingual children as disabled have been documented in different states and districts (Artiles et al., 2005). When working with bilingual children with a disability, explorations leading to processes of conscientization about the oppressive conditions they experience and the collective nature of these conditions must be designed (Freire, 1993).

Educators should explore disability identities with bilingual and bicultural children with care and consciousness of related issues, because of their possible misidentification as disabled and because a disability label can have bad consequences for minoritized children. Issues also include how children with an IEP might not realize they have a labeled disability, or how family members may not fully accept the disability label their children have been assigned. For example, Cioè-Peña (2021) in her research with Latinx mothers of children with a disability found that the mothers in her study tended to minimize their children's disability, expressed interest in keeping the label confidential, and situated their children as "different" but not "disabled" (p. 144). These aspects must be carefully navigated while offering opportunities for fluid multilayered identity exploration, and for learning about the disability rights movement and other landmarks in disability activism. These opportunities might lead to more positive views of a person with a disability that could potentially promote the development of new identities and better self-images as learners.

DSE scholars understand the issues around the mislabeling of minoritized children but also promote practices honoring disability and exploring a positive disability identity (Erwin et al., 2021). In this integrating effort, it is important that disability is associated with competence and that existing educational barriers are understood as rooted in racist and ableist processes deeply ingrained in the history of the United States (Annamma et al., 2013b). As Galvin (2003) described citing different researchers, learning to feel pride in being disabled can assist in the process of conscientization by developing a common purpose for productive change. This involves breaking away from the hierarchical processes that have dichotomized learning into mutually exclusive binaries such as language learner/language proficient or able/disabled, toward possibilities for valuing learning and agency for all students (Galvin, 2003). It also involves celebrating the "disabled identity" as much as the temporary or the permanent possibility of "existing outside of it" (Galvin, 2003, p. 686).

In summary, while labels connected to bilingualism and disability can be used to enact social oppression, they can also be signals for transformative work and become positive contributors to children's identities (Galvin, 2003). When working with bilingual children with a disability, attention must be given to factors related to the intersection of multiple labels.

TEACHING ABOUT DISABILITY AND THE DISABILITY RIGHTS MOVEMENT

Disability history and the contributions of people with a disability to securing the rights disabled people now have, have rarely been taught in schools (Bacon & Lalvani, 2019). Avoiding the topic, however, communicates the idea that ability differences might be less valuable than other forms of difference (Bacon & Lalvani, 2019). That is, as teachers continue to question the need to explore disability in the classroom, negative beliefs continue to predominate (Ware, 2005).

Researchers emphasize the importance of nurturing children's "sense of justice in the classroom and beyond" (Erwin et al., 2021, p. 1). Teaching about the way people with disability have stood out for disability rights can promote this important goal. While participating in disability related explorations, children will actively bring their own ideas, knowledge, and possible bias into these less well-known topics, and they will act upon new ideas, creating hybrid understandings (Erwin et al., 2021).

Children may not spontaneously ask questions about disability, and teachers might assume that children do not notice disability and conclude that there is no need to discuss aspects of ability diversity (Lalvani, 2015). Research, however, has shown that elementary level children are curious about disability and that they do notice their classmates' different ways of learning or moving, but that they may have learned to conceal this genuine interest about disability (Lalvani, 2015). This supports the idea from DSE scholars that discussing disability in schools is morally necessary and fundamental (Bacon & Lalvani, 2019; Connor & Gabel, 2010; Lalvani, 2015)

We need to better understand the ways bilingual children with a disability might react to invitations to explore the disability rights movement, and to learn about the rights of disabled youth learning in public schools and beyond. Likewise, while there is growing understanding around disability oppression and disability identity, more work is needed to better understand how to explore these developing ideas with elementary level children with and without a disability (Bacon & Lalvani, 2019) and with children who are bilingual and bicultural.

A part of this need is to learn how children draw and generate different forms of knowledge while involved in these kinds of explorations about disability. For instance, researchers have identified three forms of knowledge associated with movement for social change that might be important to consider as we engage in disability-related conscientization efforts: "subaltern knowledge," which refers to the knowledge that is often ignored in schools but that those who are oppressed possess; "knowledge of the system" and how it operates; and "knowledge about tactics" for resistance (Cox & Flesher Fominaya, 2009, as cited in Greenstein, 2016, pp. 58–59).

As discussed below, CHAT frameworks hold the potential to help us understand processes related to teaching and learning about disability movements and disability identity by highlighting the role of mediation and the collective and multidimensional learning that could surface through these explorations.

LEARNING AND DISABILITY IDENTITY THROUGH A CHAT AND DSE LENS

Identity is an important concept in recent literature, where it has been explored from different perspectives. Bruner (2003) explained that "we constantly construct and reconstruct a self to meet the needs of the situations we encounter" and that "telling oneself about oneself is rather like making up a story about who and what we are, what has happened, and why we are doing what we are doing" (p. 210). Bruner (2003) described identity as ever evolving and as created from our own cultural and historical experiences, memories, and knowledge, as well as our anticipation for the future.

From a CHAT perspective, identity is not focused on the individual, but rather on the individual's participation in collective activity (Roth, 2014). This fluid and collectively achieved interpretation of identity is similar to *distributed agency*, a parallel concept in DSE: the idea that children with a disability need "the opportunity to shape this essential part of their identity [disability] in the company of others who share their experience" (Linton, 1998, p. 64). As children participate in collective activity where they care about the object of the shared work and with which they are deeply invested and actively engaged, they will help shape the activity, but the activity will also progressively shape them (see Roth, 2014). That is, during participation in learning activity, there is multidirectional qualitative transformation that results in identity refinement as children bring forth their own assets and expertise (i.e., employing distributed expertise; Cole & Engeström, 1993). This dynamic relationship between the outside material work and internal development of, in this case, one's identity is what Vygotsky theorized as the dialectical relationship of learning. Dialectical thinking, a concept still embryonic at Vygotsky's time, allows for the consideration of internal aspects of learning in relation to those that are materially in the external world (Roth & Lee, 2007). Dialectical thinking is, as Glassman (2000) explained, "the most appropriate frame of reference for the study of human development" (p. 2), because thinking develops through "dialectical moments" in a series of qualitative transformations where history is a foundational component (Glassman, 2000, p. 6).

The expansive view of agency that is employed in CHAT, where it is understood as being fundamental for learning in object-oriented activity (i.e., activity oriented toward a shared motive), is important in relation to the development of identity. This more social and collaborative form of agency that leads to transformative forms of learning is a new, alternative path to the traditional psychological interpretations through which agency is understood to be exercised through self-regulation (Bandura, 1989) or the merely sociological interpretations of agency (Emibaryer & Mische, 1998). According to CHAT theorists, agency is transformative when participants take volitional actions using artifacts to mediate a way out of a "conflict of motives" that they experience while working together (Sannino, 2015, p. 2). In this process, referred to as the principle of double stimulation, the conflict or tension that surfaces acts as a first stimulus to which participants respond, drawing on artifacts that are used as second stimuli to redirect their activity and help them learn together (Vygotsky, 1978). As people engage in collective processes, they draw on forms of agency such as "relational agency," which involves the "capacity to align one's thoughts and actions with those of others in order to interpret problems of practice and to respond to those interpretations" (Edwards, 2005, pp. 169–170).

From a CHAT standpoint, therefore, agency is enacted in response to a conflict, and the efforts that participants take to redirect their activity away from the conflict are mediated with artifacts. This process is often relational, as it involves the ability to recognize that "another person may be a resource" (Edwards, 2005, p. 172), and leads to new directions and learning. Engaging in these particular forms of taking action (i.e., enacting agency) using one's expertise, as well as that of others, as assets is aligned with identity development (Edwards & Mackenzie, 2008). In fact, in examining identity, Edwards and Mackenzie (2008) have focused on those learning zones that encourage participants to "expand their interpretations of the resources available to support their actions," enabling them to explore fluid identities as capable agents of change (p. 165). In their study of identity trajectories, the researchers found that when one can transform the object of their activities, it is possible for identity to develop; they found that relational agency "is a crucial factor in the development of purposive identities" (Edwards & Mackenzie, 2008, p. 179).

The focus of CHAT on the activity system or multiple activity systems as the unit of analysis and the centrality of object-oriented activity, and its emphasis on the resolution of tensions mediated by the participants' volitional actions as a form of multidimensional learning, make this theory a fruitful tool for understanding the curricular invitations at the center of this chapter (Hancock & Miller, 2018). The curricular invitations that focused on exploring topics of the disability rights movement with the bilingual children in the VWK are described next.

EXPLORING THE DISABILITY CIVIL RIGHTS MOVEMENT AND THE RIGHTS OF PEOPLE WITH A DISABILITY

The unit of the VWK program exploring the disability civil rights movement and the rights of people with a disability is briefly described in Classroom Identity and Knowledge Exploration 7.1. The full bilingual description can be found on this book's product page at https://www.tcpress.com.

Classroom Identity and Knowledge Exploration 7.1

The Derechos de las Personas con Discapacidad (Disability Rights Movement) Project

Day 1 of the project: Introduce disability diversity using the book *¡Solo pregunta!: Sé diferente, sé valiente, sé tú* (Just ask!: Be different, be brave, be you) and exploring children's disability experience using questions.

Day 2 of the project: Discuss one of the main rights of people with a disability in schools, the Plan Educativo Individualizado (Individualized Educational Plan; IEP) and artifacts (e.g., questions, manipulatives, or other teaching materials and resources that teachers can use to mediate children's learning.

Day 3 of the project: Introduce the disability civil rights movement and two main activists who played critical roles in it (Edward Roberts and Roland Johnson), and have the children design their ideal classroom using LEGOs and clay.

Day 4 of the project: Put the book of children's disability experiences together and create videos of the children narrating their ideal classroom creations.

AGENCY AND COLLECTIVE LEARNING WHILE EXPLORING DISABILITY

The following sections illustrate the ways in which the children responded to this 4-day project exploring the disability civil rights movement and disability identity. During this collective learning experience, the children explored their disability identity as they spoke about the ways they experienced difficulties and how the social context, at times, aggravated their circumstances rather than alleviating them. The children also revealed their knowledge about the artifacts, resources, and accommodations they used in the context of learning about IEPs.

The third part of the findings illuminates how the children responded to learning about two disability rights activists who were disabled themselves. The section reports on responses to both the abstract idea of disability and specific observation of people who used wheelchairs. The last section focuses on the final classroom designs that the children created. Through the children's designs and words, the section highlights how the children enacted agency and engaged in collective learning with transformative potential.

Surfacing Aspects of Children's Disability Experiences

The first day of the Disability Rights Movement Exploration project helped us learn about ways in which the children revealed aspects of their disability experiences. For instance, one of the girls in the program, Elena, explained her difficulties with math in the following exchange:

> *Elena:* Lo que me ayudan en la clase es que en matemáticas casi todo es difícil. (What they help me with in class is that almost everything in mathematics is difficult.)
>
> *Carlos:* Matemáticas es fácil. Le pone un problema de fracciones. (Mathematics is easy. They give you a fraction problem.)
>
> *Elena:* ¡Estoy en cuarto grado, no en quinto, oye! En clase me ayudan solo un poco. (I'm in fourth grade, not in fifth, hey! In class they help me just a little)

As Elena explained that she needed help in mathematics and that it was difficult, Carlos contradicted her, stating that it was easy. Elena reacted to this comment by first explaining that she was in a grade level lower than Carlos and then, in an effort that pointed to her possible feelings of inadequacy, adding that she received only "un poco" (a little) help [not a lot]. The children seemed to feel in a safe space to share their vulnerabilities while working in these sessions. However, we see in this conversation that children might experience microaggressions as they navigate learning spaces in relation to their ability to do/learn things, and it is important to monitor these interactions and offer support for those involved, as needed.

Children also described their difficult experiences in relation to languages. For example, during this first session, Xochtil opened up about her and her family speaking Mixteco at home. She explained that she rarely used Mixteco, because when she did, others did not understand her. Another similar comment was Dorita's concern about her accent when speaking English. She described how others did not always understand what she was saying in English and that friends made fun of her when she spoke English. Marina, the teacher candidate of Mexican origin, discussed this exchange in our follow-up reflection meeting, and added that another girl had mentioned that voice could be used "to defend yourself." Marina explained that she felt this was a tool that the girl offered to follow up on the experience of Dorita, who, as she knew, was "attacked" because of her accent when speaking in English.

Apart from these descriptions, children had other ideas in relation to voice through which they expressed their disability. For example, one of the girls who always spoke very softly explained the reason behind her way of talking: "I only talk low because sometimes I'm scared [. . .] que no puedo hablar bien (that I can't speak well)." She also explained how a child "is mean" to her and so she sometimes is "speechless. Sometimes I show my feelings. I don't like to do it all the time." She then added, "They interrupt me, and I forget my words [. . .] I just put some[thing] random at times," and added, " I don't like it when I lose my words." Through this excerpt, this girl explained her awareness of the difficulties she has in expressing herself in the classroom. She expressed these difficulties that the educational system summarizes as a learning disability or as a speech and language impairment, operationalizing it for us with: being "speechless," "forget my words," "put some[thing] random," or "lose my words." In the mix, she added her feelings around these experiences and how other children might be "mean" to her, manifesting that the difficulties are not within her (i.e., biological or innate) but fostered through an, at times, non-supportive environment.

In a way, as the children expressed instances when they were not understood, or when they could not easily express their feelings or safely use their accented English, they were showing awareness of how they are restricted within the school confines. They also hinted at how, at times, they took action as a way out of an undesirable circumstance (use your voice to "defend yourself" or "put some[thing] random"). This information constitutes important knowledge, "subaltern knowledge" that is often rendered invisible in schools by those with more power but that teachers need to bring to children's consciousness when working with minoritized communities (Cox & Flesher Fominaya, 2009, as cited in Greenstein, 2016, p. 58). As children were validated as experts, this knowledge manifested more fluidly and hence was integrated into the school potentially promoting additional opportunities for collective learning and development.

It is important to create situations where children can deal with feelings of oppression by external forces within schools through the nurturing of a sense of agency where learning takes place (Greene, 1988, as cited in Greenstein, 2016). Children's ideas in this first part of the project were all expressions that can contribute to the development of a disability identity and that are important to consider while teaching and learning with all children, but particularly with bilingual children with a disability.

As the first day of the project came to an end, the teacher candidates felt they understood the children's needs and feelings better than before this lesson. The book that was used, *¡Solo pregunta!: Sé diferente, sé valiente, sé tú* (Just ask!: Be different, be brave, be you) by Sonia Sotomayor, in which children with different needs and abilities were portrayed, helped children in reflecting about their own diversity and highlighted aspects of ableism (discrimination based on ability) and linguicism (discrimination based on language) in bilingual programs. Creating spaces where vulnerabilities can be shared and discussed is very important, but to openly discuss one's vulnerabilities, children need to feel safe from criticism about their abilities, languages, and cultures.

Exploring Disability Identities: Mediating Artifacts and Resources

During the second day, Juán, the teacher candidate leading the lesson, explained to the children how some of them might have an individualized educational plan, an IEP. The teacher candidate then guided the children to name the artifacts and resources from which they benefitted in the classroom and to reflect upon them. The discussion aimed at showing that in their classroom there are artifacts and resources that are needed to accommodate everyone's learning and that some children do need specific tools that are not typically offered in educational spaces. Susan Gabel (2002) addressed this when describing a girl who, while she had been labeled with, in the author's terms, "severe mental retardation," did not identify as disabled (Gabel, 2002, p. 181). She noted that the material things and needs that must be attended to "cannot be ignored, regardless of her self-constructed identity" (Gabel, 2002, p. 184). In the VWK context, independently from the children's identities, Juán started highlighting some of the things the children used for learning in the following conversation:

Juán: ¿Qué cosas usan en clase, fidget, sillas, rockers, computadora? (What things do you use in class, fidget, chairs, rockers, computers?)

Andrés: Pero no, porque todos lo usan la computadora. (But no, because everyone uses the computer.)

Carlos: No todos a veces. Por ejemplo, Ana. (Not all always. For example, Ana.)

In this exchange, Andrés pointed out that the artifacts and resources Juán was referring to were those that were uniquely used by a particular child rather than those that were used by all children. With this comment, he demonstrated the awareness of the nature of the IEP, which addresses things that some children need that are different from what is generally provided in the classroom for learning. Likewise, as Juán offered more examples, children confirmed when they or their classmates used these different things to help them learn. Elena explained, after Juán mentioned doing exercises in the hallway, that "yo lo hago a veces" (I do it sometimes), while another girl said that "un niño de mi clase sale y hace ejercicio" (a boy from my class goes outside and exercises). Likewise, when Juán mentioned the accommodation of providing extra time, Carlos spontaneously said "a mí me dan [más tiempo]" (I am given more time). Additionally, he wrote, with the help of a teacher candidate, the following ideas that helped him learn: fidget para las manos (fidget for the hands); computadora para mi tarea (computer for my homework); Mis lentes para leer (my glasses to read); Comida para comer (food to eat); Examen para estudiar y practicar (exam to study and practice); Escuela para aprender mucho (school to learn a lot); Mis amigos, hablamos mucho (my friends, we talk a lot); A sentar para estar enfocado (to sit down to be focused); Hacer slime y otras cosas divertidas (make slime and other fun things); Mi familia para estar juntos (my family to be together); Video de juegos para enfocar (video games to focus).

Carlos's ideas add new elements to the discussion such as the role of low-level assistive tools and other mediators (i.e., fidgets, food, having the exam ahead of time, talking to friends, staying seated, and making fun things) as well as others that could be considered among high-level assistive tools (i.e., a computer, glasses, or videogames to help him focus). The ideas of Carlos and of other children showed how most of the artifacts they needed and used were easy to provide. One might wonder if an IEP should always be required in order to receive some of these "special" accommodations. This points to the way disability is fostered in a context that expects children to learn in standard ways rather than flexibly exploring what might work best without having to be labeled (Martínez & Chiang, 2020), particularly if the labels are perceived as being of a more permanent nature (van Swet et al., 2011).

In mentioning these multiple artifacts, children demonstrated their own awareness of things that were provided to them, and those that other children with IEPs also received. At the same time, the exploration that the activity facilitated helped them realize the many artifacts they use on a daily basis for learning. This was expressed through the exit ticket responding to the prompt in Spanish asking "What did you learn today about the IEP?,". Xochtil answered in writing as follows, using a different color for every two words: "Yo aprendí; *que* me *ase* relajar y *que* me ayuda a aprender" (I learned what makes me relax and what helps me learn).

Interestingly, the discussion around specific artifacts and resources expanded as the sessions continued. For instance, homework was discussed while explaining artifacts used to help them, or not, learn. One of the boys, Andrés, said, "No homework, me ayuda a aprender mejor porque no tengo que preocuparme de hacer la tarea" (No homework, helps me to better learn because then I do not have to be preoccupied about doing the homework); Elena explained that "[la tarea] tiene muchas hojas. Ayer me dieron nueva tarea para entregarla el viernes. Me preocupa la tarea un poquito" (the homework has many pages. Yesterday they gave me a new homework to deliver on Friday. The homework worries me a little). These expressions about homework showed that homework caused children to worry and that the assigned homework felt very long to them. In fact, Andrés suggested that he would be a better learner if he did not have to be continually concerned with completing homework.

While homework is assigned in most public schools, research has suggested that could be a source of inequality, as English-speaking parents have been found to provide more support with homework to their children in bilingual programs than the parents of bilingual children (Block & Vidaurre, 2019). It has also been documented that children from affluent backgrounds have more literacy confidence than those from lower socioeconomic levels, and that differences are rooted in an assortment of practices, including regular support for completing homework (Kellett, 2009). In the afterschool program, we dedicated the first part of our time together to providing support for homework, as both school staff and parents had asked us for this form of help. The completion of homework surfaced as an added source of concern for the children in the VWK.

As these bilingual children expressed when and where they needed support and talked about how they used artifacts and resources in the classrooms (artifacts that could at times be part of their experience as language learners but reflect more of their disability learning characteristics), they were discursively manifesting parts of their multifaceted identity.

Learning About Activists of the Disability Rights Movement

Days 3 and 4, during which children were introduced to the disability civil rights movement, provided the richest conversations around disability and disability identity and generated information about how children might react to these kinds of learning invitations. One interesting moment of exploration took place as Juán, the teacher candidate, showed a photograph of Edward Roberts, who was one of the pioneering leaders of the disability rights movement. In the photograph, Edward Roberts is shown using his wheelchair with a tube coming out of his mouth; the tube assisted him with breathing. Victor, one of the 3rd-grade boys in the VWK, exclaimed and laughed while repeatedly turning to another student in the room for approval. This reaction captured our attention, and it was discussed during our follow-up reflection meeting in the context of Victor's own ways of learning. Victor's reaction to the photo came up in a discussion that at first was about his reading ability. Following is an excerpt from this conversation:

Juán: Like Victor [. . .] I think he's aware that, you know? He obviously can't read. He has a hard time.

Rita: And the other kids are aware of it. Mirella was telling me [in front of] Victor, "[he] can't read" [. . .] I was like, "we all read differently. We all, you know, [learn things] differently." And she's like, "yeah, sometimes I need help with my drawing" [. . .] I don't think it came from like a bad place, I think it was just [stated] as a fact, an observation [. . .]

Patricia: I mean, I understand you see it as a fact because we're comparing Victor to an average person in his class. Which is why it doesn't work for us very well.

In this part of the discussion Rita shared the information that one of the girls had brought up Victor's disability during the session. However, Rita noticed that Victor could be a reader through other means, even if he did not decode; as she stated, "we all read differently." Then, nonetheless, she situated what Mirella was saying (i.e., "he can't read") as something that could be understood as "a fact." However, this comparison and it being situated as "a fact" is also rooted in the idea that we all should be reading in the same way and at the same level when sharing a classroom, which is a form of ableism. As explained in Chapter 2 and exemplified in Chapter 4, ableism refers to ability discrimination, or the way forms of learning and moving that do not match the image of the typical learner are devalued, or discriminated against (e.g., Baglieri et al., 2011; Freedman & Ferri, 2017; Reid & Knight, 2006). Contrary to educational systems' efforts to promote unified ways of learning, many children follow different developmental pathways from what is considered to be typical (Vygotsky, 1993).

As Mirella spoke about Victor's difficulties with learning to read in the more traditional way, she revealed that she noticed his disability and was ready to bring that forward. Research has shown that children of all ages are indeed curious about differences but are not always ready to ask questions (Lalvani, 2015). It is thus worth noticing the fact that Mirella was the one bringing up disability, and this volitional choice should be valued as an expansive action through which Mirella enacted agency. Silences around disability might reinforce ableism, but, instead, Mirella's comment was an opportunity for allowing this discussion to take place and for Victor to explore the identity of a disabled person (Bacon & Lalvani, 2019).

The conversation continued on to discuss the way Victor had reacted when the photograph of Edward Roberts was shown:

Patricia: But it was interesting to see how when the picture of Ed Roberts was shown . . .

Juán: Oh. Yeah, Victor. His reaction!

Patricia: He said several times, "Oh God!", which was interesting [. . .] He was telling [this] to Andrés and you [Juán] didn't [react to it].

And then he came to realize that he wasn't supposed to be making fun of the [photograph].

Juán: Oh, yeah. Yeah. I saw them like, when I, when the first, when the first image came up [of Ed Roberts with] the wheelchair. I think he like, he was, like, "wow!" He was like, "what is that!?" Or in a way, kind of like . . . in a negative way almost. [. . .] [And at the same time], he experiences stronger dyslexia.

In this part of the conversation, two things are worth considering. First is the acknowledgment that voice can be expressed in many ways. In this case, Victor, who is himself labeled with a disability, reacted by laughing as he saw Edward Roberts with his wheelchair and with his breathing tube in the photograph. As the work in the VWK continued, he realized that Edward Roberts was a person who had a disability and at the same time he was an activist, who contributed to advance the rights that all people with a disability enjoy today, including Victor himself. Children with a disability might express their ideas in ways that are less articulate and might be considered inappropriate as they experiment with how to explore and learn about things that surprise them (Gabel, 2002). It is important to make sure educators contextualize these initial, possibly shocking, exchanges to support children as they build hybrid understandings.

During the following sessions, when the children continued to explore the disability civil rights movement and were invited to design their ideal classroom using LEGOs and clay, there were other instances where Victor expressed comments that the teacher candidates felt were inappropriately connected to the activity (i.e., drawing reproductive organs or speaking about food like chicken nuggets while working on the initial inclusive classroom design on his notebook). The teacher candidates were ready to understand Victor and provide a supportive and an understanding environment for his exploration and learning. This is shown in the following exchange:

Patricia: Since with Victor, you know, we see his reaction when he saw the image of Ed Roberts and then just later, with, you know, playing around with the classroom design. And again, we see that Victor there is trying to get himself into the group.

Rita: Yeah.

Alicia: Absolutely [. . .]

Juán: We don't want him, just, I guess [we don't want to] dismiss him. Like usually in the classrooms. Where it's like oh like, don't do that, like, that's inappropriate or it's unnecessary. Like just go [to the peace corner until you] get it. Making them feel like they're in trouble [. . .]

Patricia: He needed time to digest [the information] at that moment. To see what's an appropriate way of reacting when he sees someone [that looks different from what he is used to].

As shown in this excerpt, there was an effort to understand Victor's responses to the project activities. The teacher candidates focused on allowing space for him to explore multiple identities, without having to discipline or control him, or as Juán said, not "making them feel like they're in trouble." It is important to understand how the rigidity of our educational institutions might constrain expressions of agency from those who are rarely encouraged to act. As Shalaby (2017) explained it, rather than controlling what is perceived as discipline problems, teachers should imagine how "*being love* might play out" (p. 176). With such a stance, learning freedom is at the center, and children's needs, even when communicated through challenging actions, are identified, understood, and addressed (Shalaby, 2017).

Instances like those that have been described in the previous paragraphs created a safe space in the VWK program, which allowed children to critically engage with the topics. In the following excerpt, an exchange that took place during the whole-group conversation while watching a video is described to further exemplify this safe space for criticality:

> *Juán:* Yeah, and I think [name of girl], when she brought up the whole thing about [Johnson being bullied]. Because in the video, I know I mentioned, based on what I found on Johnson, is that they used to call them "retarded," there's a section where it talks about people with an intellectual disability being called "retarded" [. . .] That's when she was like, "oh, yeah, he was bullied" [. . .] And I think it's because she heard the little excerpt of what I found and it said, you know, "they used to call them this. And then people would treat them as kids sometimes, even though they're adults." And I think just with that little comment [she reacted . . .] It has a negative connotation to using that word and how people get bullied and get called that [. . .] if they are outside an institution.
>
> *Patricia:* Which is an interesting point, right? That she thinks that he would be bullied [outside], if he's the only one with an intellectual disability, but if he's with other people with an intellectual disability, they're just the same [and he wouldn't be bullied . . .]
>
> *Student Teaching Supervisor:* Amazing insights. And you can see how with this exploration and these conversations. You get to see what their ideas are, what they think about. Cause I know throughout the year, we've been talking about how important it is to explore what they know and how they feel about topics. And—I think this is such a good example of just [that]!

This exchange recognizes the value in finding ways to surface children's knowledge and providing opportunities to explore their ideas while building upon them. Children in VWK clearly had knowledge about the world, including thoughts about disability, and these activities helped in creating a safe space for them to express them fluently and critically.

As shown, children's ways of expressing ideas could be interpreted as being silly or might include behavior that is, in other contexts, typically a reason for disciplining children. Children's efforts, even when these might be considered out of place, are volitional actions with learning potential. These actions must be understood as ways to try to make sense of a world that is less known to the children, particularly to many of those with a disability (Gabel, 2002).

Connected to the level of familiarity of the children with various forms of disability, during the next part of this conversation, I began the following exchange about the absence of children with a physical disability in this school:

> *Patricia:* In [School Name], they might have never seen a person using a wheelchair [. . .] they're not accustomed to people in wheelchairs, like in other schools [are].
>
> *Juán:* You can't even get inside the school [because you have to go up so many stairs].
>
> *Patricia:* You can't even bring someone to present, to talk about the experience of a physical disability. It's not accessible.
>
> *Juán:* Mmm-hmm [in agreement].
>
> *Patricia:* Talk about segregation, right? We talk about racial segregation, by colors in the city, and languages. It's the same thing with disability.

Children in the school where VWK took place were not used to seeing children in a wheelchair because, even though this is an inclusive school, it centers on non-physical disability, and it is not accessible for wheelchair users. In fact, all classrooms can be entered only after climbing multiple sets of stairs and there are no elevators or ramps, except for an alternative pathway at the back of the school to enter the first floor of the building. Children in this school where the VWK program took place did not have any opportunities to interact with children in wheelchairs and consequently did not understand their needs. However, their thinking is possibly influenced not just by the segregation taking place in schools in the United States but also by ideas they encounter in the social spaces they navigate or from the conventional information they receive from the media (Baglieri & Lalvani, 2019; Bigler & Liben, 2006). Hence, children who lack experiences with peers who are disabled in different ways might situate those with a physical disability as the "other," even when the children who manifest "othering" expressions are disabled themselves (Erwin et al., 2021).

The absence of peer models who have a physical disability, or other forms of disability depending on the representation in the particular school context, underlines the lack of opportunities for children to safely express their curiosity and ask questions about other ways of engaging with the world or making meaning (Lalvani, 2015). Unless topics of disability are centered in the class, children will not often express questions about disability. When working with children, particularly those who are bilingual and have a disability, the topic of disability is fundamental and must be included in any effort to further identity (Bacon & Lalvani, 2019; Connor & Gabel, 2010; Lalvani, 2015).

Designing an Inclusive Classroom: Volitional Actions, Learning, and Humanity

The invitation to create their ideal inclusive classroom using LEGOs and clay materials was introduced at the beginning of session 3 by asking children to think about one aspect they would like to change in their class or in their school building. Children then were to create a model/diorama to show to others and to convince them, as an activist would try to do, that their proposed model can meet the needs of people with a disability. Maybe because of the earlier talk about physical accessibility and differences, Rita noticed during our reflection meeting that the children were creating their ideal inclusive classroom designs with the LEGOs, really prioritizing the needs of wheelchair users. Multiple learning instances showed how they sought to understand the experiences and needs of wheelchair-using children. This is illustrated in the following conversation:

Rita: And I think that she was creating her [ideal classroom] with the Legos, she really had the wheelchair people in mind. Because I think she did her whole entire project having that in mind. Creating a table that was on their level, which was lower level. Having pencils on their reach so they wouldn't stretch [. . .] And then I think she created with two [pieces of Lego and] like the [playdough . . .] she created a shape of a chair. And she placed them there and she said that that's the two wheelchairs. So, she basically made it into like a reality. So, I see, kind of like the thinking process for how they were entering the building [and] how they would navigate [it . . .] So, she, I think she thought about everything. From beginning, middle and [end].

Student Teacher Supervisor: I thought [they rather needed] higher desks because I've seen [them with the] wheelchairs get under it.

Juán: I mean, for example, with Ed Roberts, he couldn't like slouch or [anything] like [that . . .] And so, he would have to have a desk right here (pointing to a higher point). Or when he's laying down, even when he would lay down, to put things for him to read was like [. . .] really high up.

Student Teacher Supervisor: So, it depends. On the type of [wheel]chair.

Juán: But I think she said like [that children] can't see or [those] who are short, are lower, that's why they're smaller. I think Luis asked, like, why do you have a bigger window and a smaller window?
Rita: [There's a reason why they're] different.
Juán: And then she's like well, someone that's lower uses the smaller window. And someone that's in a higher [chair] position can use a bigger window. So that's why she put the two different windows.

In this exchange, we witness a discussion about what type of desk, among other things, could best serve children who are wheelchair users. In the conversation, it is not only the children's learning that is discussed, but also the adults' learning as they are exploring what would be the best way to accommodate different ways of sitting in the classroom. At the same time, the intentionality behind each one of the details the children decided to include in their designs becomes clear to the teacher candidates.

At a certain point during the discussion, Juán noticed that the learning went beyond merely building their ideal classroom; he highlighted other forms of learning such as the importance of the humanity in the feelings the children manifested while working. He explained:

Juán: Like, it's not just about making the building that's for people with disabilities. But it's also about, you know, with [child from VWK], it's like "oh, yeah. They are loved." Like, "we love them." And we're like just going into that, [the love]. Like I think it's a deeper thought, not just about them creating a building. It's like the importance [of shared] space.
Rita: The [importance of the] conversation.
Juán: And the feelings about it. And I think that having an adult there and having someone with them at [each of] the tables, I think, really truly, helped make the better sense of [actual work around disability]. The physical disability and . . . sometimes [we moved into] intellectual disability as well.

This is an important noticing from soon-to-be practitioners. The children themselves expressed humanity and aspects of equity in different ways. One of the girls explained her rationale for promoting ramps and installing low windows as "porque la persona [aunque] no puede caminar o no puede hacer algo, no significa que no son tan especiales" (because the person [even when] cannot walk or cannot do something, it does not mean that they are not very special). In this context, "special" appears to be used to mean unique or particularly important, rather than as in "special education," and it points to the feelings that guided the children's work and decisions. As the children explored the topic of disability, they not only investigated the artifacts that were needed, and thought about varied ways in which children had to be allowed to learn, but also went beyond to really embrace an inclusive community, one where everyone belonged and was appreciated and loved.

In the following discussion, recognizing the importance of human connection was mentioned as being part of the activity:

> *Juán:* With Andrés and Victor how, at first, when they, when they talked about how [. . .] they had the person [represented] with the red clay. And that's a person that had the hardest time learning. They had their little chairs and they put a piece of red clay on top of [the] seat where the student who struggles the most would be [. . .] And then everyone around him, would like, I guess, support him [. . .] That they would be around him to help him. So, it is like, you know, surrounding them with people that can help the student who struggles. And then they had a—, the whole light thing where it's like, oh, when you're in a really bad mood, like it turns bright, bright red. And when you're in a really good mood, it turns, you know, bright green.

Juán described for the group the ways in which the children were thinking about the space and the humans present within it as possible mediators for learning. In this way, the group was going beyond the actual artifacts and resources that are also there to support those they feel would "struggle" the most, and who were at the center of initial discussions. Children showed a sensitivity to difference and needs, and to multiple types of support, that is probably connected to their own experiences as minoritized children with a disability. Still, there was a tendency to situate those with a disability as always being the ones needing help, and more explicit discussions about how we all need help at certain points, and in different ways, should be emphasized to avoid paternalistic ideas of unidirectional care (Kilinc, 2018; Rummery & Fine, 2012).

Other ideas that point to ableist tendencies common in schools began to come out during the following conversation, where the student teacher supervisor, who is also the mother of a child with a disability, shared her insights:

> *Patricia:* Yes. And I feel that the children are aware of differences because they are in this school. And they do notice that certain children have certain things that others don't. And they understand and allow for that. Like, you know, there's the peace corner that some children need, and some others don't. And some children need a paraprofessional. I had a conversation with [a child in VWK] about a child in particular that has someone to

help because he . . . couldn't read, also. And she [the child] said, "well, he should read more."

Rita: Yeah. [She said] read more books [laughter].

Patricia: Like this idea that we communicate as teachers sometimes [and then children replicate], that if you work harder, you are going to get better in that. But it's not always the case

Student Teaching Supervisor: In my daughter's school, she has a teacher who I like so much, and she says to her, "don't work harder. Work smarter" (laughter) But what she means is, you don't have to work harder. We just, we have to find another way of doing it, a better way that [works].

Patricia: Find a way to learn.

Student Teaching Supervisor: So, yeah. A way to learn, but not this like, I have to work harder. Because a lot of students, yeah, do think that, even the students themselves, like I just . . . I worked hard and if I do this I will learn.

This conversation could potentially start to disrupt some of the ableist ideas within our own afterschool experience.

Subtle messages about ability were constantly being communicated to the VWK participating children, who were themselves experiencing difficulty when using traditional approaches. They had experienced that they did not learn through the regular school means and we had discussed how they were better learners with certain artifacts (computers, extra time, fidgets, opportunities for movement, etc.), and when having an adult or other classmates with them. However, very often, there were comments about the need to "read more" or "work harder" which are tightly connected to the image of the ideal "average" learner, who did not really represent the children in VWK (Davis, 2006). Research has suggested that the language that teachers use while teaching reading often reflects a "dichotomy of strength and weakness, valuing individual able-bodiedness (or able-mindedness)" (Coakley-Fields, 2019, p. 258). Hence, having conversations about disability and the disability rights movement, including activists with a disability, with teacher candidates and children is fundamental if they are to be prepared for the inclusive bilingual classroom.

The process the children went through was cyclical in that they designed, revised, and redesigned their project models, changing some parts of the classroom as they continued their work. Allowing at least two full sessions for the design of the ideal inclusive classroom where everyone could learn was important so that all children had plenty of time to explore their ideas, test them against their partners' and those of other pairs of children, and redesign the model as needed. This is illustrated by the work that Andrés and Victor completed around the "light device" and that the teacher candidates shared during the reflection meeting after one of the sessions. Alicia was describing some of the items the two children had decided to include on their project model, and as she described a light placed for children with a disability to ask for assistance, Rita was curious to know more:

Rita: Red light, green light [to ask] for assistance. Did you ask where did that idea come from?

Alicia: Well, Andrés was very, very passionate about the activity. And he was really trying to think about students in a wheelchair and students who struggle the most, like the person who was in the red spot [red clay . . .]. [I]t was hard to see where that idea came from because he was thinking about technology. He was like, yeah, this is a screen, this is the air conditioning. This is the big white board. And this thing that comes off in the ceiling, and this thing is water. And it, it has like warm and cold water. [That's] where it came from, [. . .] that he wanted technology to be a huge part of [the classroom . . .] I know that they either press something or pull something and then like something turns on.

Juán: A life alert thing?

Alicia: [I]t alerts something. So probably he was like, okay. A red-light indication that you need help. Green light that they're fine [. . .] He was really . . . He changed the models so much! That first, he had a door that was coming in. Like he was like, "a wheelchair doesn't fit through here. So, the wheelchair would come through here." So, he made a round [door or hole]. And he was like, "what if there were wheels?" When Andrés saw the car wheel, he was like, "we have to use this. What could this be for? [. . .] If there are children who need to move, they can just go to that and that will be a swing." Then he was like, "this thing that used to be the air conditioner, not anymore! Now, it's the water tank [and it is] attached to the thing that tells you if a student needs help or not." Like he changed so much as he was like developing that narrative in his mind.

Patricia: Yeah. As a good designer would do.

Alicia: Yeah. He was really passionate about what was happening. And it was so good when Juán came over and said, do you want to present? [And] he was so excited. He was like, "yes!"

This excerpt clearly illustrates the enjoyment, as well as the thinking and decision-making process the children experienced while working in the design of an ideal classroom project. The final design that Andrés and Victor created is shown in Figure 7.1.

While sharing, these children explained additional ideas about their project such as Andrés explaining how they had "made a class for disabled and non-disabled [children]. Here is the entrance for the disabled [while pointing].

Figure 7.1. Classroom Design Project Created by Andrés and Victor

We made it a tongue with a happy smile [. . .] for when they walk in here." Andrés also described a "machine where they can breathe" which seemed to be inspired by their learning about Edward Roberts who used a device to assist his breathing through a technique for forcing air into his lungs. Andrés and Victor also created a place for easy water drinking, and for heating and cooling the classroom. The whiteboard they proposed would [have] signs and they "made it extra big for the people to see." They also had a special seat for those who need more time and made sure to place people around him that could help him. The children added beanbags and a couch for learning more comfortably, and a phone to use if someone needed to call someone. The classroom included, Andrés explained, "a tool for math [which] they can move around" and, honoring Victor's desire, the class had a cafeteria where as Andrés explained, "we can serve everybody chicken nuggets with milk." This shows the distributed contribution of both children to the final design, and highlights how an idea that was initially perceived as being out of place (i.e., mentioning chicken nuggets while designing an inclusive classroom), ended up expanding their thinking.

Other projects also included this idea of a place to go if one needed to go home or call home. For instance, Xochtil included an office where children could go for, as she described it, "por si quieren ir a la casa temprano o hablarle a tus papás" (in case they want to go home or speak to their parents). This idea established a connection between the home and the school, which surfaced as being highly desirable among the participating children.

Children used their own experiences and needs, as well as what they had witnessed in their classrooms, to inform their designs. For instance, Luis explained how "[P]use esto aca para que no se escondan [. . .] Quería bloques pero no había, así que usé plastilina para que no se escondieran ahí" (I put this here so that the children wouldn't hide [. . .] I wanted blocks but there were none, so I used playdough to prevent them from hiding there).

He explained how, often, there were children that would hide inside closets in playful ways (something that was also witnessed in VWK), but how he felt this was to be prevented.

With his design, Luis was, in a way, fostering the school personnel's effort to control certain behaviors or forms of action that were situated as being inappropriate. While this idea was not questioned at the time, this design choice points to an opportunity for future collective learning and development in the context of actual self-determination that is encouraged through children's agency (Petersen, 2009). For example, teacher candidates could have prompted Luis to describe what was problematic about hiding in the spaces around the classroom and why certain children might do that. Exploring multiple perspectives would possibly raise a conflict of motives and foster the generation of novel ways to address it (Sannino, 2015).

Additional agentive turns took place as the children presented their designs, when the other participants asked questions that often led to improvements of their existing designs. They also used elements that had been brought in during the initial sessions. In Elena's case, for instance, she described how she and her classmate had included a park with a swing and a slide to play and that she had named it "Everafter." At this point, Andrés asked her, "How the disabled are going to go down the slide and that (pointing to the swing)?" To this question, Elena explained that they had created "un elevador para que Ed Roberts lo suba por todos los edificios" (an elevator so that Ed Roberts could ride it to all the buildings), and added, switching to English, that the slide and the swing are "just for the kids." Further questioning Elena's design, Andrés then asked, "what if they [the children] are in wheelchairs?" These kinds of exchanges were critical in helping children to consider all needs and accessibility to all spaces rather than just a few, and hosted potential for collective learning opportunities.

The analytical ways in which the children designed their classrooms showed the potential for discussing disability and diverse needs with children who have a disability themselves. In this way, the children were allowed to explore their own knowledge, which might, under more traditional institutional circumstances, remain invisible, while at the same time building new understandings.

CONCLUSION

This chapter aimed to describe children's knowledge and forms of agency in connection to processes of conscientization that were experienced in the VWK. The chapter highlighted the work and conversations generated while participating in the Disability Rights Movement Exploration project for four of the sessions. The chapter offered a range of possible responses that can be expected. It also provided a rationale for creating safe spaces conducive of critical endeavors when discussing disabled activists and disability rights. In this way, the chapter can act as a guide for student teachers and those working to prepare them as they develop their own disability-centered lessons and explorations.

The ideas shared through the chapter are insights worth considering when teaching about the disability civil rights movement and when exploring children's disability identity, since there has been generally little attention to children's ways of constructing ideas about disability (Bacon & Lalvani, 2019; Lalvani, 2015). This work suggests that minoritized children who do not see certain forms of disability in their schools and classrooms will be surprised and curious about them when confronted with images such as those of some of the most critical disability rights activists (e.g., Edward Roberts or Roland Johnson). Having conversations about varied forms of moving and learning assisted in the process of expanding our understanding of the broad "range of human embodiments and support needs," which, as Greenstein (2016) explained, can mediate more radical inclusive pedagogies (p. 5). Such conversations about multiple forms of learning and of being able can also encourage children to talk about what they notice in class about their classmates' ways of being. This can facilitate discussions about their own needs and ways of learning as children who carry a disability label.

Identity, as has been discussed in this chapter, is ever-evolving, and is created from our own cultural and historical experiences, memories, and knowledge, as well as our anticipation for the future (Bruner, 2003). The experiences in which the children participated during the VWK and that are described in this chapter were opportunities to analyze their own learning and to notice the artifacts, resources, and relationships that were helping them learn. The collective nature of the interactions in VWK promoted transformative processes, which, as Xochtil summarized, helped the children (as well as the adults) in learning about what it was that helped them learn. Sharing about the disability rights movement and talking about the children's own IEPs mediated their collective thinking through the explorations. As children's existing knowledge and experiences surfaced and were integrated to create new sources of knowledge, their preexisting FoK began to form part of their own selves while learning, shaping strong funds of identity to continue this process (Esteban-Guitart, 2014). That is, the process of learning about the disability experiences of the activists while exploring their own also assisted in building children's identities as individuals who are labeled with a disability.

Aspects of disability are often forgotten or avoided when working with bilingual children who are labeled as having a disability. Issues of racism, inequality, and disproportionality may dominate thinking about the problems faced by children of immigrant background, leaving little energy to add disability to the mix of considerations (Martínez-Álvarez, 2018). Nonetheless, children who have immigrant roots and are growing bilingually, which might lead to being categorized with an ELL label in the United States, are sometimes also marked as disabled and receive assistance through special education services. Hence, it is important that bilingual and bicultural children, in particular, learn about disability rights, activists, and about their own positionality within the system as multiply labeled learners (i.e., ELL and disability labels). In this sense, the curricular invitations assisted in a process of conscientization. That is, for Freire (1993), we must trust oppressed children's ability to think to the highest levels about aspects of their experiential circumstances and to connect those with social pressures and forces. As children were situated in the VWK as the ones who possesed vast knowledge about learning-mediating artifacts and resources, and as those who could create a highly inclusive classroom design, they came to understand their own learning conditions and status within and beyond the classroom.

The curricular invitations here described can be conceptualized as first stimuli, which generated responses from the participating children (Vygotsky, 1978). As the children reflected, were surprised, or heard about the multiple artifacts and ideas shared in this collective space of the VWK, they enacted agency by pulling on whatever knowledge they had available, and that of others, to address the conflict of ideas they were experiencing. For example, as Andrés worked with Victor, he incorporated the idea of the cafeteria and the chicken nuggets into their design; as the children talked about the adequate height of the desks for wheelchair users, they added new ideas to the ones they had initially expressed; and as they learned about disability movements, they realized that disabled people can be activists who radically transform the world.

All throughout the explorations, the children uncovered and negotiated things that contributed to their fluid learning identities. When children draw on resources that others have, they enact relational agency, which can allow learning to take place (Edwards, 2005). This is a way of understanding learning by participating in activity with others, as labor is dynamically distributed according to interest and expertise (Cole & Engeström, 1993). This form of learning refuses to solely foster independence, and instead relies on understanding and nurturing interdependent relationships of mutual learning and expansion. Such a perspective on learning is closely aligned with the principles behind DSE (Savarese, 2020, as cited in Hastings Center, 2020). While DSE scholars understand interdependence as a way of learning and living in society, educational systems around the world often aim for independence as a required goal for progressive development (Kilinc, 2018). Interdependence is a mediator for learning, just as important as many others, and should be embraced when fostering inclusive education (Martínez-Álvarez, 2022). Unless we embrace different ways of participating and learning, bilingual children with a disability will continue to be forced into ableist systems guided by neoliberal principles that favor only one way of developing (Bacon & Pomponio, 2020).

I would like to close this chapter returning to the initial framing I proposed. We need to continue to support children "to better understand themselves, the world and their relations with others in the world" (Greenstein, 2016, p. 5), while embracing pathways of "conscientization" (Freire, 1993). Bilingual children with a disability need to discuss disability and their own labels of disability to assist in developing collective understandings using the knowledge they carry and expanding upon it (Greene, 1988). This chapter clearly highlights the importance of discussing disability with bilingual children and provides a pathway for new teachers to embrace some of those discussions with their students.

CHAPTER 8

Science Learning With Bilingual Children

Learning In-Between Boundaries in a Hybrid Space

The Varied Ways of Knowing (VWK) afterschool project documented in this study was built on an expansive understanding of learning. Inspired by CHAT frameworks, learning in VWK was understood as taking place not only vertically, following a typical developmental trajectory, but also horizontally, as children and teacher candidates worked side by side, sharing the role of experts and learning from each other along a ZPD (Vygotsky, 1978). Hence, in VWK, learning that took place through participation in meaningful collective activity (Roth & Lee, 2007) via distributed expertise (Cole & Engeström, 1993) was prioritized. Distributed expertise promotes breaking away from the more didactic, externally organized requirements and unidirectional nature of traditional forms of learning. Instead, distributed expertise aims to highlight the multiple knowledges and abilities of the different participants and to recognize and nurture their shared contribution to the learning activity.

The form of learning promoted in VWK relied on children's volitional actions as they attempted to agentively address the arising "conflict of motives" they experienced while collectively engaging in activity (Sannino, 2015, p. 2). For example, children were given the prompt of using clay to create a representation of the city where they lived as it looked like years ago (i.e., first stimulus), but they wanted to create something from their popular culture or a specific landmark from their community. While some children integrated a version of this prompt into their design, others plainly decided to explore the clay, manipulating and altering it, without creating anything concrete. The conflict of motives they experienced thus stimulated action involving the use of novel artifacts upon which they drew, based on their expertise, to inform their work with the clay. For instance, they used images they brought from home, knowledge and ideas they carried, or tools from the classroom, shifting the object of their collective activity in a slightly different, but still meaningful, direction. This process can be characterized as a form of development and growth, which Engeström conceptualized as "expansive learning" (Engeström, 2001).

This expansive view characterizes the learning taking place in less formal educational spaces like those of VWK and similar voluntary instructional settings. These informal educational spaces are prime for teacher candidates' learning about children because their flexibility allows for agentive negotiation of what counts as knowledge and learning, and they still take place within the same school children attend during the day (Martínez-Álvarez, 2017a). In this way, they can provide important information for supporting learning in and out of schools. In particular, exploring the learning taking place in settings such as VWK can contribute to efforts to move beyond the traditional hierarchical learning structures, also referred to as "the factory model," that continue to dominate educational institutions and the learning of minoritized children (Rogoff et al., 2016).

This chapter uses information from a series of four instructional sessions originally focused on science education but conceptualized from the perspective of expansive learning just described. According to this perspective, agentive participation via distributed expertise allows for conceptualizing development not only vertically but also horizontally, and can, in the process, blur the dimensions of various figurative boundaries such as those of disciplinary separations. The science explorations were purposefully designed to allow for a hybrid space where learning could take place in-between typically established boundaries (Lizárraga & Gutiérrez, 2018). As already discussed, hybrid spaces can be playful yet rigorous and are spaces that allow educators to center the knowledge and practices of bilingual children, which actually "thrive on the boundary" (Lizárraga & Gutiérrez, 2018, p. 38).

This chapter addresses the question: How does boundary crossing manifest in a hybrid science learning space with bilingual children with and without a disability, and what possibilities for expansive learning surface in this space? In exploring this question, the chapter aims to contribute to more comprehensive ways of understanding knowledge and learning with bilingual children with and without a disability. Findings explore the various dimensions along which boundary crossing took place in the hybrid space of the VWK afterschool program, manifesting the porosity of categories. The following sections provide an overview of the research addressing science education with emergent bilinguals and with children with a disability.

SCIENCE EDUCATION AND EMERGENT BILINGUALS

The demands of the most recent science teaching guidelines, the Next Generation Science Standards (NGSS; NGSS Lead States, 2013), revitalized efforts to make science learning accessible for language learners of immigrant backgrounds (Lee et al., 2013). However, concern about accessibility for diverse learners has existed for over 2 decades (Furman & Calabrese Barton, 2006). Even so, there is a need to continue to learn about the meaningful inclusion of diverse children's FoK in science for more successful and respectful learning experiences (Moll et al., 1989). The validation of children's FoK connects to the nature of science, through which children can begin to see science as a practice and as a way of knowing, and to understand that scientists employ multiple methods for doing science (National Research Council, 2012). It is now well understood in the science education research community that children must learn both about the content and about the nature of science (i.e., understand that science is embedded in social and cultural contexts) in schools (National Research Council, 2012). This idea is also present in the NGSS, which highlight, as one of their three dimensions, the need for elementary children to engage in scientific and engineering practices (NGSS Lead States, 2013).

Research suggests that science-as-practice instructional invitations can be built upon children's knowledge and practices across social spaces (Calabrese Barton et al., 2004; Martínez-Álvarez, 2017a). It has been documented how diverse children carry family knowledge and experiences about the world that can be used for science teaching and learning, but their vast legacy is often dismissed as deficit views about immigrant children prevail (Calabrese Barton & Tan, 2009; Moje et al., 2004).

The idea of *proximal representations* of science, which refers to the perceived relationship, or distance, of science to one's "personal, lived experience" (Hogan, 2000, p. 52), is central in efforts to validate and integrate children's knowledge in schools. Images of science can be more traditional, in the sense of displaying a static image of science as something very distant from the children themselves, "traditional distal" images, or they can be closer to the children's experience, or "creative proximal" (Martínez-Álvarez, 2017a, p. 27). Proximal and creative representations of science, which flourish in hybrid, less formal learning spaces, can facilitate expansive learning through horizontal patterns of knowledge-sharing and -building (Martínez-Álvarez, 2017a).

Less formal learning spaces, such as the voluntary setting of the VWK afterschool program, that tend to be "nondidactic" and "embedded in meaningful activity" and that "build on the learner's initiative," are excellent bases for understanding learning itself and ways to promote it (Rogoff et al., 2016, p. 358). These informal learning spaces can generate opportunities where, as Rogoff and colleagues (2016) explained, "anyone may take initiative as they see a way to contribute," a process that grants children permission to explore multiple identities as they meaningfully participate in collective learning experiences (p. 372).

SCIENCE EDUCATION AND CHILDREN WITH A DISABILITY

Traditionally, research looking into science education for children with a disability has supported approaches rooted in behavioral principles such as systematic instruction, particularly when working with children with intellectual or autism spectrum disability (Apanasionok et al., 2020). However, there are studies that indicated promising results when implementing practices oriented toward inquiry-based, hands-on activities, cross-curricular projects, or multiple means for representing information. Specifically, the review of research focused on science education for students with learning and other forms of disability conducted by Vavougios and colleagues (2016) highlighted that (1) inquiry-based instruction was an effective mode for teaching children with learning disability, helping to improve children's conceptual understanding and their ability of applying strategies for processing information; (2) hands-on activities can be more satisfying to children than textbook-based learning and are particularly effective when they rely less on language-related activities and when suitable material has been created; (3) methods implementing cross-curricular projects, based on constructivist principles, have been shown to generally help children with learning disabilities learn; and (4) multiple means of representation can be effective to help children with a disability acquire not only facts but also higher order thinking skills.

An instructional context that is flexibly adapted to children's needs is the essence of VWK. Learning experiences that are understood as being mediated socially and through multiple artifacts, and where various modalities are employed, can enhance the experience of learning science for all children. This is critical, given that most students perceive science as being "rational, cold, unexciting, and lacking any emotional content" (Varelas et al., 2010, p. 322). Relatedly, practices that closely align with the UDL approach (Center for Applied Special Technology [CAST], 2018), through which varied forms of engaging, representing, and expressing information for learning are prioritized have also been highlighted as means for the inclusive learning of children with a disability (Watt et al., 2013).

In conclusion, recent developments in teaching science highlight the need to reframe the discourse around the learning of children with a disability. These children have traditionally been situated as lacking the basic necessary skills for learning, resulting in the emphasis of mechanistic approaches often leading to reproductive learning (Martínez-Álvarez, 2017b). Such deficit views negatively impact children with a disability, who might be exposed to reductionist academic opportunities or lower expectations for their learning (Shifrer et al., 2013).

Contrary to this reductionism, agency-enhancing dialogical approaches to teaching science are a tool for reducing educational inequalities and promote inclusive education (Reynaga-Peña et al., 2018). Disability studies scholars demand "access to a newly imagined and newly configured public sphere where full participation is not contingent on an able body" (McRuer, 2006, p. 30). Likewise, access to the academic space should not depend on favoring "a specific style of learning, a particular language, and/or a culture that best matches the educational norm within a curricular space" (Martínez-Álvarez, 2017b, p. 527). Providing access to all children to learn science is important, and solidifying new ways of understanding what science is and what counts as learning science is a step toward that goal (Martínez-Álvarez, 2019).

EXPLORING SCIENCE WITH BILINGUAL CHILDREN WITH AND WITHOUT A DISABILITY

As the literature reviewed above suggests, inclusive bilingual education must be guided by high expectations and flexible understandings of learning, through which, given appropriate learning contexts, all children can learn science, even if in "unexpected ways" (Martínez-Álvarez, 2017b, p. 524). Appropriate science learning contexts demand support for children's learning styles through culturally and linguistically relevant pedagogies, multiple forms of engaging, representing, and expressing information, and the shared commitment to viewing education as a tool that can transform the world (see Martínez-Álvarez, 2020a). A Vygotskian understanding of the role of historical artifacts and the social context and collective efforts in mediating learning, and centering and enhancing critical forms of agency, can help in ensuring valuable learning opportunities for both teachers and the children with multiple labels whom they serve (Martínez-Álvarez, 2020a).

Opportunities for exploring multiple identities, including that of knowledgeable experts, and creating a sociocultural context for respectful learning through children's volitional actions are tools for inclusive bilingual education in science and other content areas and should be planned for and enacted while teaching (Martínez-Álvarez, 2020b). As explained in the next subsection, exploring multiple identities, knowledge, and practices takes place best in a hybrid third space (Bhabha, 1994; Gutiérrez, 2008; Gutiérrez et al., 1999; Moje et al., 2004). In hybrid spaces, learning can take place "on the boundary" (Lizárraga & Gutiérrez, 2018, p. 38), or the space that can be characterized as being in-between dichotomies or between aspects that are contradictory.

Boundary Crossing in Hybrid Spaces

Hybrid third space refers to a space in-between (Bhabha, 1996), a space where children can entertain multiple abilities, cultures, knowledges, practices, and identities, even if they contradict each other, and through which these different entities can be generated and altered qualitatively (Martínez-Álvarez, 2020b). Hybrid spaces hold rich potential to promote learning that takes place "on the boundary" (Lizárraga & Gutiérrez, 2018, p. 38), which refers to the space in between perceived dichotomies.

Boundaries have typically been examined in the social sciences as "relational processes at work across a wide range of social phenomena, institutions, and locations" (Lamont & Molnár, 2002, p. 169). Boundary crossing can be mediated by a process of knowledge sharing from those who, belonging to different disciplinary or professional groups, bring diverse artifacts, rules, or forms of division of labor. Within CHAT, boundaries are a source for learning and expansion ocurring during boundary-crossing efforts (Engeström, 2001). That is, as participants bring contrasting knowledge, practices, or artifacts that are figuratively separated by boundaries to mediate their collective activity, contradictions will surface. Attempts to solve contradictions so as to understand each other's ways of functioning promote boundary crossing.

This chapter interprets boundaries as ideational separations that, while culturally presented as dichotomies, are rather part of a continuum that have been artificially separated. For instance, in this chapter, boundaries between forms of knowledge and practices (i.e., across social spaces or carried by children or by teacher candidates), between disciplines (i.e., science education, art education, or other areas), and between formal or informal learning spaces (i.e., playful spaces outside of school times versus learning spaces while in school) were centered and analyzed. The crossing of boundaries and the learning that can take place when boundaries are blurred to form an in-between learning space are certainly complex and need to be further understood (Wenger, 1998).

THE RELEVANT CONTEXTS FOR SCIENCE AND LANDFORMS UNIT

The unit that generated the work at the center of this chapter started out with an exploration of children's ideas about what science is and then shifted to exploring geomorphology. The unit included three main lessons, which are briefly described in Classroom Identity and Knowledge Exploration 8.1 below. The full bilingual description of the lessons in this unit can be found on this book's product page at https://www.tcpress.com.

Classroom Identity and Knowledge Exploration 8.1

Contextos Relevantes para Ciencias y Accidentes Geográficos (Relevant Contexts for Science and Landforms) Lessons

Day 1 of the project: Explore the question "¿Qué es ciencia?" (What is science?) using the book *In my Family/En mi Familia* by Carmen Lomas Garza (1996) and/or *Family Pictures/Cuadros de Familia* by Carmen Lomas Garza (2005). Children draw and write to assist their narratives

Day 2 of the project: Analyze images of worldwide landmarks. Children choose one to create with clay

Day 3 (and follow up session) of the project: Paint sculptures, think of Manhattan 500 years ago (back when it was called Mannahatta), and analyze a photograph of the sculpture digitally

Day 4 of the project: Explore pebbles. Mix ingredients to create slime. Explore various consistency and optional addition of pebbles to the slime

LEARNING AT THE BOUNDARY OF KNOWLEDGES, DISCIPLINES, AND FORMAL/LESS FORMAL SPACES

An important characteristic that surfaced as the series of lessons was implemented was that while we initially aimed at exploring science, children were not restricted to the parameters of science. Rather, they could use their resources and enjoy the activities in flexible ways. As a result, the children involved themselves in the topics through varied ways and children's learning took place along ZPDs in multiple different directions. For instance, the children enjoyed the artistic part of the activities as much as the learning about landmarks. They really immersed themselves in the exploration of the clay and of colors, and enjoyed the kinesthetic pleasures of mixing the slime and achieving the right consistency. The following sections show the learning that can take place in a hybrid space where the boundaries between dimensions blur. Specifically, the sections illustrate learning (1) at the boundary of "traditional distal" and "creative proximal" knowledges and practices (Martínez-Álvarez, 2017a, p. 27), (2) at the boundary of disciplines, and (3) at the boundary of more formal and less formal spaces.

In-Between Boundaries of Distal and Proximal Knowledges: "¿Qué es Ciencia?"

The sharing of the books by Carmen Lomas Garza and the discussion that it facilitated promoted a ZPD where expansive and revealing ideas about what science is were brought to light. For instance, one girl wrote, in non-standard spelling form, how "En *ciesa aprente* para ser *sientificos*" (in science you learn to be a scientist), pointing to a view of science as something you achieve, and that eventually grants you the status of a scientist, while Jimena wrote "I think it's about learning new things," indicating that science is about learning something you do not yet know. These ideas could be interpreted as being more distal from their own experiences (Hogan, 2000).

Influenced by an idea of remedies as science knowledge that the teacher candidates conveyed while reading Lomas Garza's books (i.e., a woman burning a newspaper cone placed inside a man's ear), however, other children explained what science was by using examples of their own home remedies. This was the case of Elena, who wrote "Mi remedio es el *vaporud*" (My remedy is VapoRub), referring to a popular topical ointment made by Vicks to treat cold and flu that releases vapors to calm a cough; Dorita, who wrote "*Yotomohelo cuandome due le* la garganta" (I take ice when my throat hurts); or another girl, who explained when talking about science that they used "cremas para las heridas [. . .] aloe vera para el cabello [y] Aloe para la herida" (creams for wounds [. . .] aloe vera for the hair [and] aloe for the wound). All these suggestions, highlighting natural ways of helping people feel better through home remedies, can be described as proximal scientific representations that could be explored in science classrooms.

Similarly, there were two boys who referred to things that were important to them outside of school and they found ways to connect them to school science. One of the boys mentioned how Karate used a different language and how there was science in Karate. He explained, "se divide en katas para pasar de cinturon" (it is divided into katas to pass the belt) and added how he had to memorize the series of movements, or katas, the steps to follow, to be able to move to the next belt. In describing these examples as connected to science, this child appeared to interpret science as knowledge about discipline-related terminology and about the steps that need to be followed to accomplish a set goal (i.e., an experiment in science or the next belt in Karate).

Children also mentioned the popular fictional creatures of Pokémon, a Japanese franchise, which started as a video game but then shifted to different formats. Pokémon is now well known as a complex game of cards as well as an animated show. A boy drew and wrote to explain how the dragons and animals in the game, as well as the "características del Pokémon: Agua, fuego" (characteristics of the Pokémon: Water, fire) were part of science. As shown later, Pokémons permeated into the rest of this unit's lessons. These ideas can be understood as creative thinking that can assist in constructing proximal representations of science (in contrast to more traditional or distant views).

These connections, from more "traditional distal" to more "creative proximal," around science show the porosity that is possible while learning in-between boundaries. Children bring these contrasting forms of understanding science into the same hybrid space and, as a result, they blur the boundaries typically separating the two forms of knowledge. This is a way to potentially expand ideas around science, but also to allow children to bring into the VWK space aspects of their lives typically left outside schools. As children agentively choose what to discuss in the context of science, they embrace the task of teaching others about their existing knowledge and can imagine themselves as scientists (Stroupe, 2014). Such a process can, as I documented in a study with elementary bilingual children experiencing academic difficulties, help candidates, researchers, and children conceive a more inclusive understanding of what counts as knowledge while creating views of learners as knowledgeable (Martínez-Álvarez, 2017a).

In-Between Disciplinary Boundaries: Meaningful Agentive Participation

During the following sessions the candidates first invited children to study pictures of landforms from different places around the world. Then Isabella, the leading teacher candidate for the lesson, asked the children to think about what Manhattan looked like 500 years ago. Children thought about ideas of landmarks in the past and in the present, connecting to cities and countries where their families come from. As the children went to work with white clay in their small groups, they immersed themselves in an exploration with the teacher candidates and their classmates through which they took numerous volitional actions that were promoted by the artifacts in the lesson (first stimulus) and explored knowledge across spaces and disciplines.

Becoming Artistically Literate Through Volcanoes and Color. There were several children who chose to create landforms with the clay. Creating models of volcanoes was one of the most popular choices. This could have been stimulated by one of the images shared during session 1 showing the Isla El Tigre, a volcano in Honduras. This landmark was very important for Dorita, who excitedly stood up screaming, "¡ese es mi país!" (that is my country), when Isabella revealed the location of the volcano. It could also be connected to how children are generally more familiar with catastrophic events that result in drastic changes such as volcanic eruptions than with slow changes to the surface of the earth caused by water, wind, or ice (Cheek, 2010; Martínez et al., 2012).

Figure 8.1 displays Andrés's initial volcano design, and then his painted version. His model included a flat representation of smoke that he had created with the clay. The painted version shows a mixture of shades suggesting Andrés's dedication to finding the right colors for his design, and the textured red lava he was able to create.

Children need multiple experiences with the clay so that they start to envision the possibilities it can offer to represent things three-dimensionally. Andrés's work manifests this learning in its making as he experimented with two- and three-dimensional shapes.

Figure 8.1. Andrés First and Painted Model of a Volcano With Smoke

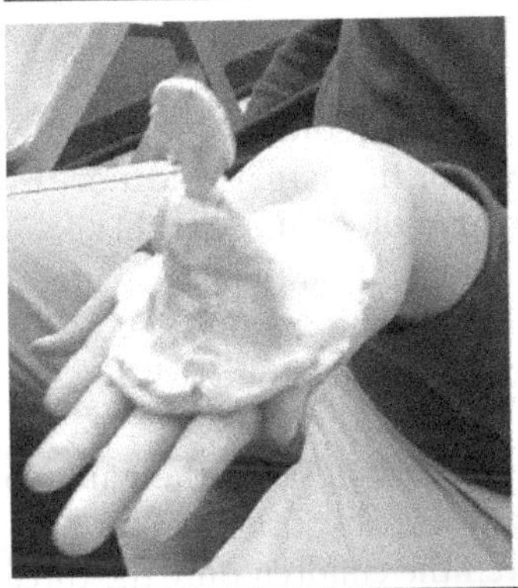

Siena (who typically had a lot of trouble during the school day in relation to behavior that was at times considered to be aggressive and to her resistance with following the rules) was very excited about this instructional invitation. She worked for an extended period of time with Cynthia, another VWK child participant, creating another volcano. The process followed by the two girls lasted for two full sessions during which they persistently worked on their model. On the second session, Siena brought in a piece of clay that she and her older sister had, in preparation for the session, mixed with red paint at home. Silvia, the teacher candidate who, like Siena, was of Dominican background, felt at the conclusion of this session that this lesson really worked for Siena. Silvia highlighted the volitional actions of the two girls, and particularly of Siena, and other aspects she noticed during the experience. She wrote in her learning notes:

> Siena took out clay that she had brought from home. Her sister and her [had] mixed it with red paint to make the lava for their volcano. I was so happy to see how engaged Siena was in the task. She even remembered to bring her clay, meaning that she was looking forward to come back to [afterschool program] to finish her and Cynthia's creation. [Silvia's Learning Notes; Day 3 of Contextos Relevantes para Ciencias y Accidentes Geográficos]

This note really emphasizes Siena's interest in bringing additional tools (i.e., the red clay) to contribute to the shared work experience. With this action, Siena also demonstrated how, even when the afterschool session was over, she continued to think about the collective activity.

In Vygotskian terms, since on the first day there was clay but no paint (first stimulus), this created a conflict for her as she wanted to add color to the volcano. She decided to bring the red clay artifact, which acted as the second stimulus, to mediate the activity she wanted to accomplish. Silvia also wrote about how the work unfolded:

> The girls went straight to work and painted their [volcano model]. We spoke about how they can make brown for the actual volcano. Siena had the idea of mixing all three primary colors and Cynthia agreed. Siena also had the idea of mixing the paint on the newspaper so we wouldn't have to waste paper. [Silvia's Learning Notes; Day 3 of Contextos Relevantes para Ciencias y Accidentes Geográficos]

Silvia's notes show the efforts of the children in working with the paint to create new shades of color, based on their interests. This became more apparent as time passed. We had purposefully given the children only the three primary colors to stimulate the color-mixing process. This choice, along with children's enjoyment and creative work, underlined the importance of the aesthetic aspect of the activity and allowed children to embrace an artistic learning experience. These aspects are part of the process of becoming "artistically literate citizens" and engage children in exploring "means of artistic expression," goals that are at the center of the New York State P–12 Learning Standards for the Arts (New York State Department of Education, 2017).

As Siena generated ideas about the mixing of the colors, Silvia praised her for her contributions, which she described as follows:

> I praised her for her smart and resourceful ideas to which [Siena] replied, "I am not smart!" I was a bit taken aback but I told her I disagreed and explicitly said when [I had seen that] she had smart ideas. After giving her the concrete examples, she didn't argue back and stayed quiet. [Silvia's Learning Notes; Day 3 of Contextos Relevantes para Ciencias y Accidentes Geográficos]

Silvia here noticed how children who are often situated as needing help or not following the rules, like Siena, who is labeled with a disability, might feel "not smart." This demonstrates how the candidates closely attended to children's identities and responded to their efforts to situate themselves as successful learners. This activity appeared to allow Siena to feel that she had something to contribute and provided her with a chance to experiment with multiple ways of being "smart" and of acting as an expert. In CHAT terms, this is an example of meaningful participation via distributed expertise (Cole & Engeström, 1993) through which different knowledges and abilities manifest.

Luis, who also included a volcano in his model, chose, on the other hand, to use it as part of a series of mini models to characterize change. He first created the mini volcano, and then a few other island-like formations that evolved from higher to lower (as if showing deposition of the lava as rock and follow-up processes of erosion that take place on the surface of the earth). As Victor joined him for the painting of his landform model, they explored different amounts of primary colors to achieve the exact shade they wanted. Silvia commented on their work with the color:

> I saw how much fun they were having making the color, but I kept asking questions about landforms to ensure they stayed on task. I asked them if the blue was a body of water. Luis said it was a color explosion and Victor agreed. I asked them "what landform is that?" And they replied, "watercolor explosion." [Silvia's Learning Notes; Day 3 of Contextos Relevantes para Ciencias y Accidentes Geográficos]

In the excerpt there are several aspects worth centering. On one hand, we witness the teacher candidate's efforts in keeping the conversation within the science aspects of the landforms, as a sign of being "on task," but also allowing children to enjoy the activity and encouraging them to make choices across other disciplines and interests. On the other hand, the excerpt also features the importance that imagination has in stimulating playful, yet rigorous, learning spaces such as the VWK.

The learning about the possibilities in mixing paint was further illustrated as Isabella also described her interaction with these two children: "We spoke a lot about which colors to mix to make colors like light purple and green." Silvia added that they were also engaging their outside of school knowledge (i.e., TV shows, video games, popular cultural elements) where "color explosions" might take place. Luis's model showing a numbered series of shapes and an image demonstrating the exploration with the colors he went through with Victor while painting the shapes are shown in Figure 8.2.

The children were exploring the change of landforms on the surface of the Earth. The work they embraced directly connected to the performance

Figure 8.2. Luis's Numbered Model and His Exploration of Colors While Painting it With Victor

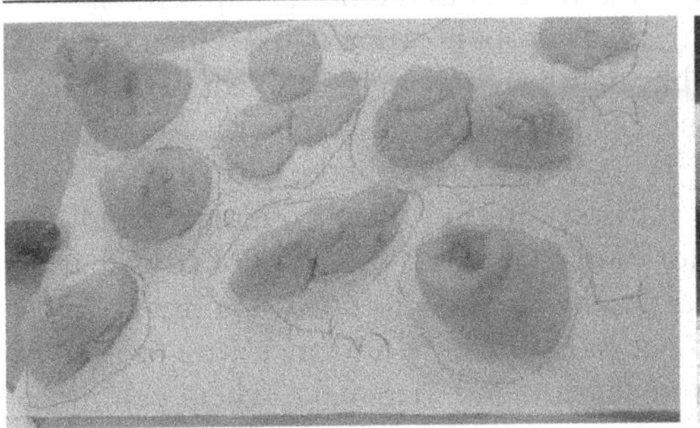

expectations in the NGSS. For example, in 2nd grade children are to "develop a model to represent the shapes and kinds of land and bodies of water in an area" and learn about the core ideas related to "earth materials and systems"; "systems and system models" is part of the NGSS crosscutting concepts (2-ESS2-2 and ESS2.A and related Crosscutting Concept, NGSS Lead States, 2013). At the same time, the children were also learning about creating new color possibilities for personal realization, part of becoming artistically literate (New York State Department of Education, 2017).

Meaningful Connections with Social Studies While Creating Other Landforms. During the landform explorations, another group of children decided to represent trees with the clay as they reasoned that there would be a lot more vegetation in the early landscape of Manhattan. This was the case of Arianna, a girl who after hearing from other children about Manhattan being an island, created a palm tree, facilitating the exploration of Manhattan as surrounded by water for the other children who could make connections to their home island (i.e., Puerto Rico or or the Dominican Republic). This idea, as Isabella recognized, was conceptually correct, even if she did not emphasize the name of the landform as an "island." Isabella explained it this way:

> I didn't want to have [a definition of what an] island is, let's review [it]. I wanted it to be whatever they could come up with. What did they see? Cause at the end of the day, it's not about me telling them what an island is. It's about them seeing what is surrounded by water, or what [is] not. So, I really liked [Arianna's ideas]. [Isabella's Learning Notes; Day 2 of Contextos Relevantes para Ciencias y Accidentes Geográficos]

As shown, Isabella valued the inquiry-based experience part of the activity and realized the value within the way through which Arianna explained, using her work with the palm tree, the idea of Manhattan being an island for others. In fact, other children had a difficult time thinking of a "city" being an island. For instance, one of the models included two buildings and trees and it was defined by his author as a city but "not an island." However, Arianna's ideas helped change the initial belief that cities couldn't be islands.

The idea of creating a palm tree was probably rooted in Arianna's mental image of islands from the Caribbean, as well as parts of Central America, having palm trees. (New York never had palm trees despite the existence of an early painting, dated around 1770, which depicted the City of New York and included a palm tree [see Carlson, 2016].) This exchange could certainly result in a follow-up exploration to find out the types of trees that do grow on the island of Manhattan, in the Caribbean (i.e., Cuba has the most species of palm trees), and in other parts of the world that are not islands. Arianna's family is actually from Mexico and Guatemala, where palm trees can be found, and her connection to palm trees built upon her FoK. In this way, Arianna's exploration manifested the type of meaningful connections children can make in flexible explorations with multimodal materials.

Laura's model represented Central Park (and also included trees, though not palms), which is part of her FoK as much as any transnational knowledge she might carry as a child of immigrant background. Marina, the teacher candidate of Mexican background, conversed with Laura about her clay model showing what appeared to be a tiger. She explained the following about Laura's model.

> Laura was being reflective about how Manhattan looked like 500 years ago, she said that probably there were Native Americans and therefore there were no buildings since they hunt in the forest. Then, I asked her what a forest looks like, she said that there is grass, trees, [and] animals to hunt for. She then created a small animal that looked like a tiger/cat. [Marina's Learning Notes; Day 3 of Contextos Relevantes para Ciencias y Accidentes Geográficos]

Laura's image of Native Americans in New York was part of her knowledge in social studies, and her reasoning of how there were a lot of vegetation and animals is probably part of that expertise in this discipline, as reflected in the New York social studies scope and sequence, as well (New York City Department of Education, n.d.). In fact, there are still many animals that share New York with humans and enjoy its urban habitat. For example, coyotes, deer, hawks, opossums, and squirrels can be found around New York City. Like other children, Laura also showed deep engagement with the artistic aspects of creating her landform model and this is suggested by the images in Figure 8.3.

Mirella was another child who decided to include trees in her clay landform. Rita, the teacher candidate whose family came from El Salvador, described Mirella's model with these words: "Mirella made two trees and crumpled clay to represent a lot of dirt. Mirella painted her árboles [trees] (brown and green), edificio [building] (pink red) and rocas [rocks] (red)." Mirella's model was motivated by a conversation that Rita documented where a boy had explained that 500 years ago "there were less buildings than today and that they were much lower in height." Mirella's and other

Figure 8.3. Laura's Model of an Early New York Animal and View of Central Park

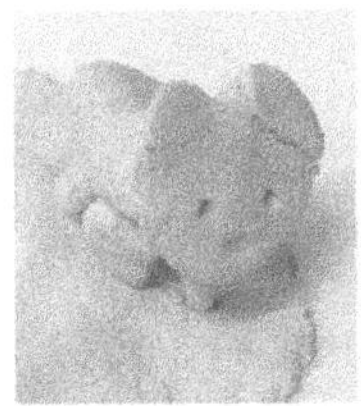

children's reaction to the idea of there being fewer buildings surprised Rita, the teacher candidate, who wrote about this in her learning notes:

> Mirella inferred that there were homeless people since there were not many places to live. In addition, they stated that since there was no medicine many people died. It was so interesting hearing how they all unanimously agreed that back in the day, times were more dark and harsh than today. [Rita's Learning Notes; Day 3 of Contextos Relevantes para Ciencias y Accidentes Geográficos]

These excerpts that the candidates wrote alongside the models show how the clay mediated collective learning experiences for the children. These projects explore not only science content but also social studies, as learning about New York City and its changes over time is part of the 2nd-grade curriculum (Unit 2, grade 2; see New York City Department of Education, n.d.). It is interesting that children thought that times were better now because before there were very harsh living conditions. However, many of the children in this study are situated as having precarious experiences themselves because of their immigrant status and low socioeconomic levels. The conversation highlights a level of perspective that is worth exploring with children, including critically engaging with the idea that Mirella generated, of homelessness and how it has evolved through history.

While some children created volcanoes or included trees and other forms of vegetation in their formations, others took a radically different approach. Their work is discussed in the next section.

Engaging the Imagination: Going Beyond Landmarks to Further Explore Social Studies. Rita engaged in a conversation with Jimena during the clay mediated exploration of landforms and of ideas about early Manhattan. She explained the novel approach Jimena took for the activity:

> In thinking about how Manhattan looked like years ago [. . .] Jimena was very intrigued in the idea of how people communicated over [500] years ago. She described the process of the telegraph and how people would use currents [electrical signals] and clicks for long distance communication. [Rita's Learning Notes; Day 3 of Contextos Relevantes para Ciencias y Accidentes Geográficos]

Rita and Jimena began an exploration about the telegraph and how it worked. They confirmed that telegraphs used coded pulses of electric current. In a volitional action, Jimena deviated from the creation of a landform and worked instead on creating a telegraph.

Rita documented Jimena's aesthetic involvement during the activity; as she wrote, "Jimena [. . .] was very focused with creating her telephone with the clay. [She] worked hard in making it stand up [and] was meticulous about painting her teléfono (telephone) brown and painted red decorations." Jimena's work shows the different pathways the activity facilitated for the children.

There were two other children who also took the activity beyond the idea of geographical landmarks. Isabella documented her conversation with the children who wanted to go back to discussing Pokémon. The discussion began with the standard proposed question, "¿Cómo era Nueva York hace 500 años?" (How was New York 500 years ago?). The children offered the following ideas explained through Isabella's words:

> We began brainstorming ideas, and I wrote them out. [A boy] said that in NY there were probably no cars but a lot of traffic. [A different child] said that he thought that there were a lot of cars y casas, no edificios (no buildings). [Isabella's Learning Notes; Day 3 of Contextos Relevantes para Ciencias y Accidentes Geográficos]

At this point, one of the boys brought up the question of whether Pokémon existed back then, and Isabella explained the child's reasoning.

> [He said] "I think there were not many humans, rather many Pokémons" and he then told me that Mew was the Pokémon that was most likely alive then. [The other child] then took out his Pokémon deck and started looking for the Pokémon he thought was alive then. He had several contenders but then agreed and said Mew was most likely alive since he is one of the strongest Pokémon. They then had a discussion of how these Pokémon probably lived in forests with lots of trees. [Isabella's Learning Notes; Day 3 of Contextos Relevantes para Ciencias y Accidentes Geográficos]

This excerpt manifested the knowledge the children possessed involving Pokémon. This knowledge could, in a different context, have remained outside of the classroom, but the VWK allowed the coexistence of knowledges of different natures. The children used painting to color trees, casas (houses), and the Pokémon this child had mentioned as being the first one existing, "Mew." Another child did not want to use colors because, as Isabella explained, "everything back then was in black and white." Isabella wrote about being "amazed by his reasoning not to paint his masterpiece and thought it was a very clever response." In fact, the world being black and white 500 years ago could be connected to children's experiences with old movies that were in black and white, and imagining the world that way.

Once again, we witness how children drove the learning experience and took on the identity of experts as they were allowed to use their imagination and their knowledge. Furthermore, Isabella said that the child had brought an artifact, a stuffed animal Pokémon, to the next session to show her. She added how she felt that her relationship with the student had improved based on the interactions during these sessions.

Capturing their model creations with the camera of the iPad was intriguing for the children, and this new modality added to their learning experience. Luis photographed part of his model and used the scribble feature in the Audio Note Lite application to draw arrows to analyze the image and share it with the group. Another child, Laura, chose to also use the scribble tool to write the names of the features in her model (Central Park, Beach). These new tools allowed for additional multimodal meaning-making and exploration of their ideas.

The work created in these different instructional invitations allowed children to use their knowledge to collectively explore ideas around the formal science topics (i.e., landmarks, changes on the surface of the Earth situated in the history of Manhattan). However, the projects also allowed the children to shift the context toward more creative/proximal representations of science (i.e., digital forms of communication or Pokémon).

Likewise, the information shows how children blurred the figurative boundaries we typically place in schools between disciplinary content areas. This took place as they agentively explored geographical landmarks, which is part of the science curriculum in the public schools in New York City, and also explored topics situated in the social studies curriculum. For instance, according to the New York City Department of Education K–8 Social Studies Scope and Sequence (2014–2015), Unit 2 for 4th-grade social studies includes learning about Native Americans as the first inhabitants of New York State; and, as already explained, studying how New York City has changed over time is part of Unit 2 for 2nd grade. Similarly, as part of Unit 5 for the 4th-grade level in social studies, children are to learn about the ways technology shapes a nation by learning about improvements and inventions, including the development of the telegraph.

The children also engaged with the arts in ways that resonated with the New York State Standards. For example, the standards state, "Through creating, performing, responding, and connecting in the arts, students generate experiences, construct knowledge, and build a more integrated understanding of self and community," and state as one of their standards in the arts the ability to "Relate and synthesize knowledge and personal experiences to inspire and inform artistic work" (Anchor Standard 10; New York State Education Department, 2017).

In-Between Formal/Less Formal Spaces: Children as Experts and Candidates' Learning

The last session of this unit invited children to work on creating slime and to explore pebbles to possibly mix them with the slime to simulate soil. Children had been asking for slime for a long time, and the candidate decided to finish the unit following their suggestion. The mixing of the slime and pebbles also provided opportunities for children to act as experts. For instance, Perla and other teacher candidates noted, during the follow-up reflection meeting, how much of an expert Dorita, one of the girls in VWK, was at what they called "amasando la mezcla" (kneading the mixture). As Perla reported, Dorita explained that she had done this a lot with her mother when cooking. Likewise, washing and sorting the pebbles was not a straightforward activity and while some children decided to count them, others coded them by color, by shape, or by size. During this lesson, rather than privileging the standard curriculum, which is a characteristic of formal learning spaces, the candidates favored children's interests and knowledge. In this way, the learning that took place can be described as occurring at the boundary between formal/less formal spaces. This section illustrates the processes through which these choices allowed children to act as experts, suggesting the permeability across labels (ability/disability; bilingual/language learner).

As the ingredients for the slime were mixed, the children explored adding different amounts of the glue and the liquid starch. Silvia, a teacher candidate who initially did not want to touch the materials, explained her own learning process, which was mediated by the work of Cynthia, one of the children.

> Cynthia [. . .] was very engaged because she enjoys making slime at home. I explained to her I've never made slime before, and she was very excited to assume the role of teacher. She said, "today I am going to be your teacher and I'll show you how to make good slime!" I stepped out of my comfort zone by touching and even creating my own slime. [Silvia's Learning Notes; Day 4 of Contextos Relevantes para Ciencias y Accidentes Geográficos]

This excerpt illustrates how children were the experts and candidates the learners during this part of the unit.

The slime ended up having different consistencies in the different groups, which made the children wonder about the role of the starch. Some children even chose to paint their slime blobs with markers. Teacher candidate Isabella summarized the experience as follows in her learning notes:

> Overall, I loved seeing how all the students made connections, observed the slime, and really had to work with their own observations to figure out how to get the right consistency of the slime. Everyone was engaged and worked the whole time. They seemed to really enjoy the slime-making process, and I felt that it was an exciting way to finalize our discussion of landforms and the earth's crust. [Isabella's Learning Notes; Day 4 of Contextos Relevantes para Ciencias y Accidentes Geográficos]

Isabella expressed the importance of the collective learning experience taking place in this final lesson of the Relevant Contexts for Science and Landforms unit. Favoring the collective learning experience and the connections across social spaces children made is also a form of allowing the boundaries between formal and less formal spaces to blur.

As part of this final lesson, the children also watched a video clip simulating the development of Manhattan from 1500 to the present (https://www.openculture.com/2015/04/timelapse-video-showing-the-creation-new-york-citys-skyline.html). One of the candidates explained Luis's ideas during the whole-group viewing:

> He LOVED the time-lapse video of Manhattan and made so many wonderful connections. First, he noted that around the time of 1700 there wasn't really a city, but there were houses. He said "fue como, fue como . . . no como ciudad, pero como town." (it was, it was . . . not like a city, but like town). I went with this and then rephrased in Spanish "Sí, sí, es como un town, es mas como pueblo, ¿no?" (Yes, yes, it is like a town, it is more like a village, no?) and he agreed, saying "sí, sí, es un pueblo" (yes, yes, it is a village). Additionally, when we watched the video one more time, which the kids asked for! he narrated over the entire thing, explaining the evolution of the island from trees and grasses to small buildings and people and then bigger buildings and skyscrapers. Even during the slime-making process, he served as a slime expert helping his group and other groups with the process of making slime. [Isabella's Learning Notes; Day 4 of Contextos Relevantes para Ciencias y Accidentes Geográficos]

The video, as shown in this excerpt, connected to many of the ideas the children had initially explored during the activities. For instance, the video showed fewer and lower buildings and more vegetation just as the children had retrodicted and confirmed that no palm trees or volcanoes existed in the Manhattan of 500 years ago. The video acted as an artifact that contributed to mediate the blurring of formal and less formal spaces. This is because the video could be seen as a more standard learning exploration that connected to the work with the slime-making, possibly perceived as being a less standard exploration.

Isabella wrote a closing reflection that also manifested the learning of the teacher candidates during this unit:

> Overall, I really appreciated the variety of responses and varied ways that students made sense of this activity [. . .] I ended up conforming my whole plan to the students (which was an area in which I was really trying to further grow as an educator—I'm so used to planning a lesson according to how my old school functioned, where there's

> a set learning goal that must be achieved, and I've been working on recreating this perspective so that I'm centering the students as the chief meaning-makers and agents in their own learning) [. . .] I really felt for the first time that I was a facilitator rather than teacher during this lesson. [Isabelle's Learning Notes; Day 4 of Contextos Relevantes para Ciencias y Accidentes Geográficos]

This excerpt powerfully demonstrates the learning that the candidate leading these lessons went through as she explored the boundary between formal and less formal learning emphases. Isabella was one of the few teacher candidates who had some prior teaching experience. She reflected on that earlier experience and how difficult it was to let go of some of the restrictions which that context had infused in her current practices. This type of practice-based learning is a process that teachers often describe as they try to grant children agency and more control of their own learning (Steele, 2001). Letting go of the restrictions placed in traditional learning settings (i.e., teacher being the expert or strictly following the standard curriculum) allows for formal and less formal spaces to coexist.

The form of learning promoted in VWK involves a collective endeavor with a "light pedagogical touch" (Gutiérrez & Calabrese Barton, 2015, p. 580). Through the VWK project, Isabella realized the importance of participation "in meaningful activity" and of building "on the learner's initiative," and revealed what we can learn as educators from these less formally controlled settings (Rogoff et al., 2016, p. 358).

CONCLUSION

This chapter used work and conversations from the Relevant Contexts for Science and Landforms unit to explore how learning takes place with bilingual children with a disability across boundaries. In a way, boundary crossing involved an effort, as Gutiérrez and colleagues (2017) explained it, of "learning to see differently" (p. 30). When working with children who learn at the intersection of ELL and disability labels, it is important we reimagine what counts as knowledge and learning and shift the focus from "what is lacking" to "seeing ingenuity in the everyday practices" they decide to share with us (Gutiérrez et al., 2017, pp. 34, 31). For such endeavor, we must explore learning that takes place (1) at the boundary of "traditional distal" and "creative proximal" knowledges and practices (Martínez-Álvarez, 2017a, p. 27), (2) at the boundary of disciplines, and (3) at the boundary of more formal and less formal spaces. For instance, "creative proximal" knowledges and practices manifested as Luis and Victor explored science topics (change on the surface of the earth with the series of mini-islands model) alongside imaginative touches like the "watercolor explosion" they created. Similarly, the rich discussions around Pokémon brought these figures from the children's outside-of-school games into the science lessons, creating a hybrid space where learning along a ZPD can be realized. Inspired by Vygotsky's 1978 notion of the playful imagination, Gutiérrez and colleagues (2017) explained how by engaging their "playful imagination, a child can move from being constrained by her situation to thinking beyond constraints," highlighting the important role imagination has in learning (p. 50).

In relation to the boundary of disciplines, it is important we allow children to enjoy the process of learning with some agency to select the direction they take, even when the chosen direction might not initially directly connect to the content objective under study. For example, Andrés needed time to explore the clay to figure out the three-dimensional potential this tool had while other children wanted to take time to mix colors and learn about the different shades they could create. This was not wasted time, as learning is taking place and children are experiencing the pleasures of being creative and engaging in being artists. Likewise, multiple possibilities for deeper science and social studies explorations surfaced during the lessons. Mirella's connection to homelessness and the Native Americans or Jimena's thinking about digital communication in early Manhattan are the sorts of topics that can help develop a child-centered curricular space across disciplines.

The VWK acted as a hybrid space also in terms of the more formal school-like environment where there is a certain goal that we targeted during the lesson, and the less formal emphasis that allowed teacher candidates to adapt to the children's ideas and interests and helped them relax, facilitating a multidirectional learning experience. While in a more formal learning space the children had been labeled with a disability, in this hybrid space of the VWK the children could experience what it is to allow different knowledges to fluidly come into being, allowing them to act as knowledgeable experts (i.e., Arianna's connection to palm trees helping her define the concept of an island). The use of multimodal materials such as clay, favored in this less-formal environment, which allowed children to use their whole bodies to create and learn, granted children opportunities to take on the responsibility to make meaning that, as Varelas and colleagues (2015) explained, can promote places for children "to assert their own epistemic authority rather than defer it to the teacher" (p. 526). Figure 8.4 visually represents the multiple dimensions where learning took place in-between boundaries, manifesting the porosity of these historical dichotomies, during the Relevant Contexts for Science and Landforms unit.

Stimulated by the instructional invitations that the teacher candidates created, the children experienced conflict as they aimed to work both within the limits of the proposed activity and toward their own interests and objects. In a sense they were constantly seeking a "new, wider and more complex object and concept for their activity" (Engeström & Sannino, 2010, p. 2). Through these activities and the responses that the teacher candidates made

Figure 8.4. Representation of the VWK Dimensions of Learning Across Boundaries

Learning In-Between Boundaries			
Between distal and proximal knowledges	Science as something you achieve giving you the status of a scientist, or as something about learning	Science in home remedies	Science in karate and in Pokémon
Between disciplines	Art (becoming artistically literate; informing artistic work by relating to knowledge and personal experience)	Social Studies (i.e., New York City has changed over time; Native Americans as its first inhabitants; the telegraph)	Science (i.e., crosscutting concepts in the NGSS of systems and system models)
Between formal and less formal spaces	Rather than privileging the standard curriculum, favoring children's interests and knowledge (i.e., slime)	Favoring the collective learning experience and the connections across social spaces children made	Letting go of restrictions in traditional learning settings (i.e., teacher as expert or adhering solely to standards)

to children's learning efforts, the VWK afterschool program embodied a hybrid space. The hybrid space embraced these multiply-marginalized children's humanity by learning what gives meaning to their school lives (Gutiérrez, 2016). This work must take place in-between boundaries across multiple dimensions such as those between distal and proximal science representations, between disciplines, or between formal and less formal spaces.

CHAPTER 9

Artifact-Mediated Science Content Learning in Inclusive Bilingual Contexts

This book has so far theorized "hybrid humanizing pedagogical moments" (Chapter 6), illustrated the need to fluidly explore children's multiple identities (Chapter 7), and discussed the expansive forms of learning that can take place in a hybrid space where the boundaries of multiple dimensions blur (Chapter 8). The present chapter builds on these ideas to center the critical role artifacts play in mediating hybrid and humanizing pedagogy for expansive content learning opportunities that can lead to identity formation, in inclusive bilingual education.

Vygotsky's (1978) idea of learning as being not just a direct response to a stimulus but rather an artifact-mediated process highlighted the importance of attending to the selection and the multidirectional use of artifacts. Artifact-mediated learning also points to the need to understand how such artifacts mediate the learning process. This is particularly important in inclusive bilingual contexts since research has shown how bilingual children with a disability often responded to artifacts used during instruction in "unexpected and surprising" ways (Martínez-Álvarez, 2017b, p. 548). In Martínez-Álvarez (2017b), children situated at the intersection of differences employed their own historically developed artifacts that were "full of purposeful and rich understandings" even when these shifted the direction of the planned lesson (p. 548).

The use of objects for mediating learning is a deeply human activity that is embedded in culture (Cole, 1998), and hence it is of fundamental importance in diverse classrooms. As teachers and children work together in hybrid spaces that incorporate various forms of speaking, learning, or interacting, they might experience contradictory situations. To break out of such situations, activity participants may draw from existing and novel repertoires of artifacts (Vygotsky, 1997). Mediators can consist of tools such as textbooks, pencils, and computers, or signs and symbols like language, ideas, or science concepts. Wertsch (2007) explained how individuals can use internal mediators such as inner speech or beliefs to implicitly (less obviously and internally) mediate their activity, or external mediators like writing on a whiteboard (more explicit or evident use of artifacts). All these artifacts have been culturally and historically developed and can transform, but are also transformed, while being used to mediate learning. For example, while early humans might have used sticks in their original form to mediate their hunting activity, these sticks eventually evolved into different specialized tools as humans transformed them into arrows, for instance. Similarly, a person's language and ideas evolve while being used to mediate learning and activity. Bilingual children and teachers acquire new terms and grammatical expressions, new meanings, and concepts for which they constantly need names and for which they might employ their multilingual resources, creatively expanding language use and learning.

While artifacts are always being employed to mediate learning, the way the same artifact mediates learning for different individuals might vary. Schools in the United States have, over the years, favored certain artifacts that have been developed to assist typically developing individuals in learning. Such artifacts might not have a comparable mediating role when used with children who are bilingual and have a disability, as they do not fit established views of the standard White, monocultural, monolingual child who learns in anticipated normalized ways (Lewis, 2017). As a result of persistent lack of successfully mediated learning opportunities, bilingual children with a disability are often portrayed as failing academically. However, succeeding in learning endeavors in schools must be understood as a cultural phenomenon directly connected to historical and social circumstances rather than as individual characteristics of any children (Trueba, 1990). Vygotsky (1993) called for the provision of additional mediational artifacts that would allow diverse children to compensate for their lack of alignment with normalized instructional practices and with the tools, signs, and symbols customarily used.

In working with bilingual children with a disability, diversity is an asset for learning and is part of what it means to be human. However, diversity acts as an asset only when the various, often contrasting, artifacts that children bring are recognized and integrated as part of the learning activity, a process that can promote a hybrid space for respectful learning (Martínez-Álvarez, 2017a).

The traditional idea of remediating bilingual children's perceived failure to learn, which relies on deficit views, dominates these children's schooling experience. Such views ignore children's repertoires of practice and situate traditional mediating artifacts as being adequate tools while individual children are to blame for their lack of learning (Lee, 2007). We need to shift this view to an understanding informed by cultural historical perspectives.

Through a cultural-historical view, the instructional environment, including the artifacts being employed, should be reorganized to expand upon children's repertoires of practice. It should respect the hybridity in human endeavors "through the conscious and strategic use of a range of theoretical and material tools" (Gutiérrez et al., 2009, p. 227). Cultural-historical embedded processes flexibly and fluidly involve "multiple forms of mediation" to emphasize *re-mediation* rather than trying to remediate (change through intervention) children and their knowledge (Gutiérrez et al., 2009, p. 227). Gutiérrez and her colleagues (2009) explain the process of re-mediation as follows:

> The basic rule of re-mediation here involves an expansive, hybrid, and additive approach to difference and diversity, in which the social rules of participation and learning and the division of labor are re-mediated by a social imagination oriented toward new forms of collective activity and new uses of the technologies of reading and writing. (p. 237)

The concept of mediating different activity elements (i.e., division of labor, artifacts, community, rules, or shared object and outcomes) repeatedly and in multiple and flexible ways can support the context for ensuing "hybrid humanizing pedagogical moments." As discussed in this volume's Chapter 6, hybrid humanizing pedagogical moments take place when hybrid and humanity-emphasizing pedagogies co-occur, cultivating and nurturing each other. Re-mediating thus can foster expansive learning opportunities as teachers and children work together to successfully mediate a hybrid humanizing learning experience where opportunities for flexible identity explorations are created.

This chapter focuses on analyzing the mediational role of artifacts while teaching science content in the Varied Ways of Knowing (VWK) afterschool program with bilingual children with and without a disability. To exemplify the process of re-mediating for hybrid humanizing pedagogies and expansive learning opportunities, this chapter explores the forms of artifact re-mediation that are generated in a bilingual science learning space and what we can learn from the analysis of artifact-mediated activity about teaching bilingual children with and without a disability. The following sections offer an overview of relevant research about artifact-mediated activity when teaching children with a disability and when teaching bilingual children. The chapter then discusses how these two bodies of research can inform the teaching of bilingual children with a disability. After this review, the chapter describes the Earthquakes, Plate Tectonics, and Ring of Fire project and presents insights from the review of the work generated in the project.

THE IMPORTANCE OF MEDIATORS WHEN TEACHING CHILDREN WITH A DISABILITY

While Vygotsky (1978) highlighted the role of artifact-mediated activity in learning, children with a disability might not respond to traditionally employed artifacts in the same ways that typically developing children do.

That is, school mediating tools and signs (i.e., lectures, worksheets, textbooks, etc.), which are most often aligned with the ways typically developing children learn, might not mediate experiences for children who differ from the majoritarian norm in language use, cultural practices, or ways of making meaning. To ensure the learning of those children who differ from expected norms and are labeled with a disability, Vygotsky (1993) argued, there is a need to explore tools and signs that more effectively help mediate their unique ways of learning. For instance, offering multimodal experiences; employing multimedia tools; or implementing embodied and kinesthetic, multilingual, multicultural, and collective (rather than individual) approaches can potentially better mediate the learning of children with a disability.

The mediation process should include opportunities for the children with a disability to compensate for their difficulties themselves. This can be accomplished by having them explore their ways of learning through different artifacts while barriers are systematically removed (Martínez-Álvarez, 2020a). Such a process provides children with opportunities to work along a ZPD, a term used to refer to the figurative space where instruction is attuned to children's knowledge, experiences, and levels so that they can best learn (Vygotsky, 1978). Recent conceptualizations of the ZPD embrace a collective understanding of this space that surfaces in collaboration with others as contradictions are addressed (Engeström & Sannino, 2010).

For example, if children have difficulty with artifacts intended to mediate learning such as a given written text because of lack of decoding fluency, they might decide to re-mediate these tools by listening to the text being read aloud or reaching out to a peer for help. That is, we need contexts where children with a disability can mediate the tools being used in schools that fail to help them in learning, using additional artifacts. This can only happen if they are allowed to take agency to re-mediate their learning following various trajectories (Gutiérrez et al., 2009). These various flexibly accessed resources function as mediating artifacts through which the child compensates for disability-related difficulties, allowing them to experience success and to learn complex material (Martínez-Álvarez, 2020a). Children with a disability benefit from this process of re-mediation (flexibly and fluidly engaging multiple forms of mediation with various artifacts) rather than remediating their learning, which often involves lowering the standards, focusing on specific uncontextualized skills, or in promoting the replication of standard procedures (Gutiérrez et al., 2009).

There is empirical work that supports this particular idea of re-mediation with children with a disability. Lewis (2017), for instance, explored how the use of novel additional mediational tools (i.e., re-mediation) helped a student with a learning disability in math gain more sophisticated understandings about fractions. The researcher described the implementation of a multimodal process of re-mediation that shifted the conceptual interpretation of fractions as linear distances (i.e., culturally used area models such as pieces of a pie or pizza) to weights (i.e., weight of portions on a scale), which helped the student understand fractional quantities. Learning in this study took place in the sense that the process bridged the child's discourse and what Lewis (2017) referred to as the "canonical discourse" (i.e., literate discourse employed in school when teaching content), while keeping the rigor of the activity (p. 327). Lewis explained that the process of re-mediation was designed for student difference and addressed issues of access by providing a design for the student with a math learning disability that could potentially benefit other students as well.

THE IMPORTANCE OF MEDIATORS WHEN TEACHING BILINGUAL CHILDREN

Content learning, particularly in the context of science, is multifaceted, and it is embedded within both culture and language (Lemke, 2001). While children have opportunities to use language to explain, read, or write, which can be very beneficial for bilingual children (Chamot & O'Malley, 1994), content learning might also pose conflicts. Researchers have found that language learners might interpret science ideas based on their knowledge and experiences, which might not be fully recognized in school or college contexts (Kortz & Murray, 2009; Kusnick, 2002). Hence, it is important that bridges are created between children's language and knowledge and ways of speaking about science in schools.

Rather than being in conflict with culturally accepted school concepts, children's knowledge and practices that are typically not recognized in school should be understood as part of cultural continuity, as students' past knowledge and practices can help with present school learning efforts (Jegede & Aikenhead, 1999). Different knowledge and practices are all part of the same continuum. Traditionally, however, research documenting children's different conceptions, rooted in a cognitive view, has often focused on their resistance to change (Kuhn, 1993). Conversely, internal (mental) conceptions should be understood within sociocultural contexts to help us move beyond the end products of science and rather focus on the process of learning and doing (Martínez-Álvarez, 2017b). Approaches such as model-based co-construction help reconcile these different perspectives. Model-based co-construction focuses on the collaborative processes through which children and teachers both contribute ideas to build shared conceptions as they together understand a certain external (material) model (Nuñez-Oviedo & Clement, 2002). In this way, engaging in the co-construction of models integrates the individual and the sociocultural context in the process of revising mental conceptions of science (Nuñez-Oviedo & Clement, 2002).

In fact, divergent ideas can be harmonized in a hybrid third space where boundaries are traversed and multiple forms of knowing coexist building on each other (Gutiérrez, 2008). This means that, children's funds of knowledge (FoK; Moll et al., 1992) can be assets for science learning in hybrid spaces. Such an approach can open opportunities for expansive transformations as the object of learning science in bilingual contexts is expanded to include knowledge and practices, which allow children to move through ZPDs. That is, in expansive learning, the object of the activity is expanded to, as Engeström (2001) explained, "embrace a radically wider horizon of possibilities than in the previous mode of the activity" (p. 137). Such expansion takes place as participants act to get out of a conflicting situation while collaborating in object-directed activity.

A sociocultural perspective of learning focuses on qualitative changes in the way learners interact with the world (Hedergaard, 2004). For learning to take place, Hedergaard (2004) suggested, the child needs to appropriate new cultural artifacts while building on their own. Language is a cultural artifact and an important mediator for learning, which is essential in making other artifacts (Puzio et al., 2013). Consequently, language needs to be attended to when working with bilingual children. Specifically, bilingual children need to employ their entire linguistic resources to learn, something that is referred to as *translanguaging* (García, 2012). Translanguaging includes the flexible use of multilingual and multimodal practices for meaning making and communication (García, 2009). Hybrid languaging is important for the recognition and integration of children's repertoires of practice (Gutiérrez & Rogoff, 2003).

Translanguaging can promote deeper understanding of content as it helps to facilitate a ZPD for bilingual children (Baker, 2006). Therefore, languages should not remain constantly separate in bilingual classrooms. At the same time, researchers recognize that it is important to respect and provide spaces for children to practice each of their languages in the classroom (Esquinca et al., 2014; Martínez-Roldán, 2015). Language is an artifact that can mediate learning, but the content learning context is also a site for children to learn language in use (DeNicolo, 2010). Esquinca and colleagues (2014) highlight the importance of studying the enactment of translanguaging at the microlevel. They explained how this can help in better understanding translanguaging within the context of the content areas, particularly when these are taught in Spanish, a minoritized language in the United States.

MEDIATING SCIENCE CONTENT LEARNING WITH BILINGUAL CHILDREN WITH A DISABILITY

Encouraging and facilitating different ways of making meaning through multimodality is critical when working with bilingual children with a disability (Martínez-Álvarez, 2017b). In a previous study analyzing the mediating tools a researcher and bilingual children with a disability employed while learning science, I found that the contextualized interpretation of children's expressions and reactions to mediators is complex and involves a culturally informed analysis (Martínez-Álvarez, 2017b). In this study, children's ideas were found to provide starting points for multidirectional expansive learning. My recommendation was to explore diverse children's mental models while analyzing them within historical contradictions as "a path for teachers to get in touch with the rediscovered intelligent person within the child" (Martínez-Álvarez, 2017b, p. 523). Model-based instruction, particularly model-based co-construction, is child-centered and mediated by teachers as it requires negotiation (Halloun, 2007). In this way, model-based co-construction aligns with CHAT principles and the process of expansive learning.

As explained in Chapter 7 in this volume, agency acquires a key relevant role in CHAT and particularly when working with bilingual children with a disability through model-based learning approaches. Rather than a cognitive perspective focused on self-regulation (Bandura, 1989), or a sociological understanding of agency as a "process of social engagement" (Emibaryer & Mische, 1998, p. 963), CHAT focuses on the subject's volitional action when experiencing conflict and the use of artifacts to mediate collective activity (Sannino, 2015).

Children will often act when they experience a "conflict of motives" while learning with others and when the elements across activity systems collide, causing tensions (i.e., conflict between artifacts or about division of labor, community, rules, object, and/or subject/s). Through their actions, they can potentially shift the object of the collective activity, enacting "transformative agency" (Sannino, 2015, p. 2). Collaboratively creating and revising models from a sociocultural perspective is also recognized as being an effective pedagogical tool for science learning as promoted in the current standards guiding the teaching of science in the United States, the NGSS, as it is included in the standards' engineering practices (NGSS Lead States, 2013).

In summary, research has suggested that contextualized understandings of bilingual children's models and science ideas, and the intentional agentive use and analysis of artifact-mediated learning when children experience difficulties, can be a pathway for improving inclusive bilingual education.

THE EARTHQUAKES, PLATE TECTONICS, AND THE RING OF FIRE UNIT

This chapter employs work generated while children participated in a unit exploring earthquakes, their location, and causes. The unit is briefly described in Classroom Identity and Knowledge Exploration 9.1. The full bilingual description can be found on this book's product page at https://www.tcpress.com.

Classroom Identity and Knowledge Exploration 9.1

TERREMOTOS, PLACAS TECTÓNICAS, Y EL CINTURÓN DE FUEGO (EARTHQUAKES, PLATE TECTONICS, AND THE RING OF FIRE) PROJECT

Day 1 of the project: Show the first 15 seconds of a National Geographic video clip showing an earthquake taking place (https://www.youtube.com/watch?v=e7ho6z32yyo). Children draw and write to show everything they know about earthquakes

Day 2 of the project: Work in small groups to trace the Ring of Fire on a map using brown playdough and explore the meaning of the Ring and the geography around it

Day 3 of the project: Show introductory video segments from two different sources using cartoons to illustrate relevant concepts (https://www.youtube.com/watch?v=9i7w7eJh3kQ and https://www.youtube.com/watch?v=yBr-D1cFmEs) and ask children to note the relationship between earthquakes and tectonic plates on post-it notes while working on two stations. Station 1: Children work with map/puzzle of tectonic plates and analyze images of earth's layers and plates; Station 2: Children work with iPad devices to explore interactive graphics at https://pbslm-contrib.s3.amazonaws.com/WGBH/conv16/conv16-int-mmes/index.html and https://d3tt741pwxqwm0.cloudfront.net/WGBH/conv16/conv16-int-tectonic/index.html

Day 4 of the project: Model the idea of tectonic plates and their dynamics using a peeled tangerine; create questions and answers to form a "pío-pío" or paper fortune teller

Day 5 of the project: Visualization of floating on water as a model to understand the way tectonic plates float on lava; create a model of the earth with the lava and the tectonic plates with the styrofoam sphere (earth), slime (lava), and felt fabric material (tectonic plates)

ARTIFACTS AND THE WAY THEY MEDIATE LEARNING IN INCLUSIVE BILINGUAL CONTEXTS

The following sections illustrate the ways in which the children responded to this 5-day project exploring earthquakes' locations and their relationship to plate tectonics, with a focus on mediating artifacts. The information presented in these sections centers on the mediators the teacher candidates chose to use to assist children in entering a ZPD and the children's reactions while engaged in the activity. The initial sections illustrate the first finding—how children took agentive volitional actions to employ their own artifacts and mediate the activity in their own ways, as they tried to re-mediate their learning. The rest of the sections address language as an artifact and illustrate the tensions uncovered by the analysis around teaching language while learning content and language as a mediator for learning the content.

CHILDREN'S VOLITIONAL ACTIONS: RE-MEDIATING USING ARTIFACTS AND VARIOUS KNOWLEDGES

As the Earthquakes, Plate Tectonics, and the Ring of Fire project began, teacher candidates wanted to learn about the children's FoK in connection to earthquakes. Three aspects surfaced in the analysis of the work in relation to teaching artifacts, re-mediation, and children's knowledge. The first subsection illustrates how the artifacts the teacher candidates decided to bring impacted the ideas and knowledge the children chose to share; the second reveals the work and conversations that unpacked how the children drew upon various forms of knowledge to mediate their own learning experience; and the last illustrates the process through which children and teacher candidates engaged in re-mediation using models.

Teaching Artifacts and Their Impact on the Knowledge Children Shared

Most children's responses during Day 1, where teachers wanted to explore their knowledge of earthquakes, centered on what was happening on the surface of the earth and saw it as related to weather, rather than explaining the underground forces causing these disasters. Focusing on this type of knowledge, the candidates explained, was mediated, or provoked, by the video artifact they had chosen. Elena's drawing in response to the invitation to explain what she knew about earthquakes included several horizontal curved lines and black shapes imitating rain clouds. Elena drew the connection between bad weather and the ground opening or breaking during an earthquake. She explained her work during a conversation with me, which clarified how her response was mediated by the video artifact:

Elena: Yo dibujé esto por el video y había muchas cosas que se estaban rompiendo y . . . (I drew this because of the video and there were many things that were breaking and . . .)

Patricia: Muéstrame qué se está rompiendo aquí. (Show me what's breaking here.)

Elena: Las rocas, aquí están—points to the lines—, y hay lluvia. (The rocks, here they are—points to the lines—, and there is rain.)

Patricia: ¿Por qué? ¿En un terremoto hay lluvia? (Why? Is there rain in an earthquake?)

Elena: Sí, hay tormetas eléctricas y nubes grises. Y causan un terremoto. (Yes, there are electric storms and gray clouds. And they cause an earthquake.)

During this conversation, Elena explained that her illustration had been mediated by the video artifact that Juán, the leading teacher candidate chose to introduce the session, saying in Spanish that she had created her drawing "because of the video." Indeed, the few seconds that were shown of the video used on Day 1 showed images that could indeed be interpreted as bad weather along with the consequences of the earthquake. Based on that video, Elena interpreted the weather as the cause for the earthquake.

The candidates reflected upon how the video had mediated the experience toward weather and the surface of the earth rather than to the actual processes causing earthquakes. For instance, Marina described Elena's work with these words:

> I was working with her [Elena] while she was doing this. And I did see that she, que ella a lo mejor confundió tornados with earthquakes (that she maybe confused tornados with earthquakes). She was elaborating so much on the sky and then the clouds [. . .] Ella me dijo, "[. . .] el cielo está azul, las nubes están grises y esa es la lluvia y cae rayos" (she told me, "[. . .] the sky is blue, the clouds are gray and that's the rain and lightning strikes"). So I was thinking that she's probably kind of mixing a hurricane rather than earthquakes that happen underground. [Marina; Planning/Reflection Meeting; Day 1 of Terremotos, Placas Tectónicas, y el Cinturón de Fuego]

Elena, like most of the other children in the group with a disability or experiencing difficulty with learning, might have focused more on the multimodal video artifact than on the teacher candidate's explanation. Since the video did not focus on the processes underneath the surface of the earth, it ended up mediating children's work toward other, while still related, ideas. Diana, the Brazilian teacher candidate, reflected upon this as follows:

> So, I think that maybe [. . .] some of the confusion came [from the video]. I don't think we showed like the cracking. It was more like the storm and rocks falling. So, I think again, technology wasn't our best friend. [Diana; Planning/Reflection Meeting; Day 1 of Terremotos, Placas Tectónicas, y el Cinturón de Fuego]

As Diana explained, the video might have misled the children toward other kinds of natural disasters, contributing to their interpretation of earthquakes as being caused by weather-related processes. Juán, the leading candidate, said that he intended to show only the first four seconds rather than the next 15 seconds, which is what he ended up showing because of technical difficulties.

> I wasn't able to let [the video] load [. . .] So, they saw the first like 15 seconds, which had [. . .] buildings falling and stuff like that. So that's

> why. And then, yeah, and then so it was rubble and stuff, like people, like the weather post the earthquake was like that. So, they assumed that it had to do with weather, too. So that's where that came [from]. [If] I had just shown them those four initial seconds, it would have been a different interpretation. [Juán; Planning/Reflection Meeting; Day 1 of Terremotos, Placas Tectónicas, y el Cinturón de Fuego]

Here Juán realized that the part of the video artifact he showed mediated children's focus on weather and how, if he had shown a different part of the clip, the responses might have been different.

Children Drawing Upon Various Knowledges to Mediate Their Learning

Children drew upon a variety of knowledges to mediate their work and think about earthquakes. One of the teacher candidates, Adriana, described for example the way Victor drew upon his knowledge of the children's show *SpongeBob SquarePants*, and how it helped him in mediating his way toward the topic of earthquakes. Adriana explained:

> We were all just talking about, like, experiences and what we thought about earthquakes. So, it felt like that was less pressure for him [Victor]. It wasn't like an interview, like so, what do you think about earthquakes? [. . .]—and on topic. And, then during the drawing part of the lesson, I was sitting with Victor, and before he started drawing the earthquake, he was starting to draw SpongeBob. So, I asked him to pause the SpongeBob so we could do the earthquake drawing. So, he did [laughter]. Reluctantly, but he put it away. [He d]id the earthquake drawing, just like awesome drawing with the street breaking [since] during the discussion at the beginning, he had described earthquakes as [happening] when the earth breaks open. This was his [drawing]. And he said, the car would be going into this crack. [Adriana; Planning/Reflection Meeting; Day 1 of Terremotos, Placas Tectónicas, y el Cinturón de Fuego]

Adriana here attempted to provide a safe space for Victor to share his knowledge about earthquakes. Using this approach appeared to lower the pressure for Victor, who typically appeared disconnected during lessons (as described by the candidates). To create such a safe space, Adriana gave him some time to draw what he had chosen himself, which was an illustration of SpongeBob. Then she asked him to produce a more closely related drawing, and in this way, she helped Victor connect back to the content.

According to Adriana, Victor described the illustration about earthquakes that he drew following her invitation as follows: "the ground is breaking, and the cars are going down cause [it] is moving a lot." Adriana also explained that he then added, "The earthquake hace que se mueva. No sé lo que hace [causa] el earthquake" (The earthquake makes it move. I don't know what makes [causes] the earthquakes). His effort marked another volitional action, after the first one of deciding to draw SpongeBob.

While Victor had decided to follow the candidate's instructions and drew something more clearly connected to the topic, he then switched back to his creation representing SpongeBob when he was done. At this point, Adriana tried once again to bring him back to the topic of earthquakes underwater, which seemed to be something that interested him. She explained it this way:

> And then he went back to his SpongeBob drawing [laughter]. So, I tried to get him back onto the conversation about earthquakes under water and, like, what would happen if there was an earthquake under water [like where SpongeBob is]? So, he started drawing the waves [on the SpongeBob drawing]. And he was like, well, the waves would shake a lot. So, I like gave him the words like, oh, big waves. They would like splash, like stuff like that. In Spanish. And we were talking a lot about that. [Adriana; Planning/Reflection Meeting; Day 1 of Terremotos, Placas Tectónicas, y el Cinturón de Fuego]

In this exchange, we witness the conflict of motives that Victor is experiencing as he wants to focus on his beloved SpongeBob, and he takes action to maintain that during class, while Adriana is experiencing her own conflict in that she wants to allow Victor to act volitionally but also make sure he addresses earthquakes. Adriana and Victor did work together to achieve a hybrid space where both forms of knowledge were welcome. Particularly, this manifested as Adriana, realizing that SpongeBob lives in the ocean, invited Victor to think about whether earthquakes took place under water, a topic that had surfaced earlier with the group. Victor accepted the invitation by adding waves to his drawing and the two generated some new terminology to describe the actions taking place. In this sense, the topics came together for Victor and Adriana as they shifted the direction of their activity toward a hybrid of their (initially separate) motives.

The transformative power of this event manifested as Adriana reflected upon Victor's renewed interest, and, in sharing while in the closing whole group, she explained:

> And then when we went back to the group circle to share, he was the first person [. . .] He right away wanted to share [. . .] That's [great] yeah, that's when I went, "good," cause like before, I'd never seen him so excited to participate. [Adriana; Planning/Reflection Meeting; Day 1 of Terremotos, Placas Tectónicas, y el Cinturón de Fuego]

Adriana was very excited to have Victor take a volitional action and volunteer to share, something we barely saw in the afterschool program. She explained how Victor described during his sharing how there is an "earthquake underneath [the water], and then it causes the waves." She realized that he did have some knowledge about earthquakes, and that his thinking with SpongeBob mediated their collaborative work. We could say Victor actually re-mediated (initially mediated by the teacher and then mediated again—re-mediated—by Victor's connection to SpongeBob toward earthquakes) their shared activity while addressing the conflicts they—Victor and the teacher candidate—both experienced.

Teacher candidates' own life experience also acted as artifacts that mediated children's thinking and exploration about the topic under study. Juán, the teacher candidate who was born in Mexico and then moved to the United States, shared how he had experienced the earthquake that took place in Mexico in 1999. He spoke about this in the following excerpt:

> When I shared my lived experience with the students, I felt warm sharing it with them [the children] and explaining to them how I felt being part of [an earthquake] especially at such a young age. They seemed really intrigued by it and I felt that they needed that connection to think more about earthquakes and the magnitude that comes with them. The earthquake I was part of in 1999 started in Mexico City, but because of their ripple effects and how strong it was it reached Puebla, and we felt it in my grandparent's ranch. [Juán; Planning/Reflection Meeting; Day 1 of Terremotos, Placas Tectónicas, y el Cinturón de Fuego]

In this part of the excerpt, Juán focused on the human aspects of sharing something from one's personal experience with the children. He described how doing so helped him feel close and connect to the children as he spoke of his life in school.

Juán then added the following description of an event taking place during this introductory session:

> One thing I do want to point out when I was sharing my lived experience of being in an earthquake when I was 3 years old, and I showed the students the map of Mexico City and its proximity to Puebla, one of the girls asked where Santo Domingo was [. . .] A fellow teaching candidate also saw this and brought the globe from the classroom to show the students where Santo Domingo was, after this students started to ask where other countries in Latin America were, which left me with a lot to think about. [Juán; Planning/Reflection Meeting; Day 1 of Terremotos, Placas Tectónicas, y el Cinturón de Fuego]

The candidate's sharing mediated children's exploration of other places that are susceptible to earthquakes. Several of the teacher candidates described Juán's description as a key mediational artifact of children's thinking and sharing about earthquakes. For instance, Marina, the teacher candidate whose family is from Mexico, explained the power in Juán's sharing as she referred to it as a "first-hand artifact" in the following excerpt:

> The more first-hand artifacts we have to show them and prove to them of the experience we had, the more interested they become about the topic. They were also asking [about] Juán's emotions during the earthquake [. . .] Questions tend to arise when we add so much vivid information to stories. [Marina; Planning/Reflection Meeting; Day 1 of Terremotos, Placas Tectónicas, y el Cinturón de Fuego]

With these words, Marina highlighted the mediational role of the experience and how it stimulated children to ask more questions connected to the topic. She also highlighted other aspects connecting to the children's humanity while working (i.e., "Juán's emotions during the earthquake").

Re-mediating Learning With Models

During the last lesson of the project, the teacher candidates proposed to create a model of the earth where the core was a styrofoam ball, the mantle was slime, and the tectonic plates were pieces of felt fabric. There were several good conversations that took place during this session, where children showed they were thinking about plate tectonics and its connection to earthquakes. The way learning was re-mediated through the tangerine model and then the styrofoam ball model is illustrated next.

The Peeled Tangerine Model. The previous week, the teacher candidates had used tangerines to model the movement of the tectonic plates. This model consisted of two pieces where the tangerine was the earth (i.e., the core and mantle) and the peeled skin pieces represented the tectonic plates. While working with the tangerine model, the candidates learned that the children were using *rotation*, or the spinning of the earth, and *translation*, or the revolution movement, the two most commonly known forms of movement of the earth, as if that was causing the movement of the tectonic plates. In fact, they felt that the model of the tangerine was helpful in uncovering how children were connecting these forms of movement. Rita explained it this way:

> When we were in the small group, I think the tangerine was helpful not just to [. . .] show them and instruct, but also for them to show us what they're not understanding. So, like when Elena was asking this question

> again in the small group, [. . .] it was difficult to understand exactly what she was saying. And then I was like, "okay [. . .] what do you think is happening?" And she started moving around the peels. And [when asked], "how are they like hitting each other?" She thought they were like coming at each other and they were like moving in space. Like not on the earth. [Rita; Planning/Reflection Meeting; Day 4 of Terremotos, Placas Tectónicas, y el Cinturón de Fuego]

Elena's explanation is illustrated in Figure 9.1, where the skin of the tangerine, representing the tectonic plates, is separating from the earth, which is, in this model, the tangerine's flesh. Rita's explanation of Elena's process suggests that the girl was implicitely mediating her learning experience. That is, Elena was trying to find ways to provide the information about the model that the teacher candidate was hoping she would generate. However, the information she chose from her knowledge repertoire, while related, was not what the candidate's lesson plan dictated.

Rita closed her reflection explaining that she was, in her words, "left with the feeling that there was something she [Elena] didn't understand about the model [. . .] she thinks that [the movement of tectonic plates] connects with the rotation of the earth." It was this event that engaged candidates in considering how difficult it is to establish new relationships between the ideas the children bring, or their existing knowledges, and new formal scientific understandings (i.e., canonical concepts and ideas) when in an inclusive bilingual education classroom.

As the candidates tried to understand their role in establishing the bridge between these multiple existing knowledges with the children, they brought into our collective space ideas that are important to consider in the context of disability and bilingualism. For instance, teacher candidate Diana said that she was having a hard time understanding that not all children will completely learn what she called "every aspect of the topic." This is an excerpt from Diana's learning notes showing her wonders about children's learning:

Figure 9.1. Elena Showing Her Thinking About How Tectonic Plates Move in Space

> During the question component, I realized Elena continued to have several misconceptions regarding plate tectonics [tectonic plates], their movement, and the rotation of the Earth. She, once again, asked how it was that the plate tectonics [tectonic plates] rotated around the Sun if the Earth was also rotating around the Earth. I would show her the tangerine version of the Earth, with the peel moving *with* the tangerine inside, and she would seem to understand that the plate tectonics [tectonic plates] were going along *with* the Earth when it rotated around the Earth but then would ask the same question again. Even despite multiple explanations, I still don't think Elena completely understood the concept. This was an ah-ha moment for me—even when we are trying our best and spending multiple sessions on a topic, it might still be that we come out at the end with some students not completely grasping every aspect of the topic. It was difficult to be okay with this. [Diana's Learning Notes; Day 4 of Terremotos, Placas Tectónicas, y el Cinturón de Fuego]

Diana here is trying to feel comfortable with allowing children to be at different levels of understanding at the same time. It is important for teachers to realize that the uneasiness that Diana felt in Elena not fully understanding the concept or the model, "even despite multiple explanations," is a form of awareness that can inform their practice and help them realize when artifacts such as the tangerine model are not mediating learning. This uneasiness can be a motivator for them to continue to try to find novel ways to help bilingual children with a disability understand in their own way.

Rita, when she realized some children were not fully understanding the ideas she was trying to teach, offered a different perspective as she turned her attention to the learning space and its design. She explained the following during the reflective meeting, "I think [. . .] if she didn't understand, then, my explanation wasn't good, because it's only good if she will understand. So, I think I should have tried different ways of explaining it for her." Rita here, as other candidates did throughout the work in the project, offered a view of learning that aligns with sociocultural understandings where development is mediated by the context. This perspective is also supported by DSE theorists where the goal is to achieve a UDL, a universal design for learning, creating a learning environment that works for all children to learn and develop.

The Styrofoam Ball Model to Re-mediate Learning. As the candidates realized that the tangerine model was not enough for all children to understand the movement of tectonic plates on the earth, they proposed an exploration with a new styrofoam model. The candidates designed the styrofoam model to help children understand that the tectonic plates (i.e., the pieces of felt material) moved slowly on lava (slime) on the earth (the styrofoam ball), as well as to follow their interest in working with slime.

Diana, the leading teacher candidate, introduced the session by inviting children into a mental visualization of herself floating on a body of water while in her native Brazil, and showed a photograph illustrating this. Diana said that the personal connection with the visualization invitation, what Marina described earlier as using "first-hand artifacts," helped the children relate to the idea of the tectonic plates floating on lava.

The styrofoam model using felt material and slime mediated new understandings among the children about the topic we were exploring. However, the candidates discussed how models are not perfect and teachers need to assist in the mediating process with other available artifacts. For instance, while working with the children, Juán explored with them how some qualities of the slime were similar to lava, like its slow motion, while others were less similar, like its stickiness. He explained during the planning/reflective meeting:

> That could be a great nature of science conversation that the models that we use are not perfect. And that, why are we using these models? Because I feel it's the liquid thing, right? It's a good comparison with lava. But it's very different in many other ways. And that is an important conversation because they have to understand that it's not a perfect comparison. [Juán, Planning/ Reflection Meeting; Day 5 of Terremotos, Placas Tectónicas, y el Cinturón de Fuego]

As Juán noticed the importance of explicitly teaching children about the nature of science, including discussing the limitations of models to represent science concepts, Marina shared ideas for improving this model with the following words:

> I think something that would have made sense, and I think it would have created probably a more graphic meaning, perhaps, is if you put the slime in red to kind of represent the lava. Then, [you put] the felt paper green for land, and then, blue for water. Just so we kind of [simulate that] the lava is right underneath what is water and the earth. Just so we can have that meaning. [Marina; Planning/Reflection Meeting; Day 5 of Terremotos, Placas Tectónicas, y el Cinturón de Fuego]

Marina demonstrated the reflective process she went through as she thought of ways to improve the styrofoam model so that it was even more effective at mediating the learning of the children. This could also be understood as part of a process of guided compensation (Martínez-Álvarez et al., 2020), and as a way to re-mediate the artifacts used when teaching in inclusive bilingual education contexts.

This final session closed with notes describing moments of discovery that took place and how the model had contributed to mediate learning. For instance, Adriana shared:

> When Xochtil's slime was ready, we placed some of her slime on the ball and added more placas (plates). She was talking about volcanos and lava, so I squished together the placas (plates) to create a volcano. Xochtil still seemed a bit lost, so I offered the example of a tube of toothpaste getting the toothpaste squished out. This seemed to help, and Dorita came over and we continued to make volcanos. Xochtil then explained that the lava goes all over the land once it comes out of the volcano. Then, unprompted, she began to question how humans are affected by natural hazards, such as lava and then snow. [Adriana; Planning/Reflection Meeting; Day 5 of Terremotos, Placas Tectónicas, y el Cinturón de Fuego]

The collaborative learning experience that Adriana shared, the way she introduced the improvised artifact of the toothpaste to, in a way, re-mediate the styrofoam ball model, and the way Xochtil used the model to then demonstrate her renewed understanding, are examples of powerful science learning with the children. An image illustrating Xochtil's styrofoam model simulating a volcano is shown in Figure 9.2.

Diana summarized Xochtil's learning when she described her exit presentation at the end of the lesson in the following way:

> I liked that all groups chose to share at least something with the whole group. Xochtil's sharing of how her tectonic plates, when she moved them, "created a volcano" because the lava moved up was so enlightening! [. . .] I hadn't even thought about that when planning this lesson and it was such an ah-ha moment for me to see students arrive at such knowledge [. . .] We create the conditions so that students can then do the learning [. . .] This is a very important

Figure 9.2. Xochtil's Demonstration of a Volcano Using The Styrofoam Model

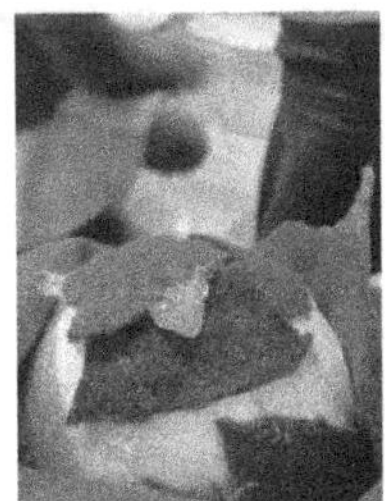

> reflection I want to keep in mind. [Diana; Planning/Reflection Meeting; Day 5 of Terremotos, Placas Tectónicas, y el Cinturón de Fuego]

The experience with the styrofoam model demonstrates collaborative learning and how the candidates and children worked together to re-mediate learning and the model itself. Through her reflection, Diana highlighted the unexpected nature of the learning that took place through the activity, rooted in children's agency with the materials, and for which she had not planned.

The learning of language, which surfaced in several instances while working in the project, is illustrated in the next section.

LANGUAGE AS AN ARTIFACT: TENSIONS ADDRESSING CONTENT LEARNING AND LANGUAGE LEARNING

The following subsections focus on illustrating the processes related to language as a mediator for content learning that manifested in the products and conversations generated during the Earthquakes, Plate Tectonics, and the Ring of Fire project. Specifically, the first subsection illustrates how content language generated conflict between everyday interpretations of terms and other, more scientifically based, or canonical, ways of understanding the terms and the related science content. The second subsection shows the tension between using language as a mediator for learning content and learning content to learn language. The information generated in the activities suggests there is a need to find a healthy balance between these two priorities when teaching in inclusive bilingual education contexts.

Mediating Multidirectional Access to Canonical Discourse and Content

During the second session of the project, the teacher candidates introduced the idea of the Ring of Fire (Cinturón de Fuego). They soon realized that the language used to describe the Ring of Fire, the active seismic region, producing both volcanoes and earthquakes, around the Pacific Ocean, was creating a tension between the candidates' ideas and the children's interpretations. Specifically, since the Ring of Fire was a "ring," or a "belt" in the Spanish translation (cinturón—belt), the children created it with the clay in the shape of a closed circle. That is, a conflict arose that can be understood as a separation between what can be called the canonical discourse and the children's everyday interpretation (Lewis, 2017). The need to bridge different understandings of terms was not only for the children but also for the teacher candidates, manifesting the multidirectionality/multidimensionality of the learning experience. That is, learning was not only vertical (i.e., from teacher candidates to children), but also horizontal (i.e., teacher candidates also learned from others and from available resources).

The candidates insisted that the Ring of Fire is open at the bottom, while most children tried closing it. Furthermore, the children were searching for evidence of "fire" since this word was used in the name. Juán described this issue as follows, "So, introducing the Ring of Fire, at first [. . .] since it is a ring, they wanted to close it. Also, since it says "fire" they focused on where the fire is too." The way most children created the Ring of Fire with clay is shown in Figure 9.3, where we not only see the closed shape they represented but also a more circular, ringlike, shape than the actual Ring of Fire.

While most of the candidates during the session were trying to convince the children that the Ring of Fire did not close at the bottom, Alicia described how she had actually explored this idea further during the session. She explained her follow-up exchange with Luis in our planning reflective meeting:

> [Luis said exclaiming], "oh, there must be plates under the water, too!" And I was like, "yes. There totally are." So, [he inferred that] there should be earthquakes there, too. And he started making little brown dots inside the Cinturón de Fuego (Ring of Fire), explaining that this was possible as well. And I wrote it on my learning notes, cause I thought it was so interesting how the [playdough] inspired his curiosity to inquire further. He was like, "oh. I have this material left. And this [extra] time. And I want to keep seeing where I can use it." So, he did that on his own [. . .] I pointed down at the map, and I was like, "yeah. Look. Look, those areas where they are, those are plates—those are the tectonic plates." And he was like, "aah!" And he changed some of it and made it into a line to show that those are like the parts of the plate. [Alicia; Planning/Reflection Meeting; Day 2 of Terremotos, Placas Tectónicas, y el Cinturón de Fuego]

Figure 9.3. Image of a Near-Circular, Closed Ring of Fire

Luis's work showed the Ring of Fire in a semiclosed shape that was less circular than those in other children's versions, and where additional seismic areas were also marked, as well as some mountain ranges, as shown in Figure 9.4.

The fact that Luis had ended up creating an unclosed representation of the Ring of Fire was initially perceived as progress. However, during our planning reflective meeting, Alicia reflected upon this idea, and shifted directions as she proposed that the Ring of Fire actually did close:

> Because Mirella was also, she drew the closed belt. And I referred to Juán [the teacher candidate] explaining, "it's a belt, but it doesn't close." And I was telling Mirella, "are you sure it closes? Remember Juán said this?" But then as I was writing my learning notes, I said to myself, "I don't know that for sure." Maybe it does close. Because the map is too [flat], but the real earth is round. So, it must continue that onto the arctic section, that must be more susceptible to movement. So maybe it does close. [Alicia; Planning/Reflection Meeting; Day 2 of Terremotos, Placas Tectónicas, y el Cinturón de Fuego]

In this excerpt Alicia shared her learning process during the lesson where she moved from the collectively accepted idea that the Ring of Fire was open at the bottom to understanding that there might also be seismic activity under water. In fact, during our reflective meeting, we investigated this idea and found out that there are volcanoes in Antarctica that can continue the figurative ring and indeed close the Ring of Fire. The moment when this shift took place is shown in the following excerpt from our reflective meeting:

> *Alicia:* I'm thinking that it, that there should be [earthquakes under the ocean], I mean logically, that whole plate is in movement

Figure 9.4. Luis's Work Expanding the Idea of the Ring of Fire

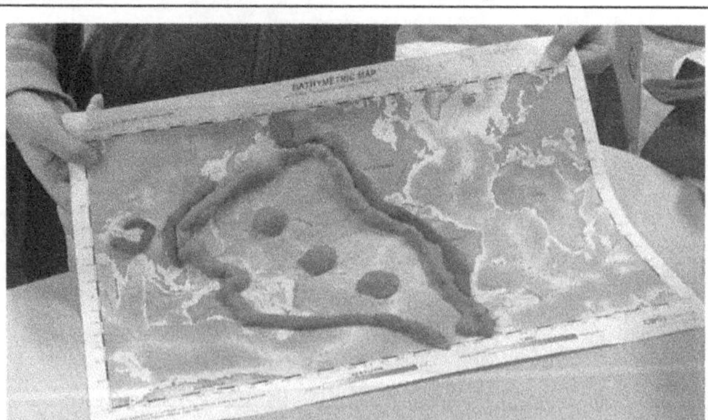

that, that edge, the lower edge of the plate must have some susceptibility of seismic [activity].

Juán: I think it's just [that is] in the middle of the ocean.

[. . .]

Rita: Yeah. It's saying here in this National Geographic article that [reading from article]—"it isn't quite a circular ring." blah, blah. And then it says, "several active and dormant volcanoes in Antarctica, however, do close the ring." That's what it said. But it's because like the Ring of Fire was, it was conceptualized as a term to like indicate where humans are more susceptible to be affected by earthquakes.

[. . .]

Alicia: Maybe I should have just like [explored] why she [Mirella] closed it. Maybe taking out my iPad and said, "hmm, that's a really interesting question that you have. Let's look." And, maybe we would have found that article.

The article that Rita was reading (National Geographic, n.d.) became at this point a mediator for the educators' learning. In this exchange we witnessed the learning of the candidates that are inquiring as they teach the children and reflect upon their experiences with them. In a sense, the mediators of the map, the playdough, the children and candidates themselves, and the reflection with the additional tools from which the candidates drew, all assisted multidirectional/multidimensional movement toward the more recognized or canonical science understanding of the Ring of Fire.

Language as a Mediator for Learning and Mediating the Learning of Language

At the end of this exploratory project, we invited the children to create posters showing their renewed understandings about earthquakes, their location, and their causes. As the children shared their work with the whole group, they made decisions about what language/s to use and the specific terminology to bring in to communicate meaning. These actions were very interesting for the teacher candidates. I share one event where we discussed language as a mediator for learning.

Marina, the teacher candidate of Mexican background, was leading the final whole-group sharing. Mirella, one of the children, came to the front of the room to share her work. While Spanish is a heritage language for Mirella, she often communicated in English and seemed to be more comfortable speaking English than Spanish in the VWK afterschool program. However, when she started to speak about her earthquake's poster, she chose to share using Spanish. This decision prompted Marina to immediately take a volitional action. She invited Mirella to switch to English to explain the science of earthquakes.

This is the event that led us to consider the mediating role of language for content learning as well as how language learning can be mediated in inclusive bilingual classrooms. The following reflection issued during the follow up meeting:

Student Teaching Supervisor: Yeah. But then when Mirella presented her poster. She started in Spanish. And I was like, yes! And then, you invited her to switch to . . .

Juán: English [laughter].

Student Teaching Supervisor: Yeah.

Marina: Why does [Mirella] feel forced to speak Spanish when she was presenting? That's something I don't . . .

Patricia: I think [. . .] it was difficult for her. But she was willing to do it.

Rita: Mmm-hmm [assenting].

Student Teaching Supervisor: I think it was because she went after Elena, that group.

Rita: And they did Spanish, right?

Juán: I think it has to do with the fact that she sees us there. And we're speaking Spanish most of the time, like mixed. So, she kind of like [feels that] connection.

Patricia: Yeah. All the presentations were mostly in Spanish.

This part of the reflection shows the supervisor pointing to the tension of Mirella choosing Spanish and Marina asking her to switch to English for her sharing, in a context where we were trying to privilege Spanish. As the conversation began, Marina gave her interpretation of why Mirella was speaking in Spanish. She thought she was feeling a conflict that "forced" her "to speak Spanish."

However, at this point, Juán offered an alternative explanation, noting that the afterschool program took place mostly in Spanish, with some translanguaging to English. He felt that the predominantly Spanish context in the VWK afterschool program had helped her connect to her Spanish. The fact that it was Mirella's decision to present in Spanish was at the center of the tension since she had not been directly invited to use that language.

Marina insisted that Mirella had felt she "had to speak Spanish." She elaborated upon this idea in the next segment:

Marina: Como que (like that) she thought she had to speak Spanish.

Patricia: Are you feeling like it's taking away from her learning or something? Or what worries you about her presenting in Spanish?

Marina: This is the first time, like throughout this whole entire after school, this is the first time I've seen her go up and present to begin with. She was the type of person that doesn't want [to share]. I'm like, "okay, [she didn't have] the motivation to go

> up there." But then the fact that she was motivated, which was already something that was a big, you know, a big milestone. And the fact that she kind of easily spoke in English, which is her comfortable language. Since I've been speaking to her in Spanish other times, and she just responds to me in English. But [I said], "speak in English if you feel comfortable" [. . .] Even with that having been said, she has to force herself to speak Spanish. I'm like [. . .], "why does she feel like she had to?" Like, what was the motivation for her to do it? Not in a bad [way but] why did she, like what were the external factors or internal?

With these words, Marina elaborated more about her reservations. For her, the fact that Mirella had decided to come up to share her work was already a big step. In her own words, it was "a big milestone." She offered anecdotal information to support her explanation that English is "her comfortable language" and felt that there were "external" or "internal" factors forcing her to choose to speak in Spanish.

Marina did not yet see the value in Mirella presenting her learning using Spanish, but rather situated it as a problem. She shared another idea as I commented on how easy it is for children to switch to English, which typically acts as the social language in the United States. This time, she drew upon her own experience to explain her interpretation of the tension under discussion.

> I didn't want her to have long pauses. Because for first-hand experience I know long pauses can feel awkward and just like I don't even want to do it anymore. And my view, being up there was already like a big, a big step. So, I didn't want her to like re-track back and like, you know, I don't want someone to say that. I didn't want her to feel that way at any point. [Marina; Planning/Reflection Meeting; Day 5 of Terremotos, Placas Tectónicas, y el Cinturón de Fuego]

As I insisted that it was out of Mirella's volitional action that she spoke in Spanish, and noticed that children's social tendency to favor speaking in English is exacerbated when children have a disability (as educators focus on learning content but inadvertedly disregard learning language), there was a shift in the direction of the conversation. As a result, Marina suggested that instead of switching to English, we could support Mirella's effort using an additional mediator:

> *Marina:* I think more preparation [as in] sentence starters. No sé (I don't know), I think that like the whole presentation, the discussion with the posters [. . .] I think that could have been a great chance for me to perhaps have like sentence starters to like how to create, how to start a presentation, pero en español

(but in Spanish). And then, cómo hacer preguntas (how to make questions) as a presenter pero en español (but in Spanish). And then definitely have that in hand. And really, of course, focus on the poster, but also in the lenguaje (language).

Student Teaching Supervisor: Like a language objective.

Marina: Yeah. So, I think if I were to like go back and do this lesson a little better, I'd definitely put more emphasis on the language part [. . .] I should've created like either strips or something for them to, like, read. They're, they're old enough. So, they can read it. And even if they can't read, nosotros (we) can read it for them and then [. . .] They start absorbing that and learning.

Here, the conversation shifted to entertain ways to create the best context to support children like Mirella in speaking in Spanish. While it seems that Marina was initially focused on helping Mirella in learning and communicating the science and in the learning of science, and in the use of language as a mediator for that learning, here she seemed to realize that the learning of language also needed to be mediated. This is shown by her realization that she had not focused on the language components and her suggestion to help children learn how to ask questions in Spanish during a science presentation, by supporting the children with "sentence starters" or "strips or something for them to like read." These different ideas about mediating artifacts for language learning suggest that Marina now had realized the need to attend to both language as a mediator to learn science and also to the learning of language itself when teaching in inclusive bilingual contexts.

The transformative potential in this reflection can be summarized by the statements that Marina made toward the end of the conversation: "I was so focused on the content, not so much on the language, but there is so much we have to take care when we get to the language part, aside from the content." With these words, Marina demonstrated once again her renewed understanding of the need to balance the teaching of content and the teaching of language. Her statement suggests that she now realized the value in Mirella choosing to share in Spanish and that she understands ways of mediating that learning with her.

CONCLUSION

The snapshots of work and conversations in this chapter revealed interesting aspects in relation to artifact-mediated activity. For instance, children naturally engaged in a process of implicit mediation using external tools. They did this as they initially focused more on the candidates' artifact (i.e., the multimodal video tool) rather than on their verbal requests and explanations. As children mediated their learning experience implicitly (i.e., guessing what candidates wanted them to focus on), they chose what knowledge to share, leaving other ideas out of the VWK space. Likewise, the information showed the humanizing pedagogies that can be mediated through what Marina described as "first-hand artifacts," meaning candidates' employment of personal experiences that mixed facts with emotions and generated feelings to mediate children's content learning in humanizing ways.

The work of the children in VWK highlighted the importance of carefully considering the materials teachers use, even when merely asking children to express their knowledge, and illustrated pathways through which hybrid and humanizing pedagogies can co-occur.

The findings also highlighted the need to understand children's interests and knowledge as central to the learning of content and as a continuation of canonical knowledge rather than separate from it. Victor's learning experience with Adriana made this apparent as the direction of the activity shifted toward a hybrid of their (initially separate) motives and the artifacts were also qualitatively transformed (i.e., Victor adding waves to his SpongeBob creation symbolizing movement in earthquakes). This is an example of a hybrid space where the boundaries across "traditional distal" and "creative proximal" knowledges and practices are blurred (Martínez-Álvarez, 2017a, p. 27), an idea that was discussed in Chapter 8.

In relation to the co-construction of knowledge using models, the information presented here demonstrated how at times the candidates needed to re-mediate the learning experience with the chosen models because they were not equally helpful to all children. Even when not fully effective, the models could still help in other processes such as surfacing children's ways of connecting knowledges (i.e., the tangerine model highlighted the areas of disconnection among these different movements related to Earth). This process of uncovering the associations the children were making using their prior experiences and knowledge from inside and outside school is important, particularly in inclusive bilingual contexts where children learn at the intersection of bilingualism/biculturalism and disability differences and identities. Uncovering the role of the artifacts in mediating learning suggests the potential permeability across educational categories (i.e., ability/disability; bilingual/language learner), and questions the adequacy of the static use of labels currently employed in educational contexts.

The last part of the findings illustrated the processes related to language as a mediator for content learning. Two main tensions surfaced in connection to language. On one hand, as shown in the work in which children engaged to learn about the Ring of Fire, language at times failed to automatically mediate pathways toward the canonical understandings in science, and purposeful redirection was important. The products and conversations also showed how explorations of language and content (i.e., the meaning of the Ring of Fire) mediated learning not just for the children, but also for the candidates, an aspect manifesting expansive learning.

Importantly, the work between teacher candidates and children during the project surfaced the second embedded tension in inclusive bilingual programs, using language to mediate content learning but also simultaneously attending to the mediation of language learning. While working with the bilingual children with a disability in VWK, teacher candidates aimed to create a context for learning content that at times took away opportunities for children to sustain their heritage language development. Through reflection, teacher candidate Marina realized the importance of not only focusing on content but also promoting learning of the minority language. She recognized the need to remove barriers with additional artifacts such as sentence starters, resources to support children's formulation of questions in Spanish, or planning for preliminary practice time, to assist children like Mirella in compensating and entering a collectively nurtured ZPD.

Teacher candidates' reflection about practice and specifically about artifacts' mediational assets and shortcomings, and their consequent actions, which are required for transforming educational contexts (Freire, 1993), were essential components for teacher learning in the VWK.

CHAPTER 10

The Varied Ways of Knowing Project

Teaching Bilingual Students With a Disability

When working with preservice and inservice teachers in my higher education program, I often engage in discussions with the teachers that comment on the added difficulty of teaching children who learn along multiple layers of difference. Teachers, directly or indirectly, feel and express that having children in their schools and classrooms who come from immigrant backgrounds, who have a disability, or both, is often inconvenient for their practice. However, that is the reality of today's classrooms, and has been for a long time now. I have high expectations for bilingual teachers' ability to manage the full complexity in their classrooms.

Classrooms are not predictably uniform anywhere around the world. The view of teaching and learning as focusing on what is most easily achieved, and the insistence on preparing teachers for addressing the generic learner, fail to adequately prepare them for public school contexts and are based on dated notions. We are experiencing a burgeoning of immigrant communities worldwide. For instance, most European countries are witnessing superdiversity and multilingualism (Gogolin & Duarte, 2017) and the U.S. immigrant population has reached peak levels (U.S. Census Bureau, 2018). Forced migration from countries like Myanmar, South Sudan, Afghanistan, Venezuela, Syria, and most recently Ukraine have resulted in 82.4 million people who, by the end of 2020, had left their home countries (United Nations High Commissioner for Refugees, 2021), which creates an influx of school-age children who bring languages and cultures different from those typically represented in the host countries.

The United States is no different, as its school population is continuing to become ever more diverse. Bilingual children already account for a quarter of the overall population with nearly 5 million children, mostly Latinx, labeled as emergent bilinguals in our public-school classrooms (Kids Count Data Center, 2019). More than one out of 10 emergent bilingual children are also identified as having a disability, most of them receiving services under the speech and language impairment and specific learning disability categories (National Center for Education Statistics, 2021). Teachers must be prepared to address the language- and disability-related needs of our schoolchildren.

The main historical contradictions related to the learning of bilingual children reside, as described in Chapter 1, in the disproportionality of minoritized children in the soft disability categories and the consequences that these labels have for immigrant children; the lack of teacher preparation programs for assisting teachers to work with children who are both emergent bilinguals and have a disability; and the lack of bilingual spaces that are inclusive of children with a disability.

As dual language bilingual education is the best option for language learners in our public schools (Genesee, 1994), these contradictions must be addressed to progress toward the vision of inclusion embraced in the 2004 IDEA special education law. Equal, free, and appropriate educational opportunities and least restrictive learning environments for children with a disability include designing bilingual spaces for all children.

Ensuring bilingual spaces that are inclusive of all learners requires that we function from several suppositions. Chapter 2 described these grounding assumptions as being, first, the belief that all children deserve to maintain their languages and grow to become biliterate; second, the recognition that learning also takes place outside formal spaces (i.e., outside schools); third, the premise that with the appropriate contextual support all children can learn bilingually.

This book aims at assisting in understanding the multiple layers involved in teaching in diverse bilingual classrooms by raising awareness of the pivotal elements that surfaced in the study around the VWK. These elements were centered on issues of assimilation and ableism, and the expansion of identity, agency, and humanistic pedagogies. While reviewing the work generated in the activities, several theoretical ideas were introduced as being potentially helpful for advancing these central elements. Chapter 2 introduced these ideas, summarized on Figure 2.1, that were then carried into the chapters to understand the collective work and to illuminate the theoretical texture of the teaching and learning endeavors in VWK.

The conceptualization of the VWK as a hybrid space in reference to language, culture, and disability gives rise to the rest of the theoretical constructs. In hybrid spaces, there are possibilities for enabling distributed expertise. Children can work with others in ways that allow them to make different but aligned contributions to the learning activity, according to the context, but in their own terms (i.e., distributed expertise; Edwards et al., 2010). This involves children compensating for possible difficulties they might encounter by performing different learning identities and acting fluidly as experts or novices within the same supportive space (Martínez-Álvarez, 2020a). The process demands opportunities for children to mediate their learning multiple times, or re-mediating, when they feel it is needed (Gutiérrez et al., 2009). That is, re-mediation makes ZPDs possible for children who can decide to take action changing the direction of the activity, a process that takes place collectively (Engeström, 1987; Vygotsky, 1978). Learning with children with a disability requires recognizing their critical ways of enacting agency and responding to their efforts to change the, often painful or difficult, situations in reassuring ways. By enacting agency in supportive learning spaces, bilingual children resist assimilationist forces and begin healing. Healing takes place in Anzaldúa's (2002) terms along the path to conocimiento (see Chapter 2).

The humanization that is required for hybrid spaces to succeed at creating inclusive spaces for bilingual children required a new concept that I introduced in Chapter 5 as "hybrid humanizing pedagogical moments." Hybrid humanizing pedagogical moments involve the mutual nurturing and cultivation of hybridity and humanizing pedagogies. That is, whereas hybridity might foster the integration of languages, cultures, and forms of (dis)ability and emphasize boundary crossing as the continuum space between related dichotomies (e.g., expert or novice, language learner or bilingual) as realized in classrooms; humanizing pedagogies center the humanity, aesthetic, emotional being over a cognitive approach to teaching children. There is a need to bond these perspectives to reinforce their mutual importance in inclusive bilingual education, which, as proposed in Chapter 5, can be accomplished through hybrid humanizing pedagogical moments.

For this last chapter I extracted the elements that surfaced in the study, and that are discussed throughout the book, on issues of assimilation and ableism and the expansion of identity, agency, and humanistic pedagogies. Each subsection below synthesizes the theoretical, alongside the practical aspects, arising from the work shared within each chapter. This final chapter also organizes the implications for progressively expanding bilingual education into spaces inclusive of children with a disability.

ABLEIST PRACTICES IN BILINGUAL EDUCATION AND IMPLICATIONS

Chapter 4 presented the construct of ableism from the perspective of bilingual education and of disability studies. Using work and conversations, and theorizing the findings, the chapter addressed the question: How does ableism manifest in bilingual education contexts with children with a disability? The exploration of the products and conversations revealed ways through which ableist beliefs guided views of the bilingual learners, and the consequences of these beliefs. Figure 10.1 synthesizes the ableist practices that surfaced through the study and the resulting experiences of three of the participating children who had a disability. The third column shows the practices that could instead assist in fostering hybrid humanizing pedagogical moments and the aligned theoretical constructs.

The analysis of the bilingual children's practices in the VWK within the context of ableism offers implications for progressing toward inclusive bilingual spaces. Bilingual teachers can learn from the experiences that Deyanira, Susana, and Jacob had, and resolve to take action to break away from ableist thinking and associated teaching practices.

bleist Manifestations, Bilingual Children's Experiences, and al Constructs

Ableist ces	Children's Practices and Experiences	Theoretical Constructs Potential Hybrid Humanizing Pedagogical Moments
	Deyanira's Experience	
Favoring traditional forms of engaging in literacy and communicating	Difficulties with writing	**Path to Conocimiento/ Re-mediation** • Telling stories multimodally (i.e., with drawings) • Learning from the expertise of family members (i.e., Deyanira learning from her mom) • Reframing identity toward competence
Pressure to learn English quickly	Struggles with English language learning	
	Susana's Experience	
Situating children who speak less as not academically developed	Really shy	**Distributed Expertise/ Collective ZPDs** • Recognizing various forms of intelligence (i.e., insightful, intrapersonal) • Valuing different patterns of being and participating in the class (i.e., verbal, nonverbal)
Early retention	Didn't get what the teacher was saying	
	Jacob's Experience	
Presuming the language skills of heritage speakers with different trajectories to be necessarily equal	Less presence of Spanish in the home	**Critical Agency/ Compensation** • Identifying the consequences of multiple simultaneous forms of oppression • Understanding and promoting children's purposeful learning actions • Honoring and supporting families' commitment to their children's bilingual development • Meeting children where they are and rejecting stereotypical expectations
Expecting rapid language mastery from heritage language speakers	Difficulties with processing written texts & limited exposure to comprehensible input	
Perceiving cultural and linguistic identities as fixed and linear	Asymmetrical expressions of linguistic and cultural identities	
Promoting independent bilingual learning	Seeking language support from classmates (i.e., translation for meaning making)	

Teachers can foster hybrid humanizing pedagogical moments, but this requires expanding the ways bilingual learners' linguistic and cultural practices are understood. Embracing the ways bilingual children with a disability decide to engage in literacy, to communicate, or to manifest their bilingual and bicultural identities and skills is one step forward. While educational systems promote more prescriptivist views of language and literacy learning, bilingual educators working with children with a disability cannot continue to judge children through this restrictive lens. It is well known that the balanced bilingual is an ideal image that differs from the actual experience of bilingual individuals. Generally, bilingual children bring varied competence in their languages based on their experiences. Bilingual children suffer the consequences of being pressured to learn in predetermined ways and to work independently, demonstrating practices they don't have while leaving the practices they do have outside of the classroom. We need to meet children where they are. This might not reflect what we typically expect bilingual children to be and to have. This is why the children with a disability are in special education in the first place (because they do not match those traditional views of what learners do). As we recognize ableism in bilingual teaching practices, we cannot continue to enact them in the same ways.

The practices shown in the last column of Figure 10.1 are examples to dismantle some of the ableist practices we have in bilingual education by fostering hybrid humanizing pedagogical moments. Individual teachers must explore the unique practices that accomplish this goal with their own students. I hope these ideas serve as a starting point for educators looking to dismantle ableism in their bilingual classrooms.

HISTORICAL ASSIMILATIONIST PRACTICES AND IMPLICATIONS FOR BILINGUAL EDUCATION

To situate the need for a humanistic approach in teaching and learning at the intersection of differences, Chapter 5 explored historical issues of assimilation in relation to the immigrant and disability experience. The chapter addressed the question: How do historical assimilationist efforts manifest when teaching bilingual children with a disability, and what opportunities toward inclusive designs might surface in a hybrid space?

Chapter 5 illuminated the forms of oppression that might surface from an analysis centered on revealing assimilation. It also offered practices that can assist in interrupting assimilationist efforts that might be taking place, even subconsciously. The chapter specifically offered information highlighting issues of inequity that take place when systems don't actively resist pressures for diverse children to assimilate.

The VWK partially functioned within limited views about the cultural and linguistic identities of the children, which promoted assimilationist efforts. For instance, children were at times situated as solely Spanish or English speakers and the children internalized some of these identities. At times, teacher candidates felt uncomfortable in providing artifacts for some children to re-mediate their learning while not giving them to all. While not all children needed to re-mediate the learning, as they were being successful with the existing resources, when possible all children could enjoy using newly available tools. If this is not possible, children who need specific tools should still be getting them. This effort to make sure everyone was equally supported promoted assimilation and forced children onto the norm they are not. Chapter 5 highlighted the importance for teacher candidates to be prepared to provide children whose unique differences require specific tools and services with what they actually need.

There were other practices that surfaced in the afterschool program that could potentially act as forces to resist assimilation. Some of these manifested in the VWK while others did not fully surface, but there was potential for shifts or turning points toward more pluralistic hybrid spaces. These were theorized in Chapter 5 and are synthesized in Figure 10.2.

Given the persistence of pressures to assimilate to a normative way of being and learning in today's educational systems, we must raise awareness and find ways to actively resist these efforts through bilingual education aiming to be inclusive. The practices synthesized in Figure 10.2 are some examples of how to dismantle assimilationist efforts that surfaced in the afterschool program. Teachers can engage in searching for these manifestations of assimilation in their own schools and even in their own classrooms, becoming aware of daily assimilation pressures placed on children who are different in multiple ways and helping dismantle these pressures to create better learning spaces for all.

HUMANISTIC PERSPECTIVES FOR INCLUSIVE BILINGUAL EDUCATION

Chapters 4 and 5 highlighted ableist and assimilationist processes as lenses that can help radically expand bilingual classrooms toward more inclusive perspectives. Chapter 6 plays an important role in illuminating the legacy of the VWK project because it underlines the need for humanistic perspectives and theorizes the idea of "hybrid humanizing pedagogical moments." This idea has been very useful in understanding the potential in the processes that take place in bilingual classrooms.

Kinloch and San Pedro (2014) explained that humanizing perspectives "privilege the co-construction of knowledge, human agency and voice, diverse perspectives, moments of vulnerability, and acts of listening" (p. 23). The VWK program strove to privilege these ideas by building on how co-construction and human agency have been helpful for humanizing our work. Working with children of immigrant background with a disability in the VWK involved diverse perspectives and required careful listening.

Figure 10.2. Productive Practices to Resist Assimilation and Theoretical Constructs

Practices with Potential to Resist Assimilationist Efforts	Turning Points Toward Hybrid Humanizing Pedagogical Moments
• Awareness about learning taking place across multiple social spaces (i.e., in school and outside of it) and throughout modalities (i.e., playing, watching, dancing as culture) • Additional language (i.e., Mixteco) as part of children's assets and learning identity	**Boundary Crossing** • Figuratively crossing boundaries about what learning looks like across experiences and abilities • Learning possibilities when crossing linguistic boundaries
• Generated ideas typically recognized as part of Mexican culture (i.e., tacos or the Mexican flag) but also others from the families' cultures (i.e., ¡Útala! [Wow!], watching Ninja show understood as a family memory, mole, Cumbia Mexicana), from popular culture (i.e., video games, Supersonic), or from additional interests (i.e., learning about China)	**Fluid Identities** **Critical Agency** • Embracing expansive perspectives of cultural and linguistic repertoires as evolving over time
• Untraditional responses to proposed invitations (i.e., drawing circles of different colors to show culture) and linguistic forms (i.e., calling a person of Chinese background "China" instead of name) • Sharing immigrant stories and feelings • Children situated as either solely English speakers or solely Spanish speakers • Making assumptions about children's linguistic competence based on limited information	**Hybrid Learning** • Attending to aspects of class, race, and culture when interpreting children's use of language and generate safe hybrid learning spaces • Understanding language as fluid and seeing bilingual children from holistic perspectives rather than as two monolinguals in one (Grosjean, 1982)
• Children as experts who, if allowed, will enact agency to teach the candidates (i.e., expressions of criticality)	**Distributed Expertise** **Collective ZPDs** • Children demonstrating critical literacy and political insights when using their personal life experiences (i.e., immigration and policies)
• Reframing agentive resistance and need of support from adults, often perceived as an inconvenience that takes time away from other children, as openings for ZPDs	**Turning Point** • Redirecting agentive energy from resistance toward collaborative spaces of possibility

(*continued*)

Figure 10.2. (*continued*)

Practices with Potential to Resist Assimilationist Efforts	Turning Points Toward Hybrid Humanizing Pedagogical Moments
• Teacher candidates providing access to new mediators when children manifest resistance & negotiating rules for access	**Re-mediation** **Compensation** **Collective ZPDs** • Generating new directions in the activity
• Questioning, and setting conditions for belonging understood as assimilationist practices	• Recognizing subtle but persistent assimilationist forces

The chapter explored the question: How can a humanistic approach assist in making bilingual programs more inclusive of children with a disability? In a way, the VWK project surfaced the need to create hybrid spaces in language, culture, and disability that were, above all, humanizing for the children. Building on Erevelles's (2005) discussion of bodily movement differences, the experiences of being of immigrant background and of having a disability cannot be divorced from the normative social spaces where children navigate their learning and their multiple identities. Prioritizing hybrid and humanistic conceptualizations worked, as we learned with the children in the VWK.

For bilingual candidates, humanistic perspectives can lead to a sense of belonging in teaching. On the other hand, the medicalized perspectives often prioritized in special education might contribute to them feeling unprepared to address the needs of children with a disability (Alderson & Goodey, 1998). Aspects of belonging arise from the "permanent relationship of dialogue" that, as Freire (1993) described in his *Pedagogy of the Oppressed*, humanistic education can establish (p. 50). It also can help bilingual teachers and candidates realize that children with a disability have the right, as much as any other person, to manifest their "creative power" and grow conscious of the multiple forces oppressing them as learners, so they can also act upon them (p. 56).

Humanizing pedagogies require principles and practical constructs that allow us to leverage bilingualism and disability as the assets that they are for learning. For instance, in a previous study (Martínez-Álvarez, 2020a), I theorized the "opportunity encounters" that can spark when, as children with a disability encounter challenges in normative educational institutions, they are able to draw on artifacts, often purposefully planned for by thoughtful bilingual teachers, to compensate and move forward toward successful bilingual learning (p. 3).

Taking the ideas from Chapter 6 forward, Chapter 10 explores: How can bilingual educators employ and build upon the realization of the need for hybrid and humanistic perspectives? How can educators transform their bilingual practice to be inclusive of children with a disability in ways that potentially expand their possibilities beyond their fixed labels? How can bilingual educators guide children with a disability into the dignified space where, as Greenstein (2016) explained, they explore the generalized knowledge and practices needed for consequential participation in the world, while building upon their own knowledge and practices?

One way to dignify the bilingual space for children with a disability, and to provide access to the normative knowledge, is to break the current "culture of control" (Monahan, 2009, p. 123). Bilingual educators must embrace children's agentive actions as potential mediators for learning that are to be encouraged and permitted. It is important to trust children with a disability in taking their own steps to think and learn, even when their actions might initially not indicate engagement in expected ways (i.e., Mirella, drawing on the whiteboard instead of joining the group on the carpet, who ended up critically participating in the discussion in this way). There is also a need to understand when diverse children take actions to resist or move away from a learning activity, as this is often an effort to redirect their work toward more successful spaces.

Accessing normative knowledge with minoritized communities can only take place respectfully if learning is understood as a mutually beneficial exchange, where the bilingual educators are learning with the children. For instance, children might understand the need to alter the context to accommodate disability, expanding opportunities for everyone's access, differently than educators, or they might express this important principle in more effective ways. During the case of the square not fitting the round door during the book discussion in the Capes and Shields project, for example, children suggested creating new shapes for the square to take or building a new house, showing the importance of all those involved taking action for accessibility.

Hybrid and humanistic perspectives involve recognizing that children's assets and ways of learning are not typically included as being helpful with academic study. Upon this realization, educators must act to welcome all assets into the classroom, opening possibilities for learning about the children. For instance, Cynthia's sharing with her cape, explained in Chapter 6, expanded once she was reassured that her powers "didn't have to be academic." She explained how she jumped rope with her grandmother. Learning this can assist educators to understand how Cynthia spends her time and how adults support her education as they shared spaces with her. Cynthia's dedication to her cape, despite having missed the initial session, showed how meaningful it was for her as a human being to engage in this work.

As illustrated with the rest of the information presented in Chapter 6, the children brought in a combination of talents connected to the academics in different ways, creating a hybrid learning space (i.e., see description of Luis's cape where he included words, symbols, and drawings portraying math and digital gaming–related ideas).

Likewise, hybrid and humanistic perspectives can help educators realize and accept that the resulting product of an activity is, as described in Chapter 6, not always the most important part of the experience. As educators, we might want to have final products that look good and provide a lot of information at first glance. This is part of the standard insistence on the collection of evidence in our education systems. For hybrid and humanistic perspectives, there needs to be a balance, however, where creating the product does not compromise the process educators go through with the children. Artistic experimentation and conversations about "knowledge, experiences, and aspirations in and out of school" are as important as the product we are inviting the children to complete. The VWK served as a space to show the value in well-designed curricular invitations that, as explained in the chapter, "evoke" instead of "prompt," and that are, in Perla's words, "the means by which we obtain a lot of the valuable information of their funds of knowledge." Such curricular invitations, which expect deviations from the initial plan, allow children to act to take the activity toward new directions without sanctions, and are built on trust in children as powerful creative human beings (Freire, 1993).

Lastly, the approach to teaching through "conversing and taking action in a mutual respectful exchange" is what makes possible, as proposed in Chapter 6, "calm and flexible hybrid humanizing pedagogical spaces." Part of the VWK hybrid humanizing pedagogical moments included creating mediators for "human agency and voice" (Kinloch & San Pedro, 2014, p. 23). For instance, the children created a video for a member of the afterschool who was absent, while another child asked the group to "be prepared" for their classmate to come into the afterschool program late, so that they could support her in learning what she had missed; and others brought into the learning spaces their academic concerns and their preoccupations about things in their lives. These processes and the "act of listening" that took place (Kinloch & San Pedro, 2014, p. 23) hybridly connected the in (i.e., our own program) and out spaces around the afterschool program and highlighted the relevance of humanistic approaches when we work in bilingual education.

The hybrid humanizing pedagogical moments in the VWK that were shared in Chapter 6 hold potential for collective creative learning. I hope the ideas here synthesized inspire bilingual educators in engaging the multiple spaces children navigate and embracing the unexpected humanizing learning that comes out of such efforts.

LEARNING ABOUT DISABILITY WITH BILINGUAL CHILDREN

Teaching about the rights of people with a disability and how these rights were earned is rarely part of the school curriculum. Chapter 7 highlighted the need to look at the history of the disability civil rights movement and to use it as an opportunity to explore different identities of bilingual children with a disability. Teaching about the rights of people with a disability can support the process of "conscientization" with the children, as Freire (1993) proposed when working with minoritized communities and which can extend to people with a disability. It can also "honor disability diversity" in ways that promote the asset-based view of disability that this book aims to inspire (Erwin et al., 2021, p. 6). The chapter explored the question: What knowledge do bilingual children with a disability manifest while engaging in identity work and learning about disability, and what forms of agency surface as children explore multiple identity possibilities? Chapter 7 also illuminated how explorations about disability history allowed children to explore their own identities while in VWK. The need to integrate children's FoK as well as disability-informed experiences into regular curricular implementations as a way to mediate children's identity formation, or funds of identity, was proposed (Esteban-Guitart, 2014).

During the VWK, children revealed their experiences with disability and bilingualism in educational contexts. Their perspectives showed the processes of oppression present in their bilingual learning spaces. For instance, the chapter described how children were verbally "attacked" because of accented English use, interrupted in ways that led to their silencing, or forced to feel inadequate when experiencing difficulty learning things that others described as being "fácil" (easy). The exploration, however, also surfaced ways through which the children took action to address these disempowering processes. These actions included things like asking teachers for additional time, or using your voice to "defend yourself." Children were very aware of their needs and the things they were receiving, or not, to accommodate their learning.

These findings have implications for teacher preparation and educators. Educators need to bring the topic of disability into their classrooms. It is important to make these discriminatory processes visible so that they can be addressed and so that the "subaltern knowledge" bilingual children with a disability acquire through experience is used to foster asset-based perspectives of disability. The chapter offered examples of how to safely engage in these explorations.

Likewise, it is important that supportive and understanding environments are created in the class for discussing disability and beliefs around what disabled people do. Chapter 7 illuminated how children, even those who have a disability themselves, might express their thinking in ways that could be seen as inappropriate and how they need time to develop language and further ideas that are new to them (Gabel, 2002). Chapter 7 shows that bilingual classrooms need to foster "trying to understand" stances without disciplining or controlling children's ways of engaging.

Furthermore, the use of mediating models, such as the classroom LEGO designs described in Chapter 7, can allow children to further their thinking about disability and ways to accommodate different needs. Such exploration advanced understandings for both children and educators in VWK. Bilingual educators can investigate how models mediate discussions about disability in their own classrooms and how they can further disability identity exploration.

In sum, it is important that disability be associated with learning competence to break away from paternalistic frameworks and that care be understood as multidirectional (Kilinc, 2018). It is particularly critical in bilingual contexts aiming to be inclusive that the ableist and assimilationist histories that have dominated educational institutions are studied and analyzed (Annamma et al., 2013b). In such a context, bilingual children with a disability must be allowed to fluidly engage in identity explorations while enacting agency for changing the oppressive circumstances they experience in schools (Edwards & Mckenzie, 2008).

A HYBRID SPACE FOR SCIENCE LEARNING IN-BETWEEN BOUNDARIES

The last two chapters, Chapters 8 and 9, explored the science learning of bilingual children with and without a disability. Chapter 8 focused on the need to understand learning as expansive (Engeström, 2001) and the need to learn in-between boundaries, and Chapter 9 on the mediational role of artifacts for hybrid humanizing pedagogical moments. Both chapters provide insights to understand bilingual science learning not only vertically, in developmentally expected ways, but also horizontally, along ZPDs created when children and educators meaningfully participate in activity. This last section of Chapter 10 reviews these chapters to draw implications from them.

Chapter 8 analyzed the crossing of figurative boundaries that have been historically established in educational contexts (Lizárraga & Gutiérrez, 2018). The question at the center of this chapter was: How does boundary crossing manifest in a hybrid science learning space with bilingual children with and without a disability, and what possibilities for expansive learning surface in this space?

The information presented in Chapter 8 explored the various dimensions along which boundary crossing took place in the hybrid space of the VWK afterschool program, manifesting the porosity of categories. Boundaries between forms of knowledge and practices (i.e., across social spaces or carried out by children or by teacher candidates), between disciplines (i.e., science education, art education, or other areas), and between formal or informal learning spaces (i.e., playful spaces outside of school times versus learning spaces while in school) were centered and consequently discussed.

In reference to crossing boundaries between social spaces, the conversation samples and descriptions illustrated the importance of having educators realize the difference between distal and proximal knowledges. At the same time, it is fundamental to uncover the many ways through which these connect with more formally recognized science knowledge. For instance, in VWK children brought in home remedies (i.e., VapoRub or aloe vera) and elements from popular fictional characters they knew (i.e., water or fire knoweldge related to Pokémon) that expanded ideas about what counts as science. The explorations in the VWK blurred the boundaries typically separating "traditional distal" and "creative proximal" science, a convergence that educators can explore in their classrooms.

Boundary crossing between disciplines will happen naturally in playful, but still rigorous, learning spaces. Educators' role would be to attend to these blurrings across disciplines and to promote the unexpected learning that will take place in multiple directions along a more integrated space. In VWK, aesthetic and kinesthetic experiences with clay and paint, aiming to promote science learning, ended up advancing children's artistic development and leading to understandings in social studies.

Lastly, boundary crossing across formal and less formal spaces allows children to engage their playful imaginations and learn beyond constraints (Gutiérrez et al., 2017). Letting go of traditional restrictions and granting children some agency to choose the direction of their learning, even when this new direction might not be directly connected to the learning objective, can prove highly productive (i.e., the work with slime in Chapter 8 that allowed science concepts to materialize).

There are implications from these findings for bilingual educators aiming to make their classrooms inclusive. Educators can benefit from designing specific spaces where explorations across formal and less formal engagements favored by the children are possible. Understanding how boundaries function to limit learning across forms of knowledge and practices, disciplines, or formal and informal spaces can help in crossing boundaries for learning that takes place in-between.

Chapter 9 discussed possibilities for creating contexts where hybrid humanizing pedagogical moments can grow during science teaching. The chapter discussed artifacts and their mediational potential. Following a Vygotskian interpretation, the chapter showed that schools tend to offer artifacts tied to normative school culture. From this view, these artifacts privilege certain forms of learning that have been "normalized" over time in the United States. There is, consequently, a need to shift instruction onto a "re-mediation" approach, for the purposeful use of an array of mediating artifacts that can benefit all children (Gutiérrez et al., 2009, p. 227). Through the analysis of work and conversations generated in the VWK, the chapter explored the question: What forms of artifact re-mediation are generated in a bilingual science learning space?

The chapter revealed how children reacted to the mediators the candidates were using for their learning by further mediating the tool (i.e., re-mediating). For instance, when candidates presented a video showing an earthquake taking place, the simultaneously occurring storm that was shown led some children to connect earthquakes to weather while disregarding internal earth processes. Other artifacts such as candidates' life experiences that were connected to the content being taught generated a multitude of reactions and feelings. Teacher candidates realized that the artifacts that connected to personal experiences mediated children's content learning, and their own teaching experience, in humanizing ways (another example of re-mediation). Both of these examples show the importance of artifacts in teaching and learning in bilingual contexts and the need to consider processes of mediation and re-mediation that take place both internally (less visibly and ideational) and externally (more visibly and material).

The chapter also highlighted the role of children's self-selected mediators, even when these seemed initially to be unconnected to the learning at hand. Teacher candidates in VWK successfully allowed children's artifacts to coexist, and at times to promote content learning (i.e., Victor's SpongeBob creation allowed him to draw the earthquake taking place as requested, and then facilitated a hybrid experience as he added waves reflecting earthquake activity to his initial creation).

Chapter 8 also included several model artifacts. These models were intended to mediate children's learning of canonical science knowledge; that is, their entry into that dignified space for consequential participation that was described in Chapter 6 (Greenstein, 2016). However, the models were not perfect at all levels, or for all children, and often need to be re-mediated using additional artifacts. Nonetheless, the models did have an important role in surfacing children's ideas and in helping them make connections with other knowledge they had, facilitating meaningful engagement.

Lastly, the work with the Earthquakes, Plate Tectonics, and the Ring of Fire project also exposed the tension between language learning and content learning and the need to attend to both, even when teaching them together. This important topic surfaced in two tensions around language. The first one centered on how language can fail to successfully mediate access to canonical understandings in science (i.e., Ring of Fire and its Spanish version, Cinturón de Fuego, which uses the metaphor of a belt). The second tension manifested in how, at times, science learning was privileged over opportunities to use the minoritized language (i.e., Spanish). Re-mediation was important in addressing both tensions to either engage in purposeful redirecting of conceptualizations (i.e., highlighting how literally interpreting the language could be misleading), or removing barriers to using language for content explorations (i.e., using additional artifacts such as sentence starters or planning for preliminary practice time).

While Chapter 8 analyzed the crossing of figurative boundaries, Chapter 9 uncovered ways through which re-mediating the artifacts typically used in bilingual classrooms can assist the "permeability across educational categories." That is, children can move from being situated as having a disability because they do not appear to be learning, to the disability not manifesting when the mediational artifacts are altered or changed for more fecund ones. Similarly, a child who experiences difficulties conveying ideas using one of the two languages of instruction (i.e., the case of Mirella presenting in science using Spanish), performing as what is defined in schools as a language learner, might act proficiently if mediating artifacts are re-mediated (i.e., altered, substituted, reimagined) in ways that work for the student.

CONCLUSION

As shown in this book, projects like the VWK reveal that we now have tools for making bilingual education inclusive of children with a disability. These include raising awareness of ableist practices and of historical assimilationist pressures that take place even in bilingual contexts as an important first step in expanding inclusivity. Hybrid and humanizing pedagogies are pivotal in leveraging bilingualism and disability as assets for learning and can help address these two persistent forms of oppression (i.e., ableism and assimilationist pressures). Learning in-between boundaries and attending to the mediation and re-mediation processes that take place constantly, both internally and externally, with cultural historical artifacts are other important tools for inclusive bilingual education manifested in VWK. Lastly, fluid understandings of culture while engaging in identity work along the different labels children in bilingual classrooms carry can promote the process of conscientization that is so important in bilingual education and must be present when working with children with a disability.

While these tools might be available, they are not being consistently implemented in bilingual classrooms. Reasons for this could be lack of awareness of the importance of these tools or systemic issues impeding innovation in our classrooms. There is a need to employ collective processes (i.e., reflection around practice, critical analysis of lessons with peers) that facilitate and monitor the consistent implementation of the inclusive tools throughout bilingual classrooms. Implementing these tools can create pathways for providing access to bilingualism and biliteracy to all learners.

However, it is important to realize that learning along pathways that work for bilingual children with a disability—particularly since the pathways are typically not those traditionally privileged in schools—takes time, persistence, and agentive work. Educators might not immediately see the transformative results of their hard efforts to create rich learning spaces for all children. Trust in one's practice and commitment to create hybrid humanizing pedagogical moments will go a long way and provide possibilities for children with a disability to continue to grow as bilingual, bicultural, and biliterate people.

Epilogue

Sharing the experience of the VWK in a way that expresses the meaningfulness of the moments we experienced is an enormous responsibility. So much teaching and learning took place in that space over time, and while some aspects are well represented in this book, I am sure I left many others out. I hope the readers can use what is in these pages while imagining what is between the lines, adding their own knowledge and experiences, to better visualize what our learning was like during the VWK project. Then maybe they will try a few of these ideas back in their own worlds. These are descriptions of the ways through which teaching and learning unfolded meaningfully for us. However, each child is different, and each group of children will bring something new every year. Discover where it is useful, select, adapt, question, and push forward to create more knowledge and better practices for your own contexts.

In closing this book, I would like to mention a few of the ways through which I hope this book can remain in your practice and research:

- The activity invitations, geared at exploring the topic at the intersection of bilingual and bicultural education and disability studies, in the form of Classroom Identity and Knowledge Exploration. These explorations are offered to assist readers in bringing these ideas into their classrooms and can help those who would like to further investigate these topics. Keep referring back to them and modify whatever you feel might not fit well for you.
- The sample products from the participating children, as well as statements generated during the learning activity, illustrate the types of responses one can expect from diverse elementary school–aged children and can help teachers and teacher educators in understanding how to create high-quality learning spaces for bilingual children with a disability. These could potentially be used for class activities to illustrate particular ideas from a practical perspective.
- The chapters of this book establish a conversation across issues such as assimilation and ableism that have been historically present in both the history of bilingual education and teaching

students with a disability and propose curriculum to expand what identity and agency look like in schools embracing more humanistic pedagogies. I believe there are other aspects that maybe did not surface in the work from the VWK but that surely cross the learning experience of bilingual children and children with a disability. It is important to uncover and explore these when working with bilingual children who have a disability.

- The central argument of this book is that while the fields of bilingual education and teaching students with a disability have been traditionally kept separate, the fact is that many of the constructs that researchers and educators in one field discuss can contribute to the others' field. I hope this is the beginning of an ongoing conversation between bilingual education and inclusive education so that we can build even stronger frameworks that enable all children as learners.
- Drawing upon critical disability and cultural historical theoretical frameworks, the book contributes to the field of inclusive bilingual education by illustrating how the histories of oppression of bilinguals of immigrant background and of people with dis/ability are aligned. Understanding how both of these forms of oppression impact children learning with different labels, and being aware of those experiences, will make a difference in their learning experience.

I end by pointing to the part of this book's title where I emphasize what I feel the chapters collectively offer: Humanizing Pedagogies to Engage Learners and Eliminate Labels. There is a need to progressively realize the limitations in using labels for categorizing children, particularly those of minoritized backgrounds, in fixed ways. Rather than so many labels, what is needed the most is the actual practices that enable learners in all possible ways. I hope the multiple examples in this book illustrate ways to do just that—enable learners with a disability in bilingual classrooms—so that teachers and teacher candidates can continue this work en su lucha diaria (in their daily fight).

References

ABC News Politics [@ABCPolitics] (2015, September 3). *WATCH @TomLlamasABC asks @realDonaldTrump to clarify his remark that Jeb Bush should speak English*. [Tweet]. Twitter. https://twitter.com/abcpolitics/status/639545119360749568

Abedi, J. (2014). English language learners with disabilities: Classification, assessment, and accommodation issues. *Journal of Applied Testing Technology, 10*(2), 1–30.

Ada, A. F. (1975). Editorial. *Bilingual Research Journal, 1*(1), 11–12. https://doi.org/10.1080/08881685.1975.10668261

Alderson, P., & Goodey, C. (1998). *Enabling education: Experiences in special and ordinary schools*. The Tufnell Press.

American Geological Institute. (2009). *Status of the geoscience workforce*. https://www.americangeosciences.org/citations/status-geoscience-workforce-2009

Annamma, S. A., Boelé, A. L., Moore, B. A., & Klingner, J. (2013a). Challenging the ideology of normal in schools. *International Journal of Inclusive Education, 17*(12), 1278–1294. https://doi.org/10.1080/13603116.2013.802379

Annamma, S. A., Connor, D., & Ferri, B. (2013b). Dis/ability critical race studies (DisCrit): Theorizing at the intersections of race and dis/ability. *Race Ethnicity and Education, 16*(1), 1–31. https://doi.org/10.1080/13613324.2012.730511

Annamma, S. A., Ferri, B. A., & Connor, D. J. (2018). Disability Critical Race Theory: Exploring the intersectional lineage, emergence, and potential futures of DisCrit in education. *Review of Research in Education, 42*(1), 46–71.

Anzaldúa, G. E. (1987, 2007). *Borderlands: La frontera. The new mestiza* (3rd ed.). Aunt Lute Books. (Original work published 1987).

Anzaldúa, G. E. (2002). Now let us shift . . . the path of conocimiento . . . inner work, public acts. In G. E. Anzaldúa & A. Keating (Eds.), *This bridge we call home: Radical visions for transformation* (pp. 540–578). New York, NY: Routledge. https://doi.org/10.4324/9780203952962

Apanasionok, M. M., Neil, J., Watkins, R. C., Grindle, C. F., & Hastings, R. P. (2020). Teaching science to students with developmental disabilities using the Early Science curriculum. *Support for Learning, 35*(4), 493–505. https://doi.org/10.1111/1467-9604.12329

Artiles, A. J., Rueda, R., Salazar, J. J., & Higareda, I. (2005). Within-group diversity in minority disproportionate representation: English language learners in urban school districts. *Exceptional Children, 71*(3), 283–300. https://doi.org/10.1177/001440290507100305

Bacon, J. K., & Lalvani, P. (2019). Dominant narratives, subjugated knowledges, and the righting of the story of disability in K–12 curricula. *Curriculum Inquiry, 49*(4), 387–404. https://doi.org/10.1080/03626784.2019.1656990

Bacon, J. K., & Pomponio, E. (2020): A call for radical over reductionist approaches to 'inclusive' reform in neoliberal times: an analysis of position statements in the United States. *International Journal of Inclusive Education*. https://doi.org/10.1080/13603116.2020.1858978

Baglieri, S., & Lalvani, P. (2019). *Undoing ableism: Teaching about disability in K–12 classrooms*. Routledge. https://doi.org/10.4324/9781351002868

Baglieri, S., & Shapiro, A. (2017). *Disability studies and the inclusive classroom: Critical practices for embracing diversity in education* (2nd ed.). Routledge.

Baglieri, S., Bejoian, L. M., Broderick, A. A., Connor, D. J., & Valle, J. (2011). [Re]claiming "inclusive education" toward cohesion in educational reform: Disability studies unravels the myth of the normal child. *Teachers College Record, 113*(10), 2122–2154. https://doi.org/10.1177/016146811111301001

Baker, C. (2006). *Foundations of bilingual education and bilingualism* (4th ed.). Multilingual Matters.

Bandura, A. (1989). Human agency in social cognitive theory. *American Psychologist, 44*(9), 1175–1184. https://doi.org/10.1037/0003-066X.44.9.1175

Barac, R., & Bialystok, E. (2012). Bilingual effects on cognitive and linguistic development: Role of language, cultural background, and education. *Child Development, 83*(2), 413–422. https://doi.org/10.1111/j.1467-8624.2011.01707.x

Bartlett, L. (2007). To seem and to feel: Situated identities and literacy practices. *Teachers College Record, 109*(1), 51–69.

Barton, D., & Hamilton, M. (2012). *Local literacies: Reading and writing in one community*. Routledge.

Beratan, G. D. (2006). Institutionalizing inequity: Ableism, racism and IDEA 2004. *Disability Studies Quarterly, 26*(2). https://doi.org/10.18061/dsq.v26i2.682

Bhabha, H. K. (1994). *The location of culture*. Routledge.

Bhabha, H. K. (1996). Cultures in between. In S. Hall & P. Du Gay (Eds.), *Questions of cultural identity* (pp. 53–60). Sage Publications.

Bialystok, E., & Martin, M. M. (2004). Attention and inhibition in bilingual children: Evidence from the dimensional change card sort task. *Developmental Science, 7*(3), 325–339. https://doi.org/10.1111/j.1467-7687.2004.00351.x

Bigler, R. S., & Liben, L. S. (2006). A developmental intergroup theory of social stereotypes and prejudice. *Advances in Child Development and Behavior, 34*, 39–89. https://doi.org/10.1016/S0065-2407(06)80004-2

Bloch, B. (1948). A set of postulates for phonemic analysis. *Language, 24*(I), 3–46.

Block, N. & Vidaurre, L. (2019). Comparing attitudes of first-grade dual language immersion versus mainstream English students. *Bilingual Research Journal, 42*(2), 129–149. https://doi.org/10.1080/15235882.2019.1604452

Bonilla-Silva, E. (2020). Color-blind racism in pandemic times. *Sociology of Race and Ethnicity*. https://doi.org/10.1177/2332649220941024

Brisk, M. E. (2006). *Bilingual education: From compensatory to quality schooling*. Lawrence Erlbaum.

Broderick, A., Mehta-Parekh, H., & Reid, D. K. (2005). Differentiating instruction for disabled students in inclusive classrooms. *Theory into Practice, 44*, 194–202.

Brown, M. (2004). *My name is Celia/Me llamo Celia: The life of Celia Cruz/la vida de Celia Cruz.* Northland Publishing.

Brown, S. E. (2017). Changing America's consciousness: A brief history of the independent living civil rights movement in the United States. In R. Hanes, I. Brown, & N. E. Hansen (Eds.), *The Routledge history of disability* (pp. 485–499). Routledge. https://doi.org/10.1201/9781315198781-32

Bruner, J. (2003). Self-making narratives. In R. Fivush & C. A. Haden (Eds.), *Autobiographical memory and the construction of a narrative self. Developmental and cultural perspectives* (pp. 209–225). Lawrence Erlbaum Associates. https://doi.org/10.4324/9781410607478

Buxton, C. A., Salinas, A., Mahotiere, M., Lee, O., & Secada, W. (2015). Fourth-Grade emergent bilingual learners' scientific reasoning complexity, controlled experiment practices, and content knowledge when discussing school, home, and play contexts. *Teachers College Record, 117*(2), 1–36.

Calabrese Barton, A., Drake, C., Perez, J. G., St. Louis, K., & George, M. (2004). Ecologies of parental engagement in urban education. *Educational Researcher, 33*(4), 3–12. https://doi.org/10.3102/0013189x033004003

Calabrese Barton, A., & Tan, E. (2009). Funds of knowledge and discourses and hybrid space. *Journal of Research in Science Teaching, 46*(1), 50–73.

Carlson, J. (2016). *Were there ever palm trees in New York City?* Gothamist. https://gothamist.com/arts-entertainment/were-there-ever-palm-trees-in-new-york-city

Cedillo, C. V., & Covert, K. S. (2016, May 23). *On the critical importance of ethnic studies.* NCTE Blog. http://www2.ncte.org/blog/2016/05/critical-importance-ethnic-studies

Center for Applied Special Technology. (2018). *The UDL guidelines. Universal Design for Learning Guidelines version* 2.2. http://udlguidelines.cast.org

Chamot, A. U., & O'Malley, J. M. (1994). *The CALLA handbook: Implementing the cognitive academic language learning approach.* Addison-Wesley.

Chang, A., Torrez, M. A., Ferguson, K. N., & Sagar, A. (2017). Figured worlds and American dreams: An exploration of agency and identity among Latinx undocumented students. *The Urban Review, 49*(2), 189–216. https://doi.org/10.1007/s11256-017-0397-x

Chaparro, S. E. (2019). But mom! I'm not a Spanish boy: Raciolinguistic socialization in a two-way immersion bilingual program. *Linguistics and Education, 50*, 1–12. https://doi.org/10.1016/j.linged.2019.01.003

Chatelier, S. (2015). Towards a renewed flourishing of humanistic education? *Discourse: Studies in the Cultural Politics of Education, 36*(1), 81–94. http://dx.doi.org/10.1080/01596306.2013.834635

Chávez-Moreno, L. C. (2020). U.S. empire and an immigrant's counternarrative: Conceptualizing imperial privilege. *Journal of Teacher Education, 72*(2), 209–222. https://doi.org/10.1177/0022487120919928

Cheek, K. A. (2010). Commentary: A summary and analysis of twenty-seven years of geosciences conceptions research. *Journal of Geoscience Education, 58*, 122–134. https://doi.org/10.5408/1.3544294

Cioè-Peña, M. (2017). The intersectional gap: How bilingual students in the United States are excluded from inclusion. *International Journal of Inclusive Education, 21*(9), 906–919. https://doi.org/10.1080/13603116.2017.1296032

Cioè-Peña, M. (2021). *(M)othering labeled children: Bilingualism and disability in the lives of Latinx mothers.* Multilingual Matters. https://doi.org/10.21832/9781800411296

Coakley-Fields, M. R. (2019). Building strong reading muscles: ableist language in a teacher's talk about reading. *International Journal of Inclusive Education, 23*(3), 245–260. https://doi.org/10.1080/13603116.2018.1432081

Cobb, C. (2015). Is French immersion a special education loophole . . . And does it intensify issues of accessibility and exclusion? *International Journal of Bilingual Education and Bilingualism, 18*(2), 170–187. https://doi.org/10.1080/13670050.2014.887052

Cochran-Smith, M., & Dudley-Marling, C. (2012). Diversity in teacher education and special education: The issues that divide. *Journal of Teacher Education, 63*(4), 237–244. https://doi.org/10.1177/0022487112446512

Cole, M. W. (1998). Can cultural psychology help us think about diversity? *Mind, Culture, and Activity, 5*(4), 291–304.

Cole, M. W. (2013) *Rompiendo el silencio*: Meta-analysis of the effectiveness of peer-mediated learning at improving language outcomes for ELLs. *Bilingual Research Journal, 36*(2), 146–166. https://doi.org/10.1080/15235882.2013.814609

Cole, M. W., & David, S. (2021). Mapping bias: A rhizomatic critique of the National Literacy Panel Report. *Bilingual Research Journal, 44*(2), 231–248. https://doi.org/10.1080/15235882.2021.1942322

Cole, M. W., & Engeström, Y. (1993). A cultural-historical approach to distributed cognition. In G. Salomon (Ed.), *Distributed cognitions: Psychological and educational considerations* (pp. 1–46). Cambridge University Press.

Collier, V. P., & Thomas, W. P. (2004). The astounding effectiveness of dual language education for all. *NABE Journal of Research and Practice, 2*(1), 1–20.

Collins, K., & Ferri, B. (2016). Literacy education and disability studies: reenvisioning struggling students. *Journal of Adolescent & Adult Literacy, 60*(1), 7–12. https://doi.org/10.1002/jaal.552

Connor, D. J., & Cavendish, W. (2020). "Sit in my seat": Perspectives of students with learning disabilities about teacher effectiveness in high school inclusive classrooms. *International Journal of Inclusive Education, 24*(3), 288–309. https://doi.org/10.1080/13603116.2018.1459888

Connor, D. J., & Ferri, B. A. (2005). Integration and inclusion—a troubling nexus: Race, disability, and special education. *Journal of African American History, 90,* 107–127. https://doi.org/10.1086/jaahv90n1-2p107

Connor, D. J., Ferri, B. A., & Annamma, S. A. (Eds.). (2016). *DisCrit–Disability studies and critical race theory in education.* Teachers College Press.

Connor, D. J., & Gabel, S. L. (2010). Welcoming the unwelcome: Disability and diversity. In T. K. Chapman & N. Hobbel (Eds.), *Social justice pedagogy across the curriculum.* Routledge.

Coplan, R. J., & Evans, M. A. (2009). At a loss for words? Introduction to the special issue on shyness and language in childhood. *Infant and Child Development, 18,* 211–215.

Crawford, J. (1999). *Bilingual education: History, politics, theory and practice* (4th ed.). Bilingual Education Services.

Crenshaw, K. (1991). Mapping the margins: Intersectionality, identity politics, and violence against women of color. *Stanford Law Review, 43*(6), 1241–1299.

Daniels, J. R., & Varghese, M. (2020). Troubling practice: Exploring the relationship between Whiteness and practice-based teacher education in considering a raciolinguicized teacher subjectivity. *Educational Researcher, 49*(1), 56–63. https://doi.org/10.3102/0013189x19879450

Davis, L. J. (2006). Constructing normalcy: The bell curve, the novel, and the invention of the disabled body in the nineteenth century. In L. J. Davis (Ed.), *The disability studies reader* (2nd ed., pp. 3–16). Routledge.

DeCapua, A., & Wintergerst, A. C. (2009). Second-generation language maintenance and identity: A case study, *Bilingual Research Journal, 32*(1), 5–24.

Delgado, R. (2008). The instructional dynamics of a bilingual teacher. *Journal of Hispanic Higher Education, 7*(1), 43–53.

DeNicolo, C. P. (2010) What language counts in literature discussion? Exploring linguistic mediation in an English language arts classroom. *Bilingual Research Journal, 33*(2), 220–240. https://doi.org/10.1080/15235882.2010.502799

Dewey, J. (1915). *The school and society* [Electronic Version] (Rev. ed.). University of Chicago Press. https://archive.org/details/schoolsociety00dewerich

Donovan, M. S., & Cross, C. T. (Eds.). (2002). *Minority students in special and gifted education*. National Academies Press.

Doyle, S. (2007). Member checking with older women: A framework for negotiating meaning. *Health Care for Women International, 8*, 888–908. https://doi.org/10.1080/07399330701615325

Drysdale, H., van der Meer, L., & Kagohara, D. (2015). Children with autism spectrum disorder from bilingual families: A systematic review. *Review Journal of Autism and Developmental Disorders, 2*(1), 26–38. https://doi.org/10.1007/s40489-014-0032-7

Dudley-Marling, C., & Gurn, A. (2010). Introduction: Living on the boundaries of normal. In C. Dudley-Marling & A. Gurn (Eds.), *The myth of the normal curve* (pp. 1–8). Peter Lang.

Edwards, A. (2005). Relational agency: Learning to be a resourceful practitioner. *International Journal of Educational Research, 43*, 168–182. https://doi.org/10.1016/j.ijer.2006.06.010

Edwards, A., & MacKenzie, L. (2005). Steps toward participation: The social support of learning trajectories. *International Journal of Lifelong Education, 24*(4), 282–302. https://doi.org/10.1080/02601370500169178

Edwards, A., & Mackenzie, L. (2008). Identity shifts in informal learning trajectories. In B. van Oers, W. Wardekker, E. Elbers, & R. van der Veer (Eds.), *The transforming of learning: Advances in cultural-historical activity theory* (pp. 163–181). Cambridge University Press. https://doi.org/10.1017/cbo9780511499937.012

Edwards, A., Lunt, I., & Stamou, E. (2010). Inter-professional work and expertise: New roles at the boundaries of schools. *British Educational Research Journal, 36*(1), 27–45. https://doi.org/10.1080/01411920902834134

Emibaryer, M. & Mische, A. (1998). What is agency? *The American Journal of Sociology, 103*(4), 962–1023.

Engeström, Y. (1987). *Learning by expanding: An activity-theoretical approach to developmental research*. Orienta-Konsultit.

Engeström, Y. (1991). Non scolae sed vitae discimus: Toward overcoming the encapsulation of school learning. *Learning and Instruction*, *1*, 243–259.

Engeström, Y. (2001). Expansive learning at work: Toward an activity theoretical reconceptualization. *Journal of Education and Work, 14*(1), 133–156. https://doi.org/10.1080/13639080020028747

Engeström, Y., & Sannino, A. (2010). Studies of expansive learning: Foundations, findings and future challenges. *Educational Research Review, 5*(1), 1–24. https://doi.org/10.1016/j.edurev.2009.12.002

Erevelles, N. (2000). Educating unruly bodies: Critical pedagogy, disability studies, and the politics of schooling. *Educational Theory, 50*(1), 25–47. https://doi.org/10.1111/j.1741-5446.2000.00025.x

Erevelles, N. (2005). Understanding curriculum as normalizing text: Disability studies meet curriculum theory. *Journal of Curriculum Studies, 37*(4), 421–439. https://doi.org/10.1080/0022027032000276970

Erste Bank (2008, December). *What would Christmas be without love?* [Video]. YouTube. https://youtu.be/okNRsJmBf_A

Erwin, E. J., Bacon, J. K., & Lalvani, P. (2021). It's about time! Advancing justice through joyful inquiry with young children. *Topics in Early Childhood Special Education*, 1–12. https://doi.org/10.1177/0271121420988890

Esquinca, A., Araujo, B., & de la Piedra, M. (2014). Meaning making and translanguaging in a two-way dual-language program on the U.S.-Mexico border. *Bilingual Research Journal, 37*(2), 164–181. https://doi.org/10.1080/15235882.2014.934970

Esteban-Guitart, M. (2014). Funds of identity. In T. Teo (Ed.), *Encyclopedia of critical psychology* (pp. 752–757). Springer. https://doi.org/10.1007/978-1-4614-5583-7_576

European Commission. (2009, July 16). *Study on the contribution of multilingualism to creativity: Final report.* European Comission. http://www.dylan-project.org/Dylan_en/news/assets/StudyMultilingualism_report_en.pdf

Fallas Escobar, C., & Treviño, A. (2021). Two Latina bilingual teacher candidates' perceptions of language proficiency and language choice options: Ideological encounters with listening and speaking others. *Bilingual Research Journal, 44*(1), 124–143. https://doi.org/10.1080/15235882.2021.1877213

Fan, S. P., Liberman, Z., Keysar, B., & Kinzler, K. D. (2015). The exposure advantage: Early exposure to a multilingual environment promotes effective communication. *Psychological Science, 26*(7), 1090–1097. https://doi.org/10.1177/0956797615574699

Flores, N., & Rosa, J. (2015). Undoing appropriateness: Raciolinguistic ideologies and language diversity in education. *Harvard Educational Review, 85*(2), 149–171.

Fountas, I. C., & Pinnell, G. S. (1996). *Guided reading: Good first teaching for all children*. Heinemann.

Fránquiz, M. E., & Salazar, M. (2004). The transformative potential of humanizing pedagogy: Addressing the diverse needs of Chicano/Mexicano students. *The High School Journal, 87*, 36–53. https://doi.org/10.1353/hsj.2004.0010

Fránquiz, M. E., Ortiz, A. A., & Lara, G. (2019). Co-editor's introduction: Humanizing pedagogy, research and learning. *Bilingual Research Journal, 42*(4), 381–386. https://doi.org/10.1080/15235882.2019.1704579

Fredricks, D. E., & Warriner, D. S. (2016). "We speak English in here and English only!": Teacher and ELL youth perspectives on restrictive language education. *Bilingual Research Journal, 39*(3–4), 309–323. https://doi.org/10.1080/15235882.2016.1230565

Freedman, J. E., & Ferri, B. A. (2017). Locating the problem within: Race, learning disabilities, and science. *Teachers College Record, 119*(5), 1–28.

Freire, P. (1993). *Pedagogy of the oppressed* (M. Bergman Ramos, Trans.) (revised 20th-anniversary ed.). Continuum. (Original work published 1972)

Furman, M., & Calabrese Barton, A. (2006). Capturing urban student voices in the creation of a science mini-documentary. *Journal of Research in Science Teaching, 43*, 667–694. https://doi.org/10.1002/tea.20164

Gabel, S. (2002). Some conceptual problems with critical pedagogy. *Curriculum Inquiry, 32*(2), 177–201. https://doi.org/10.1111/1467-873X.00222

Gallegos, A., & McCarty, L. L. (2000). Bilingual multicultural special education: An integrated personnel preparation. *Teacher Education and Special Education, 24*(4), 264–270. https://doi.org/10.1177/088840640002300403

Galvin, R. (2003) The paradox of disability culture: The need to combine versus the imperative to let go. *Disability & Society, 18*(5), 675–690. https://doi.org/10.1080/0968759032000097889

García, O. (2009). *Bilingual education in the 21st century: A global perspective.* Basil/Blackwell.

García, O. (2012). Theorizing translanguaging for educators. In C. Celic & K. Seltzer (Eds.), *Translanguaging: A CUNY-NYSIEB guide for educators* (pp. 1–6). CUNY-NYSEIB, The Graduate Center.

García, O., & Otheguy, R. (2020). Plurilingualism and translanguaging: Commonalities and divergences. *International Journal of Bilingual Education and Bilingualism, 23*(1), 17–35. https://doi.org/10.1080/13670050.2019.1598932

García, O., & Sung, K. K. (2018). Critically assessing the 1968 Bilingual Education Act at 50 years: Taming tongues and Latinx communities. *Bilingual Research Journal, 41*(4), 318–333.

García, O., & Wei, L. (2013). *Translanguaging: Language, bilingualism and education.* Palgrave Macmillan.

García, O., Kleifgen, J. A., & Falchi, L. (2008, January). *From English language learners to emergent bilinguals* (Equity Matters: Research Review No. 1). Campaign for Educational Equity, Teachers College, Columbia University. https://files.eric.ed.gov/fulltext/ED524002.pdf

Gardner, H. (2006). *Multiple intelligences: New horizons.* BasicBooks.

Gay, G. (1995). Curriculum theory and multicultural education. In J. A. Banks (Ed.), *Handbook of research on multicultural education* (pp. 25–43). Macmillan.

Gay, G. (2018). *Culturally responsive teaching: Theory, research, & practice* (3rd ed.). Teachers College Press.

Genesee, F. (1994). *Integrating language and content: Lessons from immersion* (Educational Practice Reports, No. 11). National Center for Research on Cultural Diversity and Second Language Learning, Center for Applied Linguistics.

Genesee, F. (2007). French immersion and at-risk students: A review of research evidence. *The Canadian Modern Language Review, 63*(5), 655–687. https://doi.org/10.3138/cmlr.63.5.655

Glassman, M. (2000). Negation through history: Dialectics and human development. *New Ideas in Psychology, 18*, 1–22. https://doi.org/10.1016/s0732-118x(99)00034-3

Gogolin, I., & Duarte, J. (2017). Superdiversity, multilingualism, and awareness. In J. Cenoz, D. Gorter, & S. May (Eds.), *Language awareness and multilingualism* (pp. 375–390). Springer International Publishing. https://doi.org/10.1007/978-3-319-02240-6_24

Gómez, L., Freeman, D., & Freeman, Y. (2005). Dual language education: A promising 50–50 model. *Bilingual Research Journal, 29*(1), 145–164. http://dx.doi.org/10.1080/15235882.2005.10162828

González, N., & Moll, L. (2002). Cruzando el Puente: Building bridges to funds of knowledge. *Educational Policy, 16*(4), 623–641.

González, N., Moll, L. C., & Amanti, K. (2005). *Funds of knowledge: Theorizing practices in households, communities, and classrooms*. Lawrence Erlbaum Associates.

Goodley, D. (2001). "Learning difficulties," the social model of disability and impairment: Challenging epistemologies. *Disability & Society, 16*(2), 207–231. https://doi.org/10.1080/09687590120035816

Greene, M. (1988). *The dialectic of freedom*. Teachers College Press.

Greenfield, R. (2013). Perceptions of elementary teachers who educate linguistically diverse students. *The Qualitative Report, 18*(47), 1–26. https://doi.org/10.46743/2160-3715/2013.1438

Greenstein, A. (2016). *Radical inclusive education: Disability, teaching and struggles for liberation*. Routledge.

Griffith, A. L. (2010). Persistence of women and minorities in STEM field majors: Is it the school that matters? *Economics of Education Review, 29*(6), 911–922.

Grigorenko, E. L. (2009). Dynamic assessment and response to intervention: Two sides of one coin. *Journal of Learning Disabilities, 42*(2), 111–132. https://doi.org/10.1177/0022219408326207

Grosjean, F. (1982). *Life with two languages: An introduction to bilingualism*. Harvard University Press.

Gutiérrez, K. D. (2008). Developing a sociocritical literacy in the third space. *Reading Research Quarterly, 43*(2), 148–164. https://doi.org/10.1598/rrq.43.2.3

Gutiérrez, K. D. (2016). Designing resilient ecologies: Social design experiments and a new social imagination. *Educational Researcher, 45*, 187–96. https://doi.org/10.3102/0013189x16645430

Gutiérrez, K. D., Baquedano-López, P., & Tejeda, C. (1999). Rethinking diversity: Hybridity and hybrid language practices in the third space. *Mind, Culture, and Activity, 6*(4), 286–303. https://doi.org/10.1080/10749039909524733

Gutiérrez, K. D., & Calabrese Barton, A. (2015). The possibilities and limits of the structure–agency dialectic in advancing science for all. *Journal of Research in Science Teaching, 52*, 574–583. https://doi.org/10.1002/tea.21229

Gutiérrez, K. D., Cortes, K., Cortez, A., DiGiacomo, D., Higgs, J., Johnson, P., Lizárraga, J. R., Mendoza, E., Tien, J., & Vakil, S. (2017). Replacing representation with imagination: Finding ingenuity in everyday practices. *Review of Research in Education, 41*, 30–60. https://doi.org/10.3102/0091732x16687523

Gutiérrez, K. D., Morales, P. Z., & Martinez, D. C. (2009). Re-mediating literacy: Culture, difference, and learning for students from nondominant communities. *Review of Research in Education, 33*(1), 212–245.

Gutiérrez, K. D., & Rogoff, B. (2003). Cultural ways of learning: individual traits or repertoires of practice. *Educational Researcher, 32*(5), 19–25. https://doi.org/10.3102/0013189x032005019

Hall, T. E., Meyer, A., & Rose, D. H. (Eds.) (2012). *Universal design for learning in the classroom: Practical applications*. Guilford Press.

Halloun, I. A. (2007). Mediated modeling in science education. *Science & Education, 16*, 653–697.

Hamayan, E. V., Marler, B., Sánchez-Lopez, C. S., & Damico, J. (2013). *Special education considerations for English language learners: Delivering a continuum of services* (2nd ed.). Caslon Publishing.

Hancock, C. L., & Miller, A. L. (2018). Using cultural historical activity theory to uncover praxis for inclusive education. *International Journal of Inclusive Education, 22*(9), 937–953. https://doi.org/10.1080/13603116.2017.1412517

Haque, E. (2017). Neoliberal governmentality and Canadian migrant language training policies. *Globalisation, Societies and Education, 15*(1), 96–113. https://doi.org/10.1080/14767724.2014.937403

Harwood, V., & Humphry, N. (2008). Taking exception: Discourses of exceptionality and the invocation of the "ideal." In S. Gabel & S. Danforth (Eds.), *Disability and the politics of education* (pp. 371–383). Peter Lang.

Hastings Center (Producer). (2020, December 7). *Event 3: Disrupting ableism with artful activism* [Video]. https://www.thehastingscenter.org/the-art-of-flourishing-events-series/

Heath, S. B. (1976). A national language academy? Debate in the new nation. *International Journal of the Sociology of Language, 11*, 9–43.

Heath, S. B. (1983). *Ways with words: Language, life, and work in communities and classrooms*. Cambridge University Press.

Hedergaard, M. (2004). A cultural-historical approach to learning in classrooms. *Outlines, 1*, 21–34.

Hogan, K. (2000). Exploring a process view of students' knowledge about the nature of science. *Science Education, 84*, 51–70. https://doi.org/10.1002/(sici)1098-237x(200001)84:13.0.co;2-h

Holland, D., Lachiotte, W., Skinner, D., & Cain, C. (1998). *Identity and agency in cultural worlds*. Harvard University Press.

Hollinger, A. L. (2021). *Revisiting the policy/practice gap in special education: The lived experience of teachers with ICT and RTI* (Publication No. 28154578) [Doctoral dissertation, New York University]. ProQuest Dissertations Publishing.

Hopewell, S., & Abril-Gonzalez, P. (2019) ¿Por qué estamos codeswitching? Understanding language use in a second-grade classroom. *Bilingual Research Journal, 42*(1), 105–120. https://doi.org/10.1080/15235882.2018.1561554

Howard, E. R., Lindholm-Leary, K. J., Rogers, D., Olague, N., Medina, J., Kennedy, B., Sugarman, J., & Christian, D. (2018). *Guiding principles for dual language education* (3rd ed.). Center for Applied Linguistics.

Howard, E. R., Olague, N., & Rogers, D. (2003). *The dual language program planner: A guide for designing and implementing dual language programs.* Center for Research on Education, Diversity & Excellence. https://mabene.org/resources/Documents/DLE%20Program%20Program%20Planner.pdf

Howard, E. R., Sugarman, J., Christian, D., Lindholm-Leary, K. J., & Rogers, D. (2007). *Guiding principles for dual language education* (2nd ed.). Center for Applied Linguistics.

Howard, T. C., & Milner, H. R., IV. (2014). Teacher preparation for urban schools. In H. R. Milner, IV, & K. Lomotey (Eds.), *Handbook of urban education* (pp. 199- 216). Routledge.

Huerta, T. M. (2011). Humanizing pedagogy: Beliefs and practices on the teaching of Latino children. *Bilingual Research Journal, 34*(1), 38–57. https://doi.org/10.1080/15235882.2011.568826

Individuals with Disabilities Education Act, 20 U.S.C. § 1400 (2004).

Irizarry, J. (2016). *The Latinization of U.S. schools: Successful teaching and learning in shifting cultural contexts.* Routledge.

Jegede, O., & Aikenhead, G. (1999). Transcending cultural borders: Implications for science teaching. *Research in Science & Technological Education 17*(1), 45–66.

Kangas, S. E. N. (2017). "That's where the rubber meets the road": The intersection of special education and dual language education. *Teachers College Record, 119*, 1–36.

Kangas, S. E. N. (2020) Counternarratives of English learners with disabilities, *Bilingual Research Journal, 43*(3), 267–285. https://doi.org/10.1080/15235882.2020.1807424

Kaveh, Y. M., & Sandoval, J. (2020). "No! I'm going to school, I need to speak English!" Who makes family language policies? *Bilingual Research Journal,43*(4), 362–382. https://doi.org/10.1080/15235882.2020.1825541

Kellett, M. (2009). Children as researchers: What we can learn from them about the impact of poverty on literacy opportunities? *International Journal of Inclusive Education, 13*(4), 395–408. https://doi-org.tc.idm.oclc.org/10.1080/10236240802106606

Kids Count Data Center. (2019). *Children who speak a language other than English at home in the United States.* https://datacenter.kidscount.org/data/tables/81-children-who-speak-a-language-other-than-english-at-home

Kilinc, S. (2018). 'Who will fit in with whom?' Inclusive education struggles for students with dis/abilities. *International Journal of Inclusive Education, 23*(12), 1296–1314. https://doi.org/10.1080/13603116.2018.1447612

Kim, H. U. (2017). Reflecting on a daughter's bilingualism and disability narratively. *International Journal of Whole Schooling, 13*(2), 21–34.

Kinloch, V., & San Pedro, T. (2014). The space between listening and storying: Foundations for projects in humanization. In D. Paris & M. T. Winn (Eds.), *Humanizing research: Decolonizing qualitative inquiry with youth and communities* (pp. 21–42). SAGE Publications. https://doi.org/10.4135/9781544329611.n2

Kirkland, D. E. (2014). Why I study culture, and why it matters: Humanizing ethnograhies in social science research. In D. Paris & M. T. Winn (Eds.), *Humanizing research: Decolonizing qualitative inquiry with youth and communities* (pp. 178–200). SAGE Publications. https://doi.org/10.4135/9781544329611.n10

Klingner, J., & Eppolito, A. M. (2014). *English language learners: Differentiating between language acquisition and learning disabilities.* Council for Exceptional Children.

Kohnert, K., Yim, D., Nett, K., Kan, P.-F., & Duran, L. (2005). Intervention with linguistically diverse preschool children: A focus on developing home language(s). *Language, Speech, and Hearing Services in Schools, 36*(3), 251–263. https://doi.org/10.1044/0161-1461(2005/025)

Kortz, K. M., & Murray, D. P. (2009). Barriers to college students learning how rocks form. *Journal of Geoscience Education, 57*, 300–315.

Kuhn, D. (1993). Science as argument: implications for teaching and learning scientific thinking. *Science Education, 77*, 319–338.

Kusnick, J. (2002). Growing pebbles and conceptual prisms—understanding the source of student misconceptions about rock formations. *Journal of Geoscience Education, 50*, 31–39. https://doi.org/10.5408/1089-9995-50.1.31

Kwon, K. (2021). Research with young multilingual children through child-centered interview activities. *Multicultural Perspectives, 23*(2), 101–107. https://doi.org/10.1080/15210960.2021.1914049

Ladson-Billings, G. (1995). Toward a theory of culturally relevant pedagogy. *American Educational Research Journal, 32*(3), 465–491. https://doi.org/10.3102/00028312032003465

Lalvani, P. (2015). "We are not aliens": Exploring the meaning of disability and the nature of belongingness in a fourth grade classroom. *Disability Studies Quarterly, 35*(4). https://doi.org/10.18061/dsq.v35i4.4963

Lalvani, P., & Bacon, J. K. (2019). Rethinking "we are all special." Anti-ableism curricula in early childhood classrooms. *Young Exceptional Children, 22*(2), 87–100.

Lamont, M., & Molnár, V. (2002). The study of boundaries in social sciences. *Annual Review of Sociology, 28*, 167–195.

Lee, C. D. (2007). *Culture, literacy, and learning: Taking bloom in the midst of the whirlwind.* Teachers College Press.

Lee, O., Quinn, H., & Valdés, G. (2013). Science and language for English language learners in relation to next generation science standards and with implications for common core state standards for English language arts and mathematics. *Educational Researcher, 42*(4), 223–233. https://doi.org/10.3102/0013189X13480524

Lemke, J. L. (2001). Articulating communities: Sociocultural perspectives on science education. *Journal of Research in Science Teaching, 38*, 296–316.

Lewis, K. E. (2017) Designing a bridging discourse: Re-mediation of a mathematical learning disability. *Journal of the Learning Sciences, 26*(2), 320–365. https://doi.org/10.1080/10508406.2016.1256810

Liasidou, A. (2012). Inclusive education and critical pedagogy at the intersections of disability, race, gender and class. *Journal for Critical Education Policy Studies, 10*(1), 168–184.

Liebtag, E., & Haugen, C. (2015, May 14). Shortage of dual-language teachers: Filling the gap. *Education Week.* http://blogs.edweek.org/edweek/global_learning/2015/05/shortage_of_dual_language_teachers_filling_the_gap.html

Limbos, M. M., & Geva, E. (2001). Accuracy of teacher assessments of second-language students at risk for reading disability. *Journal of Learning Disabilities, 34*(2), 136–151. https://doi.org/10.1177/002221940103400204

Lindholm-Leary, K. J. (2001). *Dual language education.* Multilingual Matters.
Lindholm-Leary, K. J. (2018). Developing Spanish in dual language programs: Preschool through twelfth grade. In K. Potowski (Ed.), *The Routledge handbook of Spanish as a heritage language* (pp. 433–444). Routledge.
Linton, S. (1998). *Claiming disability: Knowledge and identity.* NYU Press.
Lizárraga, J. R., & Gutiérrez, K. D. (2018). Centering nepantla literacies from the borderlands: Leveraging "in-betweenness" toward learning in the everyday. *Theory Into Practice, 57*(1), 38–47. https://doi.org/10.1080/00405841.2017.1392164
Lomas Garza, C. (1996). *In my family/En mi familia.* Children's Book Press.
Lomas Garza, C. (2005). *Family pictures/Cuadros de familia.* Children's Book Press.
López, J. R. (2019). Political clarity and the limitations of humanistic violence in the U.S. K–12 classroom. *International Journal of Qualitative Studies in Education, 32*(6), 632–650. https://doi.org/10.1080/09518398.2019.1609119
Lynch, A. W. (2018). Identity and literacy practices in a bilingual classroom: An exploration of leveraging community cultural wealth. *Bilingual Research Journal, 41*(2), 117–132. https://doi.org/10.1080/15235882.2018.1452312
Mackinney, E. (2017). More than a name: Spanish-speaking youth articulating bilingual identities, *Bilingual Research Journal, 40*(3), 274–288. https://doi.org/10.1080/15235882.2017.1342716
Martínez, P., Bannan, B., & Kitsantas, A. (2012). Bilingual students' ideas and conceptual change about slow geomorphological changes caused by water. *Journal of Geoscience Education, 60*, 54–67. https://doi.org/10.5408/09-145.1
Martínez-Álvarez, P. (2014). Reconceptualizing what counts as language and learning in bilingual children with disabilities. *The NYS TESOL Journal, 1*(2), 39–58.
Martínez-Álvarez, P. (2017a). Multigenerational learning for expanding the educational involvement of bilinguals experiencing academic difficulties. *Curriculum Inquiry, 47*(3), 263–289. https://doi.org/10.1080/03626784.2017.1324734
Martínez-Álvarez, P. (2017b, Published Online 2016). Special ways of knowing in science: Expansive learning opportunities with bilingual children with learning disabilities. *Cultural Studies of Science Education, 12*(3), 521–553. https://doi.org/10.1007/s11422-016-9732-x
Martínez-Álvarez, P. (2018). Dis/ability labels and emergent bilingual children: Current research and new possibilities to grow as bilingual and biliterate learners. *Race Ethnicity and Education, 22*(2), 174–193. https://doi.org/10.1080/13613324.2018.1538120
Martínez-Álvarez, P. (2019). What counts as science? Expansive learning actions for a new model of science with minoritized bilingual children. *Cultural Studies of Science Education, 14*(4), 799–837. https://doi.org/10.1007/s11422-019-09909-y
Martínez-Álvarez, P. (2020a). Dis/ability as mediator: Opportunity encounters in hybrid learning spaces for emergent bilinguals with dis/abilities. *Teachers College Record, 122*(5), 1–44. https://doi.org/10.1177/016146812012200506
Martínez-Álvarez, P. (2020b). Essential constructs in the preparation of inclusive bilingual education teachers: mediation, agency, and collectivity. *Bilingual Research Journal, 43*(3), 304–322. https://doi.org/10.1080/15235882.2020.1802367
Martínez-Álvarez, P. (2022, Published Online 2021). Teacher education for inclusive bilingual contexts: Collective reflection to support emergent bilinguals with and

without disabilities. In *Routledge Research in Teacher Education* book series. Routledge. https://doi.org/10.4324/9781003112259

Martínez-Álvarez, P. (Under Review). Inclusive bilingual education teacher preparation. In M. T. Winn & L. T. Winn (Eds.), *Encyclopedia of Social Justice (ESJ). Volume on Bodies/Abilities/Justice* (Invited Editors, T. González & A. A. Tefera). Bloomsbury Publishers.

Martínez-Álvarez, P., & Bannan, B. (2014). An exploration of hybrid spaces for place-based geomorphology with Latino bilingual children. *Journal of Geoscience Education, 62*(2), 104–117. https://doi.org/10.5408/12-407.1

Martínez-Álvarez, P., & Chiang, H. M. (2020). A bilingual special education teacher preparation program in New York City: Case studies of teacher candidates' student teaching experiences. *Equity & Excellence in Education, 53*(1–2), 196–215. https://doi.org/10.1080/10665684.2020.1749186

Martínez-Álvarez, P., & Hubard, O. (2015). Modeling change with clay: Bilingual primary students create imaginary landscapes to model slow changes to Earth's surface. *Science and Children, 52*(5), 57–63.

Martínez-Álvarez, P., Son, M., & Arana, B. (2020). Pre-service teachers' decision-making; Efforts to mediate learning with bilingual children with disabilities. *Teaching and Teacher Education, 91*. https://doi.org/10.1016/j.tate.2020.103044

Martínez-Roldán, C. (2015). Translanguaging practices as mobilization of linguistic resources in a Spanish/English bilingual after-school program: An analysis of contradictions. *International Multilingual Research Journal, 9*(1), 43–58. https://doi.org/10.1080/19313152.2014.982442

Martínez-Roldán, C., & Malavé, G. (2004). Language ideologies mediating literacy and identity in bilingual contexts. *Journal of Early Childhood Literacy*, 4, 155–180.

McCarty, S. (2012, September 14). *Understanding bilingual education 2: Analyzing types of bilingual education*. Child Research Net. https://www.childresearch.net/papers/language/2012_02.html

McDermott, R., Goldman, S., & Varenne, H. (2006). The cultural work of learning disabilities. *Educational Researcher, 35*(6), 12–17.

McRuer, R. (2006). *Crip theory: Cultural signs of queerness and disability*. New York University Press.

Medina, J. L. (2017, November 28). Qué? You don't know the 3 pillars of dual language? [Blog post]. https://duallanguageschools.org/column/3-pillars-dual-language/

Mojang (2011). *Minecraft* [Video game]. Microsoft Studios.

Moje, E. B., Ciechanowski, K. M., Kramer, K., Ellis, L., Carrillo, R., & Collazo, T. (2004). Working toward third space in content area literacy: An examination of everyday funds of knowledge and discourse. *Reading Research Quarterly, 39*, 38–70. https://doi.org/10.1598/rrq.39.1.4

Molinar-Arvizo, K. (2018, September 30). *Point: English-only laws have a disturbing history*. InsideSources. https://insidesources.com/english-only-laws-have-a-disturbing-history/

Moll, L. C. (2014). *L. S. Vygotsky and education*. Routledge.

Moll, L. C., Amanti, C., Neff, D., & González, N. (1992). Funds of knowledge for teaching: Using a qualitative approach to connect homes and classrooms. *Theory Into Practice, 31*(2), 132–141. https://doi.org/10.1080/00405849209543534

Moll, L. C., Veléz-Ibáñez, C., & Greenberg, J. (1989). *Year one progress report: Community knowledge and classroom practice: Combining resources for literacy instruction* (IARP Subcontract L-10, Development Associates). University of Arizona.

Monahan, T. (2009). The surveillance curriculum: Risk management and social control in the neoliberal school. In A. Darder, M. P. Baltodano, & R. D. Torres (Eds.) *The critical pedagogy reader* (2nd ed., pp. 123–134). Routledge.

Moore, B. A., & Klingner, J. K. (2014). Considering the needs of English language learner populations: An examination of the population validity of reading intervention research. *Journal of Learning Disabilities, 47*(5), 391–408.

Morgan, J. (2000). Critical pedagogy: The spaces that make the difference. *Pedagogy, Culture and Society, 8*(3), 273–289. https://doi.org/10.1080/14681360000200099

Mueller, T. G., Singer, G. H. S., & Grace, E. J. (2004). The Individuals with Disabilities Education Act and California Proposition 227: Implications for English language learners. *Bilingual Research Journal, 28*(2), 231–252. https://doi.org/10.1080/15235882.2004.10162815

National Academies of Sciences, Engineering, and Medicine. (2017). *Promoting the educational success of children and youth learning English: Promising futures.* The National Academies Press. https://doi.org/10.17226/24677

National Center for Education Statistics. (2019). *NAEP Report Card: Reading.* The Nation's Report Card.https://www.nationsreportcard.gov/reading/nation/achievement/?grade=12

National Center for Education Statistics. (2021). *The condition of education: Students with disabilities.* https://nces.ed.gov/programs/coe/pdf/2021/cgg_508c.pdf

National Geographic. (n.d.). *Plate tectonics and the ring of fire.* https://www.nationalgeographic.org/article/plate-tectonics-ring-fire/?utm_source=BibblioRCM_Row

National Research Council. (2002). *Minority students in special and gifted education.* National Academy Press. https://doi.org/10.17226/10128

National Research Council. (2012). *A framework for K–12 science education: Practices, crosscutting concepts, and core ideas.* National Academies Press. https://doi.org/10.17226/13165

New London Group. (1996). A pedagogy of multiliteracies: Designing social futures. *Harvard Educational Review,* 66, 60–93. https://doi.org/10.17763/haer.66.1.17370n67v22j160u

New York City Department of Education. (n.d.) *K–8 Social Studies scope and sequence (2014–2015).* https://www.weteachnyc.org/resources/resource/social-studies-scope-and-sequence-grades-k-8/

New York State Education Department. (2017). *New York State P–12 learning standards for the Arts: Guidance for implementation.* http://www.nysed.gov/common/nysed/files/programs/curriculum-instruction/2017-implementation-guide_update_final.pdf

New York State Education Department (2019, August 7). *Report—Transforming districts, schools and classrooms in New York State by prioritizing equity and academic success for multilingual learners/English language learners.* http://www.nysed.gov/common/nysed/files/programs/bilingual-ed/synthesis-report-obewl-08-07-2019-a.pdf

New York State Education Department. (2020). *NY State graduation rate data 4 year outcome as of August 2020. Graduation rate.* Available at https://data.nysed.gov

/gradrate.php?state=yes&year=2020&cohortgroup=0&lep%5B%5D=0&lep%5B%5D=1

NGSS Lead States. (2013). *Next Generation Science Standards: For states, by states.* The National Academies Press.

Nieto, S. (1999). *The light in their eyes: Creating multicultural learning communities.* Teachers College Press.

Nocella, A. (2008). Emergence of disability pedagogy. *Journal of Critical Education Policy Studies, 6*(2), 77–94.

Nuñez-Oviedo, M. C., & Clement, J. (2002). *An instructional method derived from model construction and criticism theory.* Paper presented at the NARST Conference, New Orleans, LA.

Ochoa, A. M., Brandon, R. R., Cadiero-Kaplan, K., & Ramírez, P. C. (2014). Bridging bilingual and special education: Opportunities for transformative change in teacher preparation programs. *Association of Mexican-American Educators (AMAE), 8*(1), 72–82.

Office of English Language Acquisition. (2017, May). *Demographics and State data fast facts: Students with disabilities who are English learners.* National Clearinghouse for English Language Acquisition (NCELA), U.S. Department of Education. https://www.ncela.ed.gov/fast-facts#

Ortiz, A. A., Robertson, P. M., Wilkinson, C. Y, Liu, J., McGhee, B. D., & Kushner, M. (2011). The role of bilingual education teachers in preventing inappropriate referrals of ELLs to special education: Implications for response to intervention. *Bilingual Research Journal: Journal of the Association for Bilingual Education, 34*(3), 316–333. https://doi.org/10.1080/15235882.2011.628608

Otheguy, R., García, O., & Reid, W. (2015). Clarifying translanguaging and deconstructing named languages: A perspective from linguistics. *Applied Linguistics Review, 6*(3), 281–307.

Ovando, C. J. (2003). Bilingual education in the United States: Historical development and current issues. *Bilingual Research Journal, 27*(1), 1–24.

Palmer, D. (2007). A dual immersion strand programme in California: Carrying out the promise of dual language education in an English-dominant context. *International Journal of Bilingual Education and Bilingualism, 10*(6), 752–768. https://doi.org/10.2167/beb397.0

Parrish, T. (2002). Racial disparities in the identification, funding, and provision of special education. In D. J. Losen & G. Orfield (Eds.), *Racial inequity in special education* (pp. 13–38). Harvard Education Press.

Pavlenko, A. (2002). We have room for but one language here: Language and national identity in the US at the turn of the 20th century. *Multilingual, 21*(2/3), 163–196. https://doi.org/10.1515/mult.2002.008

Peel, A. (2017). Complicating canons: A critical literacy challenge to common core assessment. *Literacy, 51*(2), 104–110. https://doi.org/10.1111/lit.12106

Peixoto, F., Monteiro, V., Mata, L., Sanches, C., Pipa, J., & Almeida, L. S. (2016). "To be or not to be retained . . . That's the question!": Retention, self-esteem, self-concept, achievement goals, and grades. *Frontiers in Psychology, 7*(1550), 1–13. https://doi.org/10.3389/fpsyg.2016.01550

Petersen, A. J. (2009). Shana's story: The struggles, quandaries and pitfalls surrounding self-determination. *Disability Studies Quarterly, 29*(2). https://doi.org/10.18061/dsq.v29i2.922

Puzio, K., Keyes, C. S., Cole, M. W., & Jiménez, R. T. (2013). Language differentiation: Collaborative translation to support bilingual reading. *Bilingual Research Journal, 36*(3), 329–349. https://doi.org/10.1080/15235882.2013.845118

Reid, D. K., & Knight, M. (2006). Disability justifies exclusion of minority students: A critical history grounded in disability studies. *Educational Researcher, 35*(6), 18–23. https://doi.org/10.3102/0013189x035006018

Reid, D. K., & Valle, J. W. (2004). The discursive practice of learning disability: Implications for instruction and parent–school relations. *Journal of Learning Disabilities, 37,* 466–481.

Reynaga-Peña, C. G., Sandoval-Ríos, M., Torres-Frías, J., López-Suero, C., Lozano Garza, A., Dessens Félix, M., González Maitland, M., & Ibanez, J. G. (2018). Creating a dialogic environment for transformative science teaching practices: Towards an inclusive education for science. *Journal of Education for Teaching, 44*(1), 44–57. https://doi.org/10.1080/02607476.2018.1422620

Rogoff, B., Callanan, M., Gutiérrez, K. D., & Erickson, F. (2016). The organization of informal learning. *Review of Research in Education, 40*, 356–401.

Román, D., Pastor, A., & Basaraba, D. (2019). Internal linguistic discrimination: A survey of bilingual teachers' language attitudes toward their heritage students' Spanish. *Bilingual Research Journal, 42*(1), 6–30. https://doi.org/10.1080/15235882.2018.1563006

Ronfeldt, M., Schwartz, N., & Jacob, B. A. (2014). Does pre-service preparation matter? Examining an old question in new ways. *Teachers College Record, 116*(10), 1–46. https://doi.org/10.1177/016146811411601002

Roosevelt, T. (1919, January 3). [Letter from Theodore Roosevelt to Richard M. Hurd.] Theodore Roosevelt Papers. Library of Congress Manuscript Division. Retrieved from https://www.theodorerooseveltcenter.org/Research/Digital-Library/Record?libID=o265602.

Roth, W-M. (2014). Activity theory. In T. Teo (Ed.), *Encyclopedia of critical psychology* (pp. 25–31). Springer.

Roth, W.-M., & Lee, Y.-J. (2007). "Vygotsky's neglected legacy": Cultural-historical activity theory. *Review of Educational Research,* 77(2), 186–232. https://doi.org/10.3102/0034654306298273

Rubin, K. H., Bukowski, W., & Parker, J. G. (2006). Peer interactions, relationships, and groups. In N. Eisenberg (Ed.), *Handbook of child psychology* (Social, emotional, and personality development, Vol. 3, pp. 571–645). Wiley.

Rudasill, K. M., Prokasky, A., Tu, X., Frohn, S., Sirota, K., & Molfese, V. J. (2013). Parent vs. teacher ratings of children's shyness as predictors of language and attention skills. *Learning and Individual Differences, 34*, 57–62.

Rueda, R., & Stillman, J. (2012). The 21st century teacher: A cultural perspective. *Journal of Teacher Education, 63*(4), 245–253. https://doi.org/10.1177/0022487112446511

Ruillier, J. (2014). *Por cuatro esquinitas de nada* (E. Bourgeois, Trans.). Editorial Juventud, S.A. (Original work published 2004).

Rummery, K., & Fine, M. (2012). Care: A critical review of theory, policy and practice. *Social Policy & Administration* 46(3), 321–343. https://doi.org/10.1111/j.1467-9515.2012.00845.x

Salazar, M. (2013). A humanizing pedagogy: Reinventing the principles and practice of education as a journey toward liberation. *Review of Research in Education, 37*, 121–148. https://doi.org/10.3102/0091732x12464032

Samson, J. F., & Lesaux, N. K. (2009). Language-minority learners in special education: Rates and predictors of identification for services. *Journal of Learning Disabilities, 42*(2), 148–162. https://doi.org/10.1177/0022219408326221

Sánchez, A. (2022, May 2). *Educación*. ConceptoDefinición. https://conceptodefinicion.de/educacion/

Sannino, A. (2015). The principle of double stimulation: A path to volitional action. *Learning, Culture and Social Interaction, 6*, 1–15. https://doi.org/10.1016/j.lcsi.2015.01.001

Schissel, J., & Kangas, S. E. N. (2018). Reclassification of emergent bilinguals with disabilities: The intersectionality of improbabilities. *Language Policy, 17*(4), 567–589. https://doi.org/10.1007/s10993-018-9476-4

Shalaby, C. (2017). *Troublemakers: Lessons in freedom from young children at school*. The New Press.

Shifrer, D., Callahan, R. M., & Muller, C. (2013). Equity or marginalization? The high school course-taking of students labeled with a learning disability. *American Educational Research Journal, 50*, 656–682. https://doi.org/10.3102/0002831213479439

Skiba, R., Simmons, A., Ritter, S., Kohler, K., Henderson, M., & Wu, T. (2006). The context of minority disproportionality: Practitioner perspectives on special education referral. *Teachers College Record, 108*, 1424–1459.

Skutnabb-Kangas, T., & Phillipson, R. (2010). Linguistic human rights, past and present. In T. Skutnabb-Kangas & R. Phillipson (Eds.), *Linguistic human rights: Overcoming linguistic discrimination* (pp. 71–110). De Gruyter. (Original work published 1994). https://doi.org/10.1515/9783110866391.71

Slee, R. (1997). Inclusion or assimilation? Sociological explorations of the foundations of theories of special education. *Educational Foundations, 11*(1), 55–71. https://eric.ed.gov/?q=education+of+special+needs+pupils+using+multiple+intelligence+theory&pg=653&id=EJ545428

Slee, R. (2001). Driven to the margins: Disabled students, inclusive schooling and the politics of possibility. *Cambridge Journal of Education, 31*(3), 385–397.

Sleeter, C. (2001). Preparing teachers for culturally diverse schools: Research and the overwhelming presence of Whiteness. *Journal of Teacher Education, 52*, 94–106.

Soja, E. W. (1996). *Thirdspace: Journeys to Los Angeles and other real-and-imagined places*. Blackwell.

Sotomayor, S. (2019). *¡Solo pregunta!: Sé diferente, sé valiente, sé tú* (Teresa Mlawer, Trans.). Penguin Random House.

Spear-Swerling, L. (2006). *Learning disabilities in English language learners*. Reading Rockets. https://www.readingrockets.org/article/learning-disabilities-english-language-learners

Steele, K. (2001). A new teacher learning to share responsibility with parents. In B. Rogoff, C. Goodman Turkanis, & L. Bartlett (Eds.), *Learning together: Children and adults in a school community* (pp. 185–187). Oxford University Press. https://doi.org/10.1093/oso/9780195097535.003.0031

Strauss, A., & Corbin, J. (1990). *Basics of qualitative research: Grounded theory procedures and techniques*. Sage.

Stroupe, D. (2014). Examining classroom science practice communities: How teachers and students negotiate epistemic agency and learn science-as-practice. *Science Education, 98*(3), 487–516. https://doi.org/10.1002/sce.21112

Suárez-Orozco, C., Suárez-Orozco, M. M., & Todorova, I. (2010). *Learning a new land: Immigrant students in American society*. Belknap Press of Harvard University Press.

Sullivan, A. L. (2011). Disproportionality in special education identification and placement of English language learners. *Exceptional Children, 77*(3), 317–334. https://doi.org/10.1177/001440291107700304

Sullivan, A. L., & Bal, A. (2013). Disproportionality in special education: Effects of individual and school variables on disability risk. *Exceptional Children, 79*, 475–494.

Tabak, I., & Radinsky, J. (2015). Educators' coaches, peers, and practices: Revisiting how teachers learn. *The Journal of the Learning Sciences. 24*(3), 343–346. https://doi.org/10.1080/10508406.2015.1065664

Thomas, W. P., & Collier, V. P. (2002). *A national study of school effectiveness for language minority students' long-term academic achievement*. Center for Research on Education, Diversity, and Excellence (CREDE). https://eric.ed.gov/?id=ED475048

Trainor, A., Murray, A., & Kim, H.-J. (2016). English learners with disabilities in high school: Population characteristics, transition programs, and postschool outcomes. *Remedial and Special Education, 37*(3), 146–158. https://doi.org/10.1177/0741932515626797

Trueba, H. T. (1990). The role of culture in literacy acquisition: An interdisciplinary approach to qualitative research. *International Journal of Qualitative Studies in Education, 3*(1), 1–13.

Tse, L. (2001). Resisting and reversing language shift: Heritage-language resilience among U.S. native biliterates. *Harvard Educational Review, 71*, 676–706.

Tyack, D. B. (1981). Governance and goals: Historical perspectives on public education. In D. Davies (Ed.), *Communities and their schools* (pp. 11–31). McGraw-Hill.

Umansky, I., & Reardon, S. F. (2014). Reclassification patterns among Latino English Learner students in bilingual, dual immersion, and English immersion classrooms. *American Educational Research Journal, 51*(5), 879–912.

United Federation of Teachers. (1999). *Special education teacher support services*. https://www.uft.org/teaching/students-disabilities/special-education-teacher-support-services

United Nations Educational, Scientific and Cultural Organization (UNESCO). (1994). *The Salamanca statement and framework for action on special needs education*. https://unesdoc.unesco.org/ark:/48223/pf0000098427

United Nations High Commissioner for Refugees (UNHCR). (2021). *Global trends: Forced displacement in 2020*. https://www.unhcr.org/60b638e37/unhcr-global-trends-2020

U.S. Census Bureau. (2018). *Selected social characteristics in the United States*. American Community Survey. https://www.census.gov/acs/www/data/data-tables-and-tools/data-profiles/2018/

U.S. Department of Education, Office of Special Education and Rehabilitative Services, Office of Special Education Programs. (2015). *37th annual report to Congress on the implementation of the Individuals with Disabilities Education Act, 2015*. https://files.eric.ed.gov/fulltext/ED572022.pdf

Valencia, R. R. (1997). *The evolution of deficit thinking: Educational thought and practice*. Falmer.

Valenzuela, A. (1999). *Subtractive schooling: U.S.-Mexican youth and the politics of caring*. State University of New York Press.

Valle, J. W., & Connor, D. J. (2011). *Rethinking disability: A disability studies approach to inclusive practices*. McGraw Hill.

Valle, J. W., & Connor, D. J. (2019). *Rethinking disability: A Disability Studies approach to inclusive practices* (2nd ed.). McGraw Hill. https://doi.org/10.4324/9781315111209

van Swet, J., Wichers-Bots, J., & Brown, K. (2011). Solution-focused assessment: Rethinking labels to support inclusive education. *International Journal of Inclusive Education, 15*(9), 909–923. https://doi.org/10.1080/13603110903456615

Varelas, M., Pappas, C. C., Tucker-Raymond, E., Kane, J., Hankes, J., Ortiz, I., & Keblawe-Shamah, N. (2010). Drama activities as ideational resources for primary-grade children in urban science classrooms. *Journal of Research in Science Teaching, 47*(3), 302–325. https://doi.org/10.1002/tea.20336

Varelas, M., Tucker-Raymond, E., & Richards, K. (2015). A structure-agency perspective on young children's engagement in school science: Carlos's performance and narrative. *Journal of Research in Science Teaching, 52*(4), 516–529. https://doi.org/10.1002/tea.21211

Vaughn, S., & Linan-Thompson, S. (2003). What is special about special education for students with learning disabilities? *Journal of Special Education, 37*, 140–147.

Vavougios, D., Verevi, A., Papalexopoulos, P. F., Verevi, C-J, & Panagopoulou, A. (2016). Teaching science to students with learning and other disabilities: A review of topics and subtopics appearing in experimental research 1991–2015. *International Journal of Higher Education, 5*(4), 268–280. https://doi.org/10.5430/ijhe.v5n4p268

Vygotsky, L. S. (1978). *Mind in society: the development of higher psychological processes*. Harvard University Press.

Vygotsky, L. S. (1993). *The collected works of L. S. Vygotsky. Volume 2: The fundamentals of defectology (abnormal psychology and learning disabilities)* (R. W. Rieber & A. S. Carton, Eds.; J. E. Knox & C. B. Stevens, Trans.). Plenum.

Vygotsky, L. S. (1997). The history of development of higher mental functions, Chapter 2: Research method. In R. W. Rieber (Ed.), *The collected works of L. S. Vygotsky. Vol. 4: The history of the development of higher mental functions* (Marie J. Hall, Trans., pp. 27–63). Plenum.

Wang, P., & Woolf, S. B. (2015). Trends and issues in bilingual special education teacher preparation: A literature review. *Journal of Multilingual Education Research, 6*(4), 35–59.

Ware, L. P. (2002). A moral conversation on disability: Risking the personal in educational contexts. *Hypatia, 17*(3), 143–172.

Ware, L. P. (2005). Many possible futures, many different directions: Merging critical special education and disability studies. In S. L. Gabel (Ed.), *Disability studies in education: Readings in theory and method* (pp. 103–124). Peter Lang.

Warikoo, N., & Carter, P. (2009). Cultural explanations for racial and ethnic stratification in academic achievement: A call for a new and improved theory. *Review of Educational Research, 79*, 366–394.

Watt, S. J., Therrien, W. J., Kaldenberg, E., & Taylor, J. (2013). Promoting inclusive practices in inquiry-based science classrooms. *Teaching Exceptional Children, 45*(4), 40–48. https://doi.org/10.1177/004005991304500405

Wei, L. (2011). Multilinguality, multimodality and multicompetence: Code- and mode-switching by minority ethnic children in complementary schools. *The Modern Language Journal, 95*, 370–384.

Wenger, E. (1998). *Communities of practice: Learning, meaning and identity.* Cambridge University Press.

Wertsch, J. V. (1998). *Mind as action.* Oxford University Press.

Wertsch, J. V. (2007). Mediation. In H. Daniels, M. Cole, & J. V. Wertsch, (Eds.), *The Cambridge companion to Vygotsky.* (pp. 178–0192). Cambridge University Press.

Williams Fortune, T., & Tedick, D. J. (2008). One-way, two-way and indigenous immersion: A call for crossfertilization. In T. Williams Fortune & D. J. Tedick (Eds.), *Pathways to multilingualism: Evolving perspectives on immersion education* (pp. 3–21). Multilingual Matters. https://doi.org/10.21832/9781847690371-004

Woumans, E., P. Santens, A. Sieben, J. Versijpt, M. Stevens., & W. Duyck. (2015). Bilingualism delays clinical manifestation of Alzheimer's disease. *Bilingualism: Language and Cognition, 18*(3), 568–574.

Yoshida, M. (1999). *Lesson study: A case study of a Japanese approach to improving instruction* (Publication No. 30454255) [Doctoral dissertation, University of Chicago Department of Human Development]. ProQuest Dissertations Publishing.

Yu, B. (2013). Issues in bilingualism and heritage language maintenance: Perspectives of minority-language mothers of children with autism spectrum disorders. *American Journal of Speech-Language Pathology, 22*(1), 10–24. https://doi.org/10.1044/1058-0360(2012/10-0078)

Zapata, A., & Laman, T. T. (2016). "I write to show how beautiful my languages are": Translingual writing instruction in English dominant classrooms. *Language Arts, 93*(5), 366–378.

Zimmerman, A., & Gonen, Y. (2022, January 20). *Pre-K for all? NYC's Universal Preschool push leaves students with disabilities behind.* The City. https://www.thecity.nyc/education/2022/1/20/22892557/universal-preschool-students-disabilities

Zisselsberger, M. (2016) Toward a humanizing pedagogy: Leveling the cultural and linguistic capital in a fifth-grade writing classroom. *Bilingual Research Journal, 39*(2), 121–137. https://doi.org/10.1080/15235882.2016.1167137

Index

About the Author

Patricia Martínez-Álvarez is an associate professor in the program in bilingual/bicultural education in the Department of Arts and Humanities at Teachers College, Columbia University, in New York. She obtained her PhD in instructional technology and multilingual/multicultural special education from George Mason University, and her master's degree in bilingual special education from George Washington University. Her research interests lie at the intersection of bilingualism/biculturalism and disability within cultural-historical perspectives. Dr. Martínez-Álvarez employs cultural historical activity theory (CHAT) to problematize the ways minoritized children with a disability are situated in schools and promote bilingual education for all children. Dr. Martínez-Álvarez is a former chair of, and an Early Career AERA awardee from the Bilingual Education Research SIG and the current co-chair of the AERA Cultural-Historical research SIG. She serves as an associate editor for *Teachers College Record* and is an editorial board member for *Bilingual Research Journal*. Her publications appear in venues such as *Curriculum Inquiry, Equity & Excellence in Education, Race Ethnicity and Education, Teachers College Record, Teaching and Teacher Education*, and *Urban Education*. She is author of the book *Teacher Education for Inclusive Bilingual Contexts* (2022, Routledge).